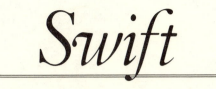

Swift

and the English Language

Swift

and the English Language

Ann Cline Kelly

upp

UNIVERSITY OF PENNSYLVANIA PRESS

PHILADELPHIA

Library of Congress Cataloging-in-Publication Data

Kelly, Ann Cline.
  Swift and the English language.

  Bibliography: p.
  Includes index.
    1. Swift, Jonathan, 1667–1745—Knowledge—Language
and languages.   2. Swift, Jonathan, 1667–1745—Language.
3. English language—18th century—History.   4. English
language—18th century—Style.   5. Language and
languages in literature.   I. Title.
PR3728.L33K45   1988   828'.509   87-19234
ISBN 0-8122-8084-9

To the best of parents
Howard F. and Mary W. Cline

Contents

Acknowledgments

For my initial acquaintance with Swift, a relationship that has intensified over the years, I am indebted to my graduate professors, Maurice Johnson and Arthur H. Scouten. Their scholarship inspired me and their generosity with assistance sustained me. Financial aid for early stages of this project came from the Faculty Research Program in the Social Sciences, Humanities and Education at Howard University through the Office of the Vice-President for Academic Affairs. I am also grateful to my students at Howard University, whose intelligent and passionate responses to Swift revealed to me the degree to which he hated oppression and sought to promote liberty.

The editors of *ELH*, *Studies in Philology*, *South Atlantic Review*, and *Neophilologus* have graciously given me permission to use material previously published in their journals. Brief excerpts from "After Eden: Gulliver's (Linguistic) Travels," *ELH* 45 (1978): 33–54, appear in Chapter 4; brief excerpts from "Swift's *Polite Conversation:* An Eschatological Vision," *Studies in Philology* 73 (1976): 204–24, appear in Chapter 3; brief excerpts from "Swift's Satires against Modern Etymologists in *The Antiquity of the English Tongue*," *South Atlantic Review* 48 (May 1983): 21–26, appear in Chapter 5; and several paragraphs from "Why Did Swift Sign His Name to *A Proposal for Correcting . . . the English Tongue?*" *Neophilologus* 63 (1979): 469–80, appear in Chapter 6.

Many individuals have contributed to the completion of this manuscript, some in practical, definable ways and some in more abstract, undefinable ways. At the risk of omitting some, let me try to itemize. A very kind and candid group read the manuscript and offered advice—Stephen Ackerman, Doris Adler, Vincent Carretta, Hugh Ormsby-Lennon, Leland Peterson, Arthur H. Scouten, Pamela Volkman, Charlotte Watkins, and Calhoun Winton. Conversation with these friends and colleagues immeasurably improved the manuscript, but no doubt flaws remain, for which I am responsible. Paul Korshin encouraged and facilitated the book's publication. At the University of Pennsylvania Press, Ruth Veleta and Trudie Calvert felicitously edited the manuscript. Charles and Mildred Nilon made my sabbatical in Colorado pleasantly productive. The Folger Library staff were both congenial and efficient. The services of Linda Mumma, my excellent baby-sitter, allowed me to work without guilt.

Without my family I would have been able to accomplish very little. I want especially to thank Henry Kelly, who has made me very happy for the past twenty-seven years, and Alice and Sophie Kelly, who have added greatly to that happiness since their births in 1981 and 1982. My most long-standing debt of gratitude, though, is to my parents, to whom I dedicate this book.

Chronology of Swift's Life

1667 Born in Dublin of English parents, November 30. His father had died a few months before his birth. Shortly after his birth, he was kidnapped by his nursemaid and taken to England, where he remained for three years.

1686 B.A., Trinity College Dublin.

1689 First entered the household of Sir William Temple, where he met Stella.

1692 M.A., Oxford University.

1695 Ordained as a priest.

1702 D.D., Trinity College Dublin.

1704 *Tale of a Tub* published.

1710–14 In London. Became friends with the Tory ministers and helped them by writing *The Examiner, Conduct of the Allies*, and other political pieces. Joined Pope, Gay, Arbuthnot, and Parnell to form the Scriblerus Club. Wrote *Journal to Stella* and met Hester Vanhomrigh.

1712 Published *Proposal for Correcting, Improving, and Ascertaining the English Tongue*.

1713 Made Dean of St. Patrick's after being disappointed in his hopes of being rewarded with an English bishopric.

1724 *The Drapier's Letters* published.

1726 *Gulliver's Travels* published.

1731 Began composing "Verses on the Death of Dr. Swift," which was not published until 1739.

1738 *Polite Conversation*, collected over Swift's life, published.

1742 Declared mentally unsound; a guardian appointed.

1745 Died in Dublin, October 19.

Abbreviations for Swift's Works

C   *The Correspondence of Jonathan Swift*, ed. Harold Williams, 5 vols. (Oxford: Clarendon Press, 1963–72)

JS   *Journal to Stella*, ed. Harold Williams, 2 vols. (Oxford: Blackwell, 1948; rpt. 1974)

P   *The Poems of Jonathan Swift*, 2d ed., ed. Harold Williams, 3 vols. (Oxford: Clarendon Press, 1966)

PW   *The Prose Works of Jonathan Swift*, ed. Herbert Davis, 14 vols. (Oxford: Blackwell, 1939–62)

Introduction

. . . they see that this [world]
Is crumbled out again to his atomies.
'Tis all in pieces, all coherence gone;
All just supply, and all relation:
Prince, subject, father, son, are things forgot,
For every man alone thinks he hath got
To be a phoenix, and that there can be
None of that kind, of which he is, but he.
John Donne, "The First Anniversary"

This book focuses on an important and somewhat neglected aspect of Jonathan Swift's thought: his fascination with language in general and his commitment to the English language in particular. Swift's linguistic concerns structured his vision of the world and determined his strategies for altering it.[1]

As John Donne laments, "all coherence" seemed to dissolve in the seventeenth century, the age into which Swift was born. The monoliths of church, monarchy, and society had been fragmented and reformed. Perhaps one of the greatest shocks in a century full of trauma was the growing perception that words did not have a fixed and orderly relationship to the objects they signified. Fears of linguistic insignificance haunted the period, causing Clarendon to worry that once clear and unifying ideas like "Religion, Law, Liberty, and Parliaments" were now a source of argument because their agreed-upon meanings had been lost. For Swift the problem of meaning had an existential dimension. He continually fought to define himself, rather than be defined by others. Words were the medium through which he determined his presence in the world, for he was a man without family, without title, without wealth. But he had an intellect that expressed itself forcefully in language, and he hoped through language to

I

make a lasting improvement in the world. With his writing, Swift sought to create something worthwhile, something permanent, something explicitly valuable, something transcendent—but these verbal monuments, he feared, might sink into the swamp of oblivion if the forms and definitions of words continued to shift. Swift was not alone in this concern. Edmund Waller, in "On English Verse," asks, "Who can hope his lines should long / Last in a daily changing tongue," and Alexander Pope predicts that "such as *Chaucer* is, shall *Dryden* be," unless some measures are taken to stabilize English.

Swift's fascination with language led him to questions about practice and theory that are still being considered by linguists today: What is the relation of language to thought? Can a universal language be developed? Does current language adequately convey new or complex ideas? How should words be defined? What standard should be used for spelling? Why do certain people reject everyday language and speak in jargon or peculiar argots? What intelligence and training are necessary to produce clear discourse? Should all members of a nation speak the same language? What interconnection exists between politics and the English language? What forces cause linguistic change? Are all of these changes undesirable? Should the development of language be controlled? By whom? These serious, abstract issues apart, Swift was naturally attracted to all varieties of verbal expression and reveled in their possibilities.

Swift's famous definition of style as "Proper Words in proper Places" summarizes his theory of language but does not communicate very much without the "ample . . . Disquisition" he would have added if he had time (*A Letter to a Young Gentleman Lately entered into Holy Orders*, PW 9:65). This book supplies that "ample Disquisition" by exploring Swift's linguistic premises in a systematic way so that one can answer the question, What is linguistically proper? As much as possible, I have used Swift's language to discuss the issues he implicitly raises rather than to paraphrase or to impose modern linguistic terminology. Swift's ideas, therefore, are conveyed in his own terms, and although those ideas are embedded in diverse rhetorical strategies and in works on a wide range of topics, nonetheless certain consistent principles emerge. Swift's view of language did not vary over his career but was a fixed frame of reference. Swift's linguistic ideas were not original with him but derived primarily from the classical tradition of rhetoric and the interpretation of that tradition by the early humanists. The purpose of the study is not, however, to trace the genesis of these ideas but to see how they fit into Swift's ambitious agenda for improving the world (he set out to do no less). Swift's concern with language was at the center of his life and work, and so this book provides some interpretation of biography, but that is not its focus. Nor does the book treat in any detail contemporary linguistic theory, other than to provide a context sufficient to understand Swift's reactions to it.

Although Swift is not usually viewed as a utopian thinker, perhaps he should be. With the early humanists, he entertained a vision of a world bound together by the clear and honest use of language—a vision epitomized in his ideal of conversation, a subject that preoccupied him throughout his life. Swift believed that in conversation with other minds, both through reading and talking, people could winnow out error, establish common ground, and come to know one another. Examination of Swift's ideas on language and its social use in conversation (broadly defined) reveals a very different view of the man usually characterized by "savage indignation" and a disgust for mankind. That "savage indignation" certainly existed; it was generated not by hatred of people but by disappointment that they could not or would not achieve the possibilities of which they were capable. Those possibilities could be realized only through the use of what he called "Proper Words" to create a society that fostered the best in human nature. One of Swift's friends laughingly mocked his idealism: "How came you to frame a System (in the Times we Live in) to govern the world by Love" (*C* 1:235).

Chapter 1 demonstrates Swift's involvement in all aspects of language and lays out a general pattern of contradiction manifest in his life and thought. He sought definition within a historical context, consisting of what he called "the common forms," but at the same time he chafed at confinement and relished renegade freedom. Thus although Swift deeply yearned for a "corrected, improved, and ascertained language" and the cultural benefits it might ensure, he was nonetheless fascinated by nonstandard, ephemeral, bizarre, arcane, and mendacious modes of discourse. Using the guises of various personae, he eagerly entered different linguistic demimondes and played with their possibilities.

However much Swift delighted in aberrant discourse, he fervently believed that a permanent linguistic standard was necessary for any advancement in human affairs. Chapter 2 analyzes Swift's fundamental premise that language must serve a social function, an argument he reinforced through his persistent use of discourse-as-cloth imagery. The ideal operation of language to promote human society can be seen in microcosm when congenial and informed people converse. The paramount importance of conversation to Swift is the subject of Chapter 3. Chapter 4 examines Swift's hopes that the dynamics of good conversation might operate in national discourse as well.

The first half of the book, then, establishes the preeminent importance of "Proper Words" to Swift. His interest in the improvement of discourse was part of a general concern at the end of the seventeenth century with making language a less ambiguous mode of communication. Chapter 5 outlines some linguistic remedies current in Swift's time and discusses in detail his satiric judgment of them. Efforts by theorists to reform language or to provide new modes of definition rested on the implicit assumption that English was somehow inadequate, an idea Swift wholly rejected.

Swift was convinced that traditional English could convey any truths or ideas that men could understand, but if vitiated by "improper" discourse, the language would lose its ability to serve as a medium for conversation, and then civilization would sink into a Hobbesian pit where only naturalistic forces operate. Life would become "solitary, poore, nasty, brutish, and short."[2] To control linguistic change, Swift publicly advocated the establishment of an English academy in his *Proposal for Correcting, Improving, and Ascertaining the English Tongue* (1712), the only prose document he ever signed. Chapter 6 discusses Swift's sponsorship of the academy and his simultaneous subversion of it.

Swift's discomfort with an academy emanated in part from his conviction that discourse can be improved only by individual will, not by institutional fiat. He believed that everyone has a moral responsibility and the innate ability to put "Proper Words in proper Places." Exactly what the concept "Proper Words" entails, both in private and public discourse, is spelled out in Chapter 7. The "Proper Words" for private colloquy are those that draw the participants close to one another. If the participants are intimately acquainted, they may not even converse in standard English but in some personal, ersatz language, like the "little language" Swift used with Stella and the Anglo-Latin in which he joked with Thomas Sheridan. In more public discourse, especially in written discourse, "Proper Words" has a more confined definition. The failure of secular and ecclesiastical leaders to adhere to "Proper Words" was viewed by Swift as a serious moral flaw, symptomatic of profound antisocial, even inhuman, tendencies. Polluting the language of public discourse, Swift believed, was comparable to poisoning the intellectual well of the entire English-speaking community.

Chapter 8 shows, through example, how Swift associated the use of "Proper Words" with the sustenance of two common forms—the Established Church and the constitutional monarchy—that shaped British life. Swift believed that stylistic decisions are existential decisions and showed that by violating established verbal decorums, people such as Matthew Tindal and Richard Steele proclaimed their rejection of communal, civilizing values. Referring back to the imagery of discourse-as-fabric, Swift characterized them as "shredders"—agents of entropy.

Chapter 9 focuses on Swift's summary thoughts on the lasting value of his writing—and his life—because for him writing and living were almost one and the same. He had a faith that by exposing error and promoting rational norms, some social progress might be made, an idealism he mocks when he has Gulliver lament that even six months after the publication of the *Travels* he sees little improvement in the world. The success of *The Drapier's Letters*, however, dramatized the ability of clear expression to unite men in pursuit of their common interests. Because the Drapier epitomized Swift's faith in writing as a social force, Swift came more and more to identify himself with this character. In a final attempt to define himself for posterity, Swift memorialized himself in "Verses on the Death of Dr. Swift" as a powerful writer, who though forgotten by the London elite, was valued and remembered by the average man, a fate he welcomed yet disdained. Above all, he was involved in a search for lasting meaning, both in his own life and in human life in general—a search that led him deep into the nature of the language, the medium by which, he believed, the best of the human spirit is expressed and conveyed.

1

The Wild Dean

Rais'd up on Hope's aspiring Plumes,
The young Advent'rer o'er the Deep
An Eagle's Flight and State assumes,
And scorns the middle Way to keep. . . .
      "The Bubble," *P* 1:252, 32–36

J onathan Swift, a natural-born linguist, displayed an interest in verbal
manifestations of all kinds and developed a coherent theory of language that shaped his response to the events surrounding him. Nowhere does he elaborate his theory in a comprehensive manner, but it
is implicit in everything he wrote. From a close reading of his entire canon,
Swift's linguistic principles emerge and reveal their logical connection and
their consistency over decades. The multiple citations in this book illustrate how Swift's ideas on language regulated his expression and provided
the foundation of his intellectual outlook. As detailed analyses reveal, linguistic concerns govern the meaning of Swiftian texts to a surprising
extent.

Pervasive in Swift's canon is his concern with man-in-society, a relationship whose sine qua non is language. Verbal coherence and social
coherence were causally linked in his mind. Yet, though in theory he supported the need for a standard, traditional language, he resented limits and
boundaries; he always wanted to see how far he could go before actually
"going too far." He enjoyed treading the line between acceptable and unacceptable, not wanting to lose the blessing of the establishment but feeling besmirched if its members embraced him too heartily.[1] Although he
craved the stability of a humanist utopia and acknowledged its superiority
to existing social structures, he knew he would be oppressed by the con-
formity it required.[2] Knowing his own individualistic urges, he feared
them in other people. His irony and satire allowed him to play with anti-

social, subversive possibilities yet at the same time support the status quo. Thus although deviant language attracted and excited him, he advocated the establishment of a national linguistic standard because he dreaded the ascension of what he describes in *A Tale of a Tub* as a "new Deity . . . by some called *Babel*, by others, *Chaos*" (*PW* 1 : 124), another emanation of Alexander Pope's "Great Anarch," Dullness.

Swift was born into an age fascinated with linguistic inquiry.[3] Tracts poured off the presses on, among other things, cryptography, education of the deaf, shorthand, mystical or religious interpretations of words and letters, universal languages, pedagogical techniques, long distance communication, the physiology of speech production, and spelling reform. As one of its first actions, the Royal Society sponsored John Wilkins's ambitious enterprise of constructing a new language more suitable for scientific discourse. Daniel Defoe, John Evelyn, John Dryden, and the Earl of Roscommon publicly urged the creation of an English version of L'Académie Française. Linguistic theories and reforms were in the air.

Swift early demonstrated an interest in the world of words. In an autobiographical fragment, he brags that "by the time he was three years old he could read any chapter in the Bible" (*PW* 5 : 192). His deep interest in language is clear from his wide-ranging references. He studied everything from the eccentricities of individual dialect to abstract concepts of definition. Allusions in his writing testify to his extensive knowledge of current ideas on language, and many of his satires become clearer when read against this background.

On a practical level, Swift, like a modern ethnologist, took notes on the different types of speech he heard around him. He studied and recorded the patois of the underculture—balladmongers, beggars, journeymen, servants.[4] Fascinated by the calls of streethawkers, he writes Stella: "We have an abundance of our old criers still hereabouts. I hear every morning your woman with the old sattin and taffata, &c. the fellow with old coats, suits, or cloaks" (*JS* 2 : 570). He transcribed his own calls, echoing the originals: "Come buy my fine Wares, / Plumbs, Apples and Pears," "Charming Oysters I cry, / My Masters come buy," "Come, follow me by the Smell, / Here's delicate Onyons to sell" (*P* 3 : 951–52). To amass his *Complete Collection of Genteel and Ingenious Conversation*, known as *Polite Conversation*, he continually jotted down over the years the trite and unchangeable expressions that make up unimaginative parlor talk. The ephemeral argots of the political world also intrigued him. During his stay in London he assiduously remarked on the latest usage, speaking, for example, of "that Race of Politicians, who in the Cant Phrase are called Whimsicalls" (*Some Free Thoughts on the Present State of Affairs*, *PW* 8 : 82); or of rival periodicals, "which, in the Phrase of *Whig Coffee-Houses*, have *Swinged off* the *Examiner*" (*The Examiner*, PW 3 : 35); or of Lord Ranelagh, who "*dyed hard*, as the Term of Art is here, to express the woeful State of Men who discover no Religion at their Death" (*C* 1 : 285). Swift had a linguist's ear, which caught the verbal nuances around him.

When he traveled, Swift delighted in the varieties of language that he encountered. As a young man, he stayed in cheap inns, according to Lord Orrery, because he enjoyed listening to the "vulgar Dialect."[5] Swift himself speaks of conducting "several Experiments" in which he analyzed language in the rural areas of England and Ireland. He observed from "travelling over both Kingdoms . . . [that] the poor Cottagers here [in Ireland], who speak our Language . . . have much better natural Taste for good Sense, Humour, and Raillery, than ever I observed among People of the like Sort in *England*" (*C* 4 : 51). When Stella planned a trip to Wexford, of interest linguistically because the inhabitants spoke what was thought to be the English of Chaucer's time (*JS* 1 : 311, n. 17), Swift advised her to do the same kind of informal research he must have conducted: "They are old English; see what they have particular in their manners, names, and language" (311). His attention to indigenous languages can also be seen in the interest, which he shared with his friend Thomas Sheridan, in the Irish and Scots dialects. He writes Sheridan, for example, that "the Scotch mean the same thing by *Minding* that we do by *remembring*. Sirrah [said] I to a Scots foot man, why did [you] not go that Arrand? Because I did no *mind* it quo' Sawny" (*C* 4 : 350). Swift and Sheridan traded collections of Irish idioms, and Swift's *Dialogue in Hibernian Style* and *Irish Eloquence*, despite their sarcastic titles, are not satires but records of the syntax and diction peculiar to the Irish countryside. ("He keeps none but Garrauns, and he rides on a Soogaun with nothing for his Bridle but Gadd. In short, he is a meer Spawleen, and a perfect Monaghen, and a Munster Crack into the Bargain"—*PW* 4 : 279).[6] Joshing Swift, Sheridan describes him as one who loves to converse with

> ev'ry Irish Teague he spies . . .
>
> .   .   .   .
>
> Conforming to the tatter'd Rabble
> He learns their Irish Tongue to gabble. . . .
>   (*P* 3 : 1040, 28, 31–32)

How well Swift knew Gaelic is debatable, although he put forward as his own "The Description of an *Irish-Feast*, translated almost literally out of the Original *Irish*."[7] Despite his interest in the Irish language, he believed that if Ireland were ever to be given decent political treatment, English must be made the official public language, "so far at least as to oblige all the natives to speak only English on every occasion of business, in shops, markets, fairs, and other places of dealing" (*Answer to Several Letters from Unknown Hands, PW* 12:89). In his ironical *On Barbarous Denominations in Ireland*, Swift modestly proposes that the Irish language "might easily be abolished, and become a dead one in half an age, with little expence, and less trouble" (*PW* 4:280); this, he slyly suggests, would greatly convenience the "English lawyers" who look after the interests of the absentee landlords (281–82), whom Swift detested for their part in deepening Ireland's misery.[8]

Although at times he was an impartial observer, for the most part Swift actively challenged what he considered the serious threat to the social order posed by nonstandard, untraditional, or uncommon discourse. Swift's obsession with the particularities of language and the moral dimensions of an individual's linguistic choices determined his frequent use of parody as a satiric method. The stylistic idiosyncrasies of *Meditation on a Broomstick, Directions to Servants, Discourse Concerning the Mechanical Operation of the Soul, An Argument against Abolishing Christianity*, the Introduction to *Polite Conversation*, and, of course, *Gulliver's Travels* imply certain criticisms of their "authors." Swift habitually ventriloquizes through various perspectives, often several within a single work, as a way of presenting moral alternatives.

The norm against which one measures linguistic deviations is an unaffected, conversational style, such as people have customarily used for everyday communication. Enriched for generations, traditional English expresses the time-tested verities of British civilization, which Swift called the common forms. As the persisting elements of culture, the common forms provide a historical structure that binds men together and makes their lives meaningful. Without common forms, barbarity reigns, and so Swift devoted his energies to preserving cultural fixtures such as the Established Church, the constitutional monarchy, and the English language. Sometimes his defenses of these institutions were so ironic and unorthodox that he was mistaken for a subversive—with good reason. Undeniably, he enjoyed flirting with the uncommon forms he ostensibly condemned. Repeatedly Swift walked the boundary between the proper and improper, deriving deep pleasure from the balancing act. Swift's critics were right: *A Tale of a Tub* is blasphemous. Yet it also reinforces Christian orthodoxy. Swift is the master of mixed assertions; he hated to foreclose any possibilities.

Swift's polarities are bound in the oxymoronic epithet "wild Dean," which he applied to himself on hearing that Queen Caroline had requested a visit from him as well as from an *enfant sauvage* on the Continent; he delightedly notes the parallel: "having sent for a wild Boy from Germany, she had a curiosity to see a wild Dean from Ireland" (*C* 4:98). Swift's self-characterization as a "wild Dean" lightheartedly expresses his desire to be known as one who upholds cultural values as well as one who follows a defiantly individualistic path ("wild").[9] This dualism is nowhere more evident than in his attitudes toward discourse in general and the English language in particular, concerns that governed his life and art.

The Common Forms

Ironically, the clearest statement of what Swift meant by the "common forms" comes in his most obscure work, *A Tale of a Tub*. Although he speaks through many different mouthpieces in the *Tale*, Swift occasionally assumes a voice that espouses ideas consonant with opinions thought to be his own. Such an instance seems to occur when he declares that "the Brain, in its natural Position and State of Serenity, disposeth its Owner to pass his Life in the common Forms, without any Thought of subduing Multitudes to his own *Power*, his *Reasons* or his *Visions;* and the more he shapes his Understanding by the Pattern of Human Learning, the less he is inclined to form Parties after his particular Notions" (*PW* 1:108). In this sense, the "common Forms" represent the stabilizing expectations of the group that control the disruptive or domineering impulses of the individual. These cultural forms, including the English language, have evolved over time and transcended particular places and persons. They have become permanent elements of civilized life.

On the surface Swift, the only son of an Anglo-Irish family, seems to have lived his life within traditional confines. Although not without some faltering, he completed his academic training and was ordained as a priest. While in London on a mission for the Church of Ireland, he became involved in politics and was enlisted by the Tory ministers to aid their cause. With the fall of the ministry in 1713, his hopes for preferment in England evaporated, and he had to settle for Dean of St. Patrick's in Ireland, a move that he considered an "exile." Throughout his life he fought to preserve the prerogatives of the Established Church, an institution he believed was essential in giving form and value to British life. He was a conservative in politics (an argument exists as to whether he was an "Old Whig" or a Tory)[10] and was drawn to leaders who were dedicated to preserving the power of the church and who shared a nostalgia for the stability of England before the moneyed interests destroyed the old hierarchies. Swift had an allegiance to tradition and believed that a person's potential was fully realized only within its context. He condemned, therefore, the "Moderns" who discarded the inherited wisdom of the past and who searched for enlightenment in the dark, narrow caves of their own minds. One side of Swift's nature, then, was guided by an instinct to protect the common forms of English culture.[11]

Swift believed that the common forms were primarily preserved by the natural inertia of the general populace. Typically rustic and uneducated, they were divorced from metropolitan culture that feeds on the excitement of newness. They were not tempted by innovations that would deflect them from traditional habits and values. Preaching to his flock, Swift noted that "Men of common Understandings, if they serve God and mind their Callings, make fewer Mistakes in the Conduct of Life than those who have better Heads" (*The Duty of Mutual Subjection*, PW 9:148–49). Those with "better Heads" often disdain the "common Forms" and the "Pattern of Human Learning" because they embody "the stubborn Ignorance of the People" (*Tale*, PW 1:108), who know nothing and care to know nothing about the peculiar visions of a self-styled elite. In linguistic matters, Swift believed that the common people have an instinctive urge to preserve customary usage against faddish revisionism. In Laputa, for instance, the masses resist the academicians' attempts to ban discourse in "the Manner of their Forefathers: Such constant irreconcileable Enemies to Science are the common People" (*PW* 11:185). Similarly, the Drapier repeatedly rallies the untutored Irish to resist the "Terms of Art" used by the London politicians.

The pollution of ephemeral, nonstandard usage typically emanates from the city, where uncommonness is prized. Because urban slang is so short-lived, it cannot convey any transcendent truths. Swift notes in *The Tatler*, "It is manifest, that all new affected Modes of Speech, whether borrowed from the Court, the Town, or the Theatre, are the first perishing Parts in any Language. . . . The Writings of *Hooker*, who was a Country Clergyman . . . in the Reign of Queen *Elizabeth* . . . are in a Style, that with very few Allowances, would not offend any present Reader; much more clear and intelligible than those of . . . several others, who writ later; but being Men of the Court, and affecting Phrases then in Fashion; they are often either not to be understood, or appear perfectly ridiculous" (*PW* 2:177). Thus Richard Hooker, who had to accommodate his meaning to rural listeners, wrote in English whose clarity has a permanent claim. Swift's allusions to the admirable qualities of Elizabethan discourse recur in his canon. As he argues in his *Proposal*, the Elizabethan period represented the high point of modern English, a time before the fanaticism of the Civil War and subsequent "Licentiousness which entered with the *Res-*

toration . . . fell to corrupt our Language" (*Proposal*, *PW* 4:9–10). The linguistic usage that would endure, Swift believed, was that which had already endured, unless—as he profoundly feared—the babel of competing jargons were to displace standard, traditional language so that nothing could be communicated across time or space. Although Swift did not advocate a return to Elizabethan English, he yearned for the seeming unity of Elizabethan England, where the common forms still seemed to regulate national life.

Perhaps because of the simple immediacy of their lives, the common people did not feel the need to alter the common, or traditional, linguistic forms and thus were able to speak in a way intelligible to all. Writing to a young Anglican priest, Swift wonders "how it comes to pass, that Professors in most Arts and Sciences are generally the worst qualified to explain their Meanings to those who are not of their Tribe: A common Farmer shall make you understand in three Words, *that his Foot is out of Joint, or his Collar-bone broken;* wherein a *Surgeon,* after a Hundred Terms of Art, if you are not a Scholar, shall leave you to seek" (*Holy Orders, PW* 9:66). George Faulkner, Swift's Dublin printer, describes how Swift himself used the understanding of the common man as a stylistic touchstone by reading his works aloud to "two Men Servants present for this Purpose; and when he had any Doubt, he would ask them the Meaning of what they heard; which, if they did not comprehend, he would alter and amend until they understood it perfectly well, and then would say, *This will do; for I write to the Vulgar, more than to the Learned*" (*Faulkner's Preface, PW* 13:202–3). He applied this standard to others, criticizing Pope's *Epistle to Bathurst* because "some parts of it are not so obvious to midling Readers" (*C* 4:134–35). Similarly, he reprimanded Thomas Tickell for creating confusion in a poem, "which will make some difficulty to a common reader" (*C* 3:481).

Although the voyage to Laputa contains satire on the Royal Society, Swift supports in theory the society's linguistic goals as expressed by Thomas Sprat, its historian, in particular, the need "to reject all the amplifications, digressions, and swellings of style; to return back to . . . primitive purity . . . a native Easiness . . . preferring the language of artizans, countrymen, and merchants, before that of wits, or scholars."[12] This "primitive purity," Swift would agree, is a rarity among persons who profess to education and culture, such as courtiers, poets, university men, and those "who, under the Character of Men of Wit and Pleasure, pretended to give the Law. Many of [their] Refinements have already been long antiquated, and are now hardly intelligible; which is no Wonder, when they were the Product only of Ignorance and Caprice" (*Proposal, PW*

4:10). Like Sprat, Swift praised the naturalness and easiness of unaffected discourse that was generally more prevalent in common, as opposed to elite, circles. Although Swift applied a few more strictures to written discourse than to informal conversation, his criterion of "Proper Words in proper Places" generally governed both. (Discussion of the full meaning of "Proper Words" in relation to written and oral discourse is contained in Chapter 7.)

The attachment of the common people to the common forms of both language and political order is presumed by Mr. Examiner, Swift's spokesman in the periodical he created to bolster the Tory administration of Oxford and Bolingbroke under Queen Anne. To suit his rhetorical purposes, Swift, of course, carefully aligned the common people and the common forms on his side in contrast to the artful, iconoclastic orators of the opposition. In *Examiner* 24, Swift says that some people are misled about the nature of government, "But, the Body of People is wiser; and by the Choice they have made, shew they do understand our Constitution, and would bring it back to the old Form; which if the new Ministers take care to maintain, they will and ought to stand" (*PW* 3:66). In another *Examiner*, Swift argues that the consensus of the majority contradicts the Whig application of the term *faction* to the Tory party:

> IT is usually reckoned a *Whig* Principle to appeal to the People; but that is only when they have been so wise as to poison their Understandings before-hand: Will they now stand to this Appeal, and be determined by their *Vox Populi*, to which Side their Title of *Faction* belongs? And that the People are now left to the natural Freedom of their Understanding and Choice, I believe our Adversaries will hardly deny. They will now refuse this Appeal, and it is reasonable that they should.
> (*PW* 3:105)

The idea that the common people are the defenders of common sense and common forms is used for propagandistic purposes in the passages above, but politics notwithstanding, Swift indeed thought that the common people represented an invaluable bulwark of cultural conservatism. If left in a "natural" state—unmolested by verbal manipulation—they would choose to understand the proper meaning of a word, that is, its commonly accepted, historical definition. In his *Examiner* essay on *faction*, quoted above, Swift demands that the opposition "tell us by what Figure of Speech they pretend to call so great and unforced a Majority, with the QUEEN at the Head [the Tories], by the Name of *the Faction*" (*PW* 3:103–4). Because the Whigs' definition of *faction* is opposite to that which the average person would offer, Swift designates it as a "Figure of Speech."

Swift did not romanticize simple, rural life, nor did he believe great art would emanate from thresher poets and milkmaid poetesses. Swift thought that the routine, basic life of the countryside was boring. To his friend John Arbuthnot he sent a humorous account of a rustic conversation, whose verisimilitude, incidentally, reflects Swift's ability to render individualized voices:

> Farmer Tyler says, the white Mead at Chawdry has not been so bad in the memory of Man, and the Summer Barley is quite dryed up; but we hope to have a pretty good Crop of Wheat. Parson Hunsdon tis thought must stick to his Bargain, but all the Neighbors say the Attorney was an arrand Rogue. We cannot get a good Bitt of Butter for Love or Money. I could tell you more of the State of our Affairs, but doubt your Tast is not refined enough for it.
> (*C* 2:47–48)

It is clear that Swift's life was far from that of the common man; he wrote from an urban and urbane perspective. Yet he believed that whatever was worth expressing could be put in words that ordinary, even uneducated, people could understand (which is not to say they would fully comprehend the subtleties of the work itself). In Swift's canon, language the common man can understand, therefore, is the norm against which one measures the often bizarre utterances of the self-annointed elite that he delighted in parodying.[13] Uncommon language, in his view, is "improper" because it threatens to rend the social fabric by preventing communication among men in the present and cutting them off from their cultural legacy.

One is never comfortable in Swift's presence. His perennial power to disturb derives in part from the unpredictable mixture of orthodoxy and heterodoxy that informed his life, his works, and his attitudes toward language. Although he wanted power in the English establishment, he led the Irish crusade against English tyranny. Although he detested indirection, he was the master of irony, which he claimed to have invented. Although he hoped for preferment from the powers-that-be, he calculatedly offended them with his satire. Although he undertook his ecclesiastical duties with great seriousness, he tainted himself with the "Sin of Wit." Thus although he was confined by the common forms, or customary expectations, in some things, he disdained them in others. To understand his linguistic theories and practice one needs to explore the other pole of his personality—his urge to violate the common forms.

Violation of the Common Forms

Swift differentiated, often idiosyncratically, between the common forms integral to English civilization and social conventions, such as manners, "intended for regulating the conduct of those who have weak understandings" (*On Good Manners, PW* 4:214). Which common forms Swift upheld and which he ignored were sometimes unpredictable and variable. In "Cadenus and Vanessa," for instance, the Swiftlike speaker argues to the lady that their relationship cannot continue because it violates conventional propriety, yet the poet allows her to retort "that common Forms were not design'd / Directors to a noble Mind" (*P* 2:706, 12–13). Small wonder that the real-life Vanessa (Esther Vanhomrigh) was confused about his intentions. Swift's relationship with Stella (Esther Johnson), too, was such a strange mixture of conventional propriety and impropriety that tongues wag into the twentieth century.

Much of Swift's identity depended on the idea that he was above or beyond rules and decorums. In social matters, for instance, Swift prided himself on treating all persons alike and ignoring conventional social distinctions. An exception illustrates the rule. To obtain some documents for a history he was preparing, Swift was forced to write an ingratiating letter to the Duke of Chandos. It was full of the common forms one would ordinarily expect in such a situation—"I writ him with all the civility in my power, and with compliments on the fame of his generosity, and in a style very different from what I use to my friends with titles" (*C* 4:259).

Swift's delight in defeating expectation is evident in his predilection for mock literary forms. He took the genres of travelogue, essay, elegy, drama, pastoral, georgic, and love lyric and played off against their conventions to create the greatness of *Gulliver's Travels, Modest Proposal*, "Verses on the Death of Dr. Swift," *Polite Conversation*, "A Beautiful Young Nymph Going to Bed," "Description of a City Shower," and the birthday poems to Stella. In his first major production, *A Tale of a Tub*, he says he resolved to "proceed in a manner, that should be altogether new, the World having been too long nauseated with endless Repetitions upon every Subject" (*PW* 1:1; italics omitted). Swift succeeded in his goals. The *Tale* certainly falls into no recognizable genre. It is unlike anything else in English literature, a distinction Swift obviously aspired to. Charged that he had borrowed from other works, Swift reacted violently. Of all the criticisms against the *Tale*—blasphemy, vulgarity, impertinence—the one that hurt the most, that "touches the Author in a very tender Point" (6; italics omitted), was the allegation that he had plagiarized. He never thought it would be "disputed to be an Original, whatever Faults it might have" (7;

italics omitted). Swift wanted to leave his unique mark on the world; to have his identity confused or conflated with another's damaged his sense of self. In a way he wanted to be the author of his own being, a phoenix "that there can be / None of that kind, of which he is, but he" (John Donne, "The First Anniversary"). At the beginning of his life his father was dead and his mother absent, and so he had the responsibility early on of defining himself, which he did in part by compliance with the common forms and in part by rejection of them.

Swift's self-image as a "wild Dean," an upholder/violator of the common forms, coincides with the definition of "true Genius" included in his *Proposal for Correcting, Improving, and Ascertaining the English Tongue*. No doubt he wished Robert Harley and others to note the similarities. By "true Genius" Swift does "not mean . . . any bold Writer, who breaks through the Rules of Decency to distinguish himself by the Singularity of Opinions; but one, who upon a deserving Subject, is able to pen new Scenes, and discover a Vein of true and noble Thinking, which never entered into any Imagination before." Here Swift makes his own distinction between what he considers the important forms, such as "the Rules of Decency," and the unimportant forms that "plodding, servile, imitating Pedants" tyrannically impose (*PW* 4:19). His determination of which forms were important and unimportant did not always agree with what others thought, a fact of which he was acutely aware and not a little proud.

Swift's enemies enjoyed pointing out the contradiction between his theoretical support of the common forms and his violation of them in practice. John Oldmixon, for instance, when attacking Swift's *Proposal* for an academy, gleefully paraded the ungrammatical burbling of Mrs. Harris (of "Mrs. Harris's Petition") and the piquant swearing of Peter in *A Tale of a Tub* as proof of Swift's unsuitability to be "Chairman of a new Academy to reform and improve our Stile."[14] Oldmixon further asserts that Swift's use of nonstandard language is evidence of his antisocial tendencies, a charge Swift opened himself up to because of the dualities in his nature and his use of irony, which might allow him to explore forbidden realms without relinquishing the benefits of the sanction.

Swift's attitudes toward language reflect the basic schisms in his outlook, for despite his ostensible condemnation of it, Swift was as fluent in uncommon language as he was in common, traditional language. Jargon, argot, cant, and dialect all seemed to have a compelling interest for him. His study of these linguistic deviations is evident in his skillful parodies of them. Frederik Smith, in *Language and Reality in Swift's* A Tale of a Tub, points out that in the *Tale* Swift satirizes the Modern mentality by using a genuinely Modern vocabulary, much of which he generated for the occasion. Smith calls attention to a study of the illustrative quotations Samuel Johnson used in compiling his dictionary: Swift is quoted 1,761 times in the first edition, a figure that places him third in prose citations behind Joseph Addison (2,439) and the Authorized Version of the Bible (2,270). Moreover, the *Oxford English Dictionary* is replete with quotations from Swift, an indication of his use of words in "rare, old-fashioned, new, or peculiar ways."[15] Most of these usages occur when Swift is ventriloquizing through various perspectives he wanted to condemn. Ironically, Swift out-coined many of the Moderns he attacked. His linguistic creativity is a type of "wildness" that cannot abide constraint, yet the norm at the center of all his works is the clear, direct talk of everyday conversation in which the common forms of traditional language prevail.

Swift's dual tendencies are evident in his fun with language games and punning. Many critics have wondered how the man who wanted to "ascertain" language could take such delight in willfully distorting it, yet the two can be compatible. Swift's linguistic play vents his rage for chaos yet simultaneously asserts his loyalty to the conventional linguistic expectations that make the pun's surprise possible. Deviation cannot exist without firmly established norms. Puns are doubled-edged in another way. On one hand, punning is a social activity that creates a sense of intimacy among participants. On the other, manipulation of language shows a mastery of it, a superiority, Pope notes, that often brings the witty under suspicion because they seem to have a disturbing arrogance toward conventional form (*C* 4:115). In addition, puns were widely considered to be "false wit" that should be, as Addison notes, "subdued by Reason, Reflection, and good Sense."[16] Punning, therefore, can be construed as both social and antisocial. Puns, by definition, bring into play different meanings of the same word and free it from literal strictures; the inclusion of widely separated meanings, rather than the sacrifice involved in either/or choice, must have appealed to Swift. Puns, like the irony he loved, allow meaning to oscillate between possibilities, just as he himself loved to keep all options open.

For whatever reasons, Swift wished to be recognized as a punster. The *Journal to Stella* repeatedly emphasizes his *jeux d'esprit* in conversations with the London crowd. Swift's pride in his wit is evident; when he thinks he has perpetrated a good pun, he boasts of it to Stella and repeats it for her delectation: "I'll tell you a good thing I said to my lord Carteret. So, says he, my lord ——— came up to me, and askt me, &c. No, I said, my lord ——— never did, nor ever can *come up* to you. We all pun here sometimes. Lord Carteret set down Prior t'other day in his chariot, and Prior thanked him for his *Charity*. . . . I don't remember I heard one good one from the ministry, which is really a shame" (*JS* 1 : 153). In their exchange of correspondence, Stella responds in kind—"So Stella puns again" (33), Swift remarks—weaving the punning into the other language games that he played with her and Sheridan.[17]

Swift's interest in variations from the common forms of language can be seen in some of the other linguistic games he played. In *The Proposal for Correcting . . . the English Tongue*, for instance, Swift illustrates his point about English sounds by citing the results of a parlor amusement he devised: "More than once, where some of both Sexes were in Company, I have persuaded two or three of each to take a Pen, and write down a number of Letters joined together, just as it came into their Heads" (*PW* 4 : 13), the women producing Italianlike gibberish and the men, pseudo–high Dutch. That Swift played this game "more than once" shows his "serious" interest in play of this sort, which, of course, aided him in creating the sound patterning of the languages of *Gulliver's Travels*.

It is evident that Swift had enormous fun fabricating the languages in the *Travels*. He calls particular attention to them when writing Pope from Ireland after depositing the manuscript with his London publisher: "You will find what a quick change I made in seven days from London to the Deanery, through many nations and languages unknown to the civilized world" (*C* 3 : 158). The construction of these languages is elaborate and extended enough to have encouraged numerous critics to "decypher" them, although no consensus has been reached as to their "meaning."[18] Swift clearly enjoyed voyaging beyond the bounds of standard English into linguistic realms of his own invention.

As "Dean," Swift could write compellingly simple expository prose; he could also be "wild" and write in arresting fashions, particularly when he created a voice emanating from a sensibility he wished to ridicule. The use of nonstandard, oddly juxtaposed, or intensely private language can be a symptom of insanity, yet madness and creativity are linked in that both are characterized by the free play of the mind. Frederik Smith argues persuasively that the linguistic brilliance of *A Tale of a Tub* results from Swift's "opting to deliver himself through the mind of a madman, and thus tie himself to that persona's digressiveness, illogicality, and layered metaphors. . . . [This] has, paradoxically, liberated his own mind."[19] Swift's game-playing is directly linked to the freewheeling verbal invention that characterizes not just the *Tale* but most of his other works. Although the cultivated lawn of traditional discourse represented all that was safe and civilized, Swift had an irresistible urge to explore the jungle beyond. Swift's anti-Augustan qualities—his fascination with the lowlife, the tentative, the evanescent, the unstable—have been highlighted by Carole Fabricant's

Swift's Landscape, in which she argues that the Irish consciousness of chaos deeply imbued Swift's outlook. Swift's linguistic eclecticism reflects, in her words, "an awareness of the inability of established, officially sanctioned modes of expression to deal with certain kinds of reality, certain kinds of experience" that he did not want to ignore or miss.[20]

Writing may have led Swift into the madness that is allied to genius, yet he himself saw discourse as a way of regulating the mental chaos that he always feared might overpower his rational faculties. He recounted that someone "us'd to tell me, that my mind was like a conjur'd spirit, that would do mischief if I would not give it employment,—'Tis this humor, that makes me so busy when I am in Company to turn all that way" (*C* 1:4). Discourse in general and writing in particular were Swift's way of channeling his life's energies into orderly, concrete enterprises.

Swift's need to write arose in part from a desire to control not just his own mind but the minds of others. He asks in the *Tale,* "What Man in the natural State, or Course of Thinking, did ever conceive it in his Power, to reduce the Notions of all Mankind, exactly to the same Length, and Breadth, and Heighth of his own?" (*PW* 1:105). Swift ostensibly believed that the values he thought should be universal were not "his own" but the common forms that made up the legacy of British culture. Those in the bully pulpits of position should be guiding the nation in accordance with communally-inherited ideals, but such people, in Swift's view, were too often indifferent or self-seeking. He would agree with Yeats' assessment that "the best lack all conviction, while the worst / Are full of passionate intensity." Swift's aim was to remind men, by appealing to their reason, of the common forms that fostered civilized behavior in their society.

Although he was an Anglican divine, Swift's focus was not religion or the hereafter. Rather, he was preeminently a social and political thinker who had a consuming desire to improve man's lot on earth; he believed that men were capable of a better existence than the one they accepted by default. Improved language and discourse would uncover the roots of many present evils and allow them to be dug out. Only by standardizing traditional English to allow men to garner the best ideas of the past and the present could any social progress be made.

Not being born to power, how could Swift make others share his vision? Writing to Pope and Bolingbroke, he explains that, in the absence of wealth or title, his powers of discourse give him the force of authority: "All my endeavors from a boy to distinguish my self, were only for want of a great Title and Fortune, that I might be used like a Lord by those who have an opinion of my parts . . . the reputation of wit or great learning does the office of a blue riband, or of a coach and six horses" (*C* 3:330–31).

Knowing that his writing was the key to the influence he wanted to wield, Swift sought recognition of his ability from those around him. He soon learned, though, that the principles ideally governing British civilization had little to do with contemporary politics, and even though he wanted power, he was not willing to check himself in the ways that would increase his chances of preferment.

Swift's unnerving urge to probe nasty truths (not just excrement) offended people who believed that civility demanded silence on certain issues. He was driven by the need to push ideas into clarity, a disturbing tendency in a world in which unspoken assumptions are the most powerful and unreality is more comfortable than a full recognition of the facts. For Swift, however, secrecy, vagueness, abstraction, euphemism, self-reflexivity, and silence were types of Chaos and Old Night swallowing up glimmers of human light.

Even as a young man, Swift was profoundly discomfitted by a lack of articulation. He asks Stella, "Don't you remember how I used to be in pain when Sir William Temple would look cold and out of humour for three or four days, and I used to suspect a hundred reasons? (*JS* 1:231). In his relationship with Harley, Swift says there was "one thing I warned him of, Never to appear cold to me, for I would not be treated like a school-boy; that I had felt too much of that in my life already . . . that I expected if he heard or saw anything to my disadvantage, he would let me know in plain words" (*JS* 1:230). Truth, delivered in bold language, was to Swift the beginning of any constructive human response. This premise runs counter to the way of the world.

Swift was particularly amused by the "civilized" desire to euphemize, a symptom perhaps of humankind's general desire to live with comfortable delusions rather than to face uncomfortable facts, to achieve happiness by a *"perpetual Possession of being well Deceived"* (*Tale*, *PW* 1:108). The reality that *"Celia, Celia, Celia* shits" ("The Lady's Dressing Room," *P* 2:529, 118) is one which Strephon, Celia's lover, and most readers would like to reject, yet Swift often translated polite euphemisms into blunt Anglo-Saxon words that clearly convey their meaning. For instance, in his *Remarks upon . . . Rights of the Christian Church*, written by Matthew Tindal, Swift annotates the use of the word *executioner:* "He is fond of this Word in many Places, yet there is nothing in it, further than it is the Name for the hangman" (*PW* 2:91); in *History of the Rebellion*, Clarendon uses the phrase *natural son*, which Swift amends in the margin to *bastard* (*Marginalia*, *PW* 5:297); and Swift, attacking Bishop Gilbert Burnet's indirect condemnation of people, says, "for my own Part, I much prefer the plain *Billingsgate* Way of calling Names, because it expresseth our Meaning full as well, and

would save an abundance of Time which is lost by Circumlocution . . .
I hope his Lordship doth not think there is any Difference in point of
Morality, whether a Man calls me *Traitor* in one Word, or says I am one
hired to betray my Religion, and sell my Country" (*A Preface to Burnet's Introduction, PW* 4:69–70).

Although Swift claimed to "prefer the plain *Billingsgate* Way of calling
Names," he habitually attacked through indirection. Whether Swift con-
fronted his audience outright with uneuphemistic words for unpleasant
truths or whether his irony insinuated these truths into the reader's perception, the results are the same. In Swift's view, words should facilitate
communication among men for mutual enlightenment, a classical concept
of discourse that the Horse Master explains to Gulliver: "He argued thus;
That the Use of Speech was to make us understand one another, and to
receive Information of Facts" (*PW* 11:240). The second function of language—to convey the "Information of Facts"—is dependent on the first—
"to make us understand one another." Knowledge is gained only through
collective effort because an individual's partial reason is inadequate. A
common language is the medium that allows the flow of ideas in society—
conversation—to occur. Through clear, lively intercourse the "Information of Facts" can be established by consensus. In Chapter 3, I will fully
elaborate Swift's belief in the epistemological and social importance of
conversation. Swift no doubt looked around him and was appalled to see
how seldom language was used as it should be, to reinforce rather than to
fray the social fabric.

Swift's faith in the salutary effects of exposing the "Information of
Facts," even at the cost of giving offense, can be seen in his treatment of the
Duke of Schomberg's family. After they refused him money to refurbish
the duke's monument in St. Patrick's Cathedral, Swift publicly blazoned
their parsimony by recording it on the memorial stone, an act that enraged
the duke's heirs as well as Queen Caroline (*C* 3:468, 480). Swift had an
ulterior motive here, of course, and was in essence blackmailing other
nobility to give money for cathedral improvements. Such exposure, it
seemed, was necessary to get them to do the proper thing or to behave
according to the common forms of decency.[21]

Swift describes the force of explicitness when he has a publisher print
a story about a man who maliciously fired his gun and scared the horses
that Swift and a friend were riding. He explains that

> if a tradesman cheats me, I put him immediately into a newspaper, with
> the bare matter of fact, which the rogues are grown so afraid of, that they
> are often ready to fall on their knees for pardon.

I began this scheme with a long record upon a large peice of black marble in my own Cathedral . . . whereon I put a Latin inscription which I took care to have published in 7 London news papers. The grand-daughter of the old Duke of Schomberg w^d not send 50 [pounds] to make him a Monument over his burying-place; upon which I ordered the whole story to be engraved. . . . Thus I endeavor to do justice in my station, and give no offence.

> (*C* 4:409–10)

Swift, of course, is being disingenuous when he says he hoped to "give no offence." He is clearly exulting in his own personal powers to disturb the universe. And one of the best ways to prod the world toward improvement is, through lively and sometimes unsettling language, to provoke man's reason into operation.

Swift's dislike of vagueness inspired his project to give badges to the Dublin beggars so that passersby would know who were true objects of charity. An urge toward clarity can be seen, too, in his annoyed letter to the Council of Cork, which presented him with a silver box lacking any inscription: he complained that "there is not so much as my Name upon it, or any one Syllable to shew it was a Present from your City. Therefore, I have . . . sent back the Box . . . leaving to your Choice, whether to insert the Reasons for which you [gave it to me], or bestow the Box upon some more worthy Person, whom you may have an Intention to Honour, be-cause it will equally fit every Body" (*PW* 13:190–91). His need for ex-plicitness is evident even in the smallest details of his life; for instance, arranging a dinner engagement, he tells his guest, "Name your most con-venient hour to dine, and do not say, when you please" (*C* 4:529). Despite Swift's love of explicitness, his own writing is often ambiguous. Readers continue to debate the meaning of the fourth voyage of *Gulliver's Travels* and "Verses on the Death of Dr. Swift" because in certain crucial ways they contain mixed signals and may represent Swift's unwillingness to fal-sify by simplifying or his desire to wallow in the richness of all alternatives.

Part of Swift coveted a place in the hierarchy of power—he wanted to be much more than an Irish dean—yet he could not restrain the urge to-ward wildness that forced him to rip away the veils. In "Verses on the Death of Dr. Swift," he notes more with pride than rue, "HAD he but spar'd his Tongue and Pen, / He might have rose like other Men" (*P* 2:567, 355–56). Swift, indeed, seemed to gain self-definition by angering those in control: he boasts at one point that he has "the perfect illwill of every creature in power, [which he] take[s] to be a high point of merit" (*C* 4:53). All along, his aim was "to vex the world rather than divert it," which, of course, is no way to get ahead in any establishment. His embrace of satire, by his own admission, "hath been an absolute Bar to my Rising in the World" (*C* 4:53), and it is generally agreed that Queen Anne's dislike of *A Tale of a Tub* cost Swift the ecclesiastical preferment in England he wished for.

As punishment for his sins against orthodoxy, he was exiled to Ireland, where, Swift explained, he was "forced to play at small game, to set the beasts here a madding, meerly for want of a better game." He compares himself to a monkey throwing crockery all over the kitchen, just to hear the clatter, a better choice, he says, than dying "here in a rage, like a poisoned rat in a hole" (*C* 3:383). This reductionist explanation of his efforts as mere game-playing belies the idealistic passion that motivated his assault on tyrannies of all sorts. But Swift was suspicious of abstractions, even the ones he believed in.

Shoving against the world and having it shove back is a way of affirming one's power. A reaction, however hostile, is more comforting than indifference. Thus Swift delighted in setting "the beasts . . . a madding" with his writing. Swift says to Pope that he is "not content with despising [the world], but . . . would anger it if [he] could with safety" (*C* 3:117), though he was never really concerned with "safety." He loved to walk along the precipice. No matter how great the risks he encountered as a satirist, Swift is not really envious of another poet who he claims "is wiser than I, because he writes no Satyrs, whereby you know well enough how many great People I disobliged, and suffered by angering great People in Favor" (*C* 5:86). Swift wanted to be noticed, to have his life make a difference in the world. He sought for lasting meaning and located it in the strength of the English language.

2

Language as a Social Fabric

. . . Wit and Weaving had the same beginning. . . .
"Epilogue at the Theatre-Royal,"
P 1 : 276, 37

S wift's fundamental assumptions about language were rooted in the tradition of classical rhetoric and its reinterpretation by the Renaissance humanists. He believed that formulation of ideas into proper language demonstrated man's capacity for reason, that through language men could join together for improvement, that language had an ability to affect men's actions and thoughts, that language is a historical and social institution, and that the meaning of the present is dependent on a remembrance of the past.[1] More than a humanist's pride in the vernacular, Swift's attention to the English language was motivated by the fear that linguistic degradation would result in the destruction of contexts needed for the full sustenance of human liberty,[2] a view he held with unique fervor. His commitment to liberty—"Fair LIBERTY was all his Cry," he says of himself in "Verses on the Death of Dr. Swift" (*P* 2 : 566, 347)—led him to act as well as think. He was not content to be a passive observer[3] but needed to be an active agent in shaping the world the next generation would inherit. The legacy of common forms, particularly those of the church and state,[4] could not be conveyed to posterity unless another cultural artifact, the English language, was preserved and strengthened.

Swift's ideas on the nature of language are implicit in the imagery of cloth and clothing that he persistently associates with verbal expression. Through his use of the cloth-as-discourse metaphor, he demonstrates the interconnection of the common forms of language (traditional, generally accepted usage) with other common forms or patterns inherent in British culture. The social nature of language is evident in his division of the world into "weavers"—those who use language to strengthen historical continuities—and "renders"—those who discard the legacy of the past because they think it limits pursuit of their personal goals. Although Swift does not actually use the terms "weavers" and "renders" (they are my coinages), they accurately label the polarities of language practice he describes.

The image of cloth and clothes is woven into the English language: one talks of manufacturing stories out of whole cloth, following the thread of a narrative, spinning a tale, embroidering an account, sewing up the loose ends of exposition. The metaphor of clothing one's thoughts in suitable (so to speak) language is an ancient one, but probably the best-known example of the image is Alexander Pope's "True wit is Nature to advantage dress'd," an idea also expressed by Lord Chesterfield's dictum that "Style is the dress of thoughts."[5] Just as civilized men must cover their nudity with appropriate clothes to suit them for society, so must they clothe their raw ideas in proper language. As Paul Fussell points out, the Augustan view of language is embodied in the clothing metaphor: "As often as not, style is conceived of as a social symbol like clothing which derives from a sort of public wardrobe. . . . To the Augustan humanist, clothes, like buildings, are static, public, social, completely controllable, and devoid of mysteries. They thus constitute an almost inevitable image for suggesting the humanist sense of the nature and purpose of expression."[6]

Swift exemplifies the proper and improper use of language in the Drapier and the *Tale*-brothers respectively. The Drapier's view of language, as one will see, is that of the humanist described by Fussell—"static, public, social, completely controllable, and devoid of mysteries." The *Tale*-brothers, on the other hand, see language in an opposite way. In their hands it is infinitely mutable, antisocial, self-reflexive or private, and full of mysteries to be "decyphered" when expedient. In the end they do not have control over language; possessed by it, they become insane.

Swift sees language as a fabric woven through a history of usage in which certain patterns are established. Using the common forms of language, therefore, affirms the meaning of culture and the society that fosters it. "Weavers" intuitively understand the importance of cultural continuity and use language in a way that strengthens established values, whereas "renders" shred language to advance their peculiar interests and thereby weaken it. A typical render in Swift's canon is the coxcomb who, "because Words are the Cloathing of our Thoughts, cuts them out, and shapes them as he pleases, and changes them oftner than his Dress" (*The Tatler*, PW 2:176); or the uninspired preacher who uses commonplace books to create a sermon, the result being a "manifest incoherent Piece of Patchwork" (*Holy Orders*, PW 9:76); or the bad playwright who assembles "the unravelld Shreds [with] which / The Under-wits adorn their Speech"

("Vanbrug's House," *P* 1:80, 47–48). Renders' violence against the fabric of language injures not only themselves, by failing to communicate their meaning, but society as a whole, by damaging its medium of collective expression. And renders' lack of concern for the common forms of language reveals their enmity to the other cultural values that Britons have traditionally shared.

Observation persuaded Swift that the renders have the advantage in the Manichean struggle between order and chaos, since, in his view, the world has a natural tendency toward disorder. In particular, the linguistic "ties that bind" are very fragile. These ties need constant reinforcement to hold men together. If the ties fail, men cannot talk to one another and are isolated in their ignorance; no human progress can ensue and their culture will deteriorate. The relation of effective language to the development of civilization is a classical theme, found for instance in Cicero's *De Inventione*, which describes men wandering "at large in fields like animals and liv[ing] on wild fare" until common speech is instituted.[7] One might see the degraded Yahoos as examples of creatures without any common forms of culture. Lacking both fabric and language, they run around naked and express themselves in excrement. They embody the sordid fate of those who cannot communicate with their fellows for mutual improvement.

Swift believed that language, evolved over time, comes to comprise the cultural, intellectual, and spiritual values of the nation, since each word, by continuous usage, grows with accretions of meaning. Speakers of succeeding generations inherit an ever richer lexicon of words and ideas. As the analyses below will demonstrate, Swift assumed that the cloth of language and discourse is composed of threads tying person to person and past to present, binding society together, and cloaking underlying animalism with civilization.

To Swift, renders of language were a general danger because they threatened the very existence of civilization. He felt that Britain was especially in peril because its northern climate is hostile to any enlightenment. As Swift notes in *Hints towards an Essay on Conversation*, "All the little Decorum and Politeness we have are purely forced by Art, and are so ready to lapse into Barbarity" (*PW* 4:92). That Britain's environment is inimical to cultural development is evident, for example, by the disintegration of words: "This perpetual Disposition to shorten our Words, by retrenching the Vowels, is nothing else but a Tendency to lapse into the Barbarity of those *Northern* Nations from whom we are descended. . . . We struggle with an ill climate to improve the nobler Kinds of Fruits" that grow so easily in more southern countries (*Proposal, PW* 4:12–13). Britons must take particular care, therefore, not to let their language fray. Preserving language intact is a constant battle against eroding forces, but all that is humane depends on making the effort.

The contrasting effects of linguistic rending and weaving are dramatized by Peter and Jack in *A Tale of a Tub* and M.B., Drapier in *The Drapier's Letters*. In both works, language or discourse is identified specifically with cloth. At the center of the *Tale* is a father's bequest, with the following provisos, of three identical coats to his three sons: "Their Father's Will was very precise, and it was the main Precept in it, with the greatest Penalties annexed, not to add to, or diminish from their Coats, one Thread, without a positive command in the Will. Now, the Coats their Father had left them were . . . of very good Cloth, and besides, so neatly sown, you would swear they were all of a Piece, but at the same time, very plain, and with little or no Ornament" (*PW* 1:49). Analogously, the language of the will, like the coats, initially is "all of a Piece," having a plain, explicit integrity. As the narrative progresses, however, Peter and Jack alter their coats—the one destroying his by additions, the other by reductions—and at the same time they alter the words of the will to justify their actions. Thus the fabric of the coats is directly correlated to the semantics of the will. And although critics have interpreted the will as the Bible, or the Word, it also can represent the word (lowercase), or traditional language and discourse in general. Swift firmly connects the maintenance of England's linguistic heritage with the perpetuation of the church and the state.

A Tale of a Tub plunges the reader into a nightmarish world controlled by radical amnesiacs, who cannot even remember the cultural forms that their mindless energies endanger.[8] Without a stable cultural context, Swift implies, no lasting meaning is possible, an idea he intricately develops in the "Epistle Dedicatory, to His Royal Highness Prince Posterity," in which the hack narrator imagines a future conversation when the Prince is asked where Modern productions are: "What is become of them. . . . Not to be found! Who has mislaid them? Are they sunk in the Abyss of Things? . . . Is their very Essence destroyed? Who has annihilated them?" (*PW* 1:19). The narrator accuses Posterity of cruelty for killing these undeveloped progenies "before they have so much as learnt their *Mother-Tongue* to beg for Pity" (20). Not only does the narrator continually complain about his lack of memory, he lives in a world in which no one else remembers anything either and there are no transcendent common forms but only transitory, self-referential ones. In a doomed attempt to show Prince Posterity that Modern literature has some enduring value, the narrator tries to compose a list of titles: "The Originals were posted fresh upon all Gates and Corners of Streets; but returning in a very few Hours to take a Review, they were all torn down, and fresh ones in their Places:

I enquired after them among Readers and Booksellers, but I enquired in vain, the *Memorial of them was lost among Men, their Place was no more to be found*" (21). "Truth" in this world is compared to the shapes of clouds in the sky: "In a few Minutes . . . they would all be changed in Figure and Position, new ones would arise, and all we could agree upon would be, that Clouds there were" (21). "*Modern* form[ ]" (27) is an oxymoron. To be Modern is to lack form, structure, logic, permanence, and meaning.

The Preface of the *Tale* continues the vision of a world without permanent frames of reference, a place where words, not being of the mother tongue, do not soar and bind but fall resoundingly into the "Abyss of Things." Language without common forms imperils the other common forms of British life so that, according to the narrator, "the Grandees of *Church* and *State* begin to fall under horrible Apprehensions" (24) of annihilation (a word used repeatedly in the *Tale*). The narrator offers the *Tale* as a temporary means of salvation—it will divert the "Wits" trying to "pick Holes in the weak Sides of Religion and Government" (24)—until "a large Academy [can] be erected," which will contain schools of spelling, pederasty, looking glasses, swearing, criticism, poetry, salivation, hobbyhorses, tops, spleen, gaming, "with many others too tedious to recount" (25). Such an academy, a Modern jumble itself, has little prospect of protecting the church and state against annihilation by Modern forgetfulness of traditional forms and meanings. In the infinitely plastic world of the *Tale*, even such well-known English folk tales as Dick Whittington and his cat can be construed as "the Work of that Mysterious *Rabbi, Jehuda Hannasi*, containing a Defence of the *Gemara* of the *Jerusalem Misna*, and its just preference to that of *Babylon*, contrary to the vulgar opinion" (41). In the devouring sands of the *Tale*, the stable, enduring common sense of the average person—called by the Modern "vulgar opinion"—is anathema because it curbs the "freedom" of the individual to eradicate accrued values and meanings that give form to individual lives within the general context of English culture.

The Epistle Dedicatory to Prince Posterity and the Preface establish the interrelationship of the common forms of British culture, putting special emphasis on the importance of the "*Mother-Tongue*," without which the church and state cannot survive. These key ideas recur in the allegory of the three brothers whose formative years were influenced by the ascendancy of the tailor god (46), an incarnation of the forces that rip and cut the social fabric: materialism, individualism, and faddism. The result—"Clutter and Revolution" (75). The father of the three brothers tried to prevent such waste and chaos by designing coats that never needed a tailor's attention because of their everlasting fabric and their automatically adjusting fit (44). The coats are analogous to the common forms of culture that persist through time yet suit the needs of each age. Only Martin (representing the Church of England) ultimately complies with the conditions of the will and brings his coat into a "State of Innocence" (88), thereby restoring the original pattern and shape.

In contrast, Peter, who is characterized as a scholar and critic, persistently ignores the commonly accepted meaning of the will and substitutes his own fantasies. When the brothers, mesmerized by the dictates of the tailor god, believe they must wear shoulder knots on their coats, Peter examines the authorizing document. Not surprisingly, the will contains no such words, so Peter must fragment other words of the will to form them. Rummaging through the document to collect S,H,O,U,L,D,E,R, K,N,O,T,S, Peter focuses on the isolated letters of the will, not its spirit, as he should.[9] Peter embellishes the will and the coats with his own inventions, which are contrary to the wishes of his father. He distorts the will and the coats simultaneously, for instance, when he adds a codicil to justify his desire to decorate the coats with "*flame coloured Sattin*" (53) lining. The essence of the will is quickly obliterated by Peter's "additions" to its meaning and in a like manner he ruins his coat: "There was hardly a thread of the Original Coat to be seen, but an infinite Quantity of *Lace*, and *Ribbands*, and *Fringe*, and *Embroidery*, and *Points*" (84).

By this extended analogy, Swift implies that altering the common forms with self-inspired embellishment will weaken and ultimately destroy them. The unifying fabric will be rent, and only a heap of odd decorations will remain. Once traditional English, the "*Mother-Tongue*," is displaced as a standard, individual dialects will proliferate until no common tongue prevails. Swift seems to believe in the linguistic version of Gresham's law, that bad or ahistorical usage will drive out the good. Thus Peter's eccentricities represent a serious social danger that cannot be dismissed. If the English language perishes, so will the other common forms fundamental to English life.

Jack, reacting against Peter, destroys the will and his coat in another way: instead of rending their symbolically interrelated fabrics by excessive ornamentation, Jack believes that one should "for the Love of God; Strip, Tear, Pull, Rent, Flay off all" (87; italics omitted). He, therefore, "rent the *main Body* of his *Coat* from Top to Bottom" (86). Simultaneously, Jack destroys the will in a similar fashion, among other things "when he had Fits, burn[ing] two Inches [of it] under his Nose; or if any Thing lay heavy on his Stomach, scrap[ing] off, and swallow[ing] as much of the Powder as would lie on a silver Penny" (122). Jack's habits of interpretation are as eccentric as Peter's, but whereas Peter totally ignores the words in the will, finally locking it out of his sight so he need not waste time circumventing it, Jack follows the document with unnatural literalness. Limiting himself to the letter of the will for all matters, Jack runs into difficulty when he needs to do anything that the will does not specifically mention. He, for instance, ignores "the united Rhetorick of Mankind . . . to make himself clean again" after defecating because that is not spelled out in the will (122). Peter locks the will up; Jack bandages his toe with it. Neither uses language as most people commonly do.

Jack and Peter fail to understand that the common forms are a precious legacy to be shared by all people within the culture. Instead, both see doctrine, policy, and language as their personal property, which they may alter as one alters a garment. In the particular case of language, the *Tale*-brothers embody the prime linguistic corruptions of language against which Swift inveighs: Peter illustrates the dangers of cant and jargon—idiosyncratic additions to the lexicon—and Jack illustrates the dangers of curtailing the traditional range and form of words. In both cases, the result is discourse that is remote from the common linguistic forms that most people in society accept. It is no wonder, then, that both Peter and Jack are referred to as "mad," for madness is typically characterized by socially inappropriate utterance. As the "Digression on Madness" suggests, madness is the normal state of the Modern, who clearly prefers "*Things conceived*" to "*Things past*" and the imagination ("the *Womb* of Things") to the memory, which is "no more than the *Grave*" (108). Altogether there is nothing in the Modern world but *things*.

Cut off from common sense and a memory of the common forms, Peter and Jack degenerate mentally and in their madness come to resemble each other: "Their Humours and Dispositions were not only the same, but there was a close Analogy in their Shape, their Size, and their Mien" (127). Peter's swearing and cursing cause all his neighbors to complain, and Jack offends not only man but God when he sets up an altar to a "new Deity . . . by some called *Babel*, by others, *Chaos*" (124). Even though Peter destroys his coat by additions and Jack destroys his by reductions, the results are the same, "For, as it is the Nature of Rags, to bear a kind of mock Resemblance to Finery, there being a sort of fluttering appearance in both" (128). Jack and Peter, then, are characterized as disturbers of the peace, flouters of social norms. Through them Swift stresses the threat of linguistic rending to religious and secular consensus.[10]

In contrast to renders such as Peter, Jack, and the Modern narrator, M.B., Drapier, as his profession suggests, is a promoter of weaving. (The *Oxford English Dictionary* notes that a draper can weave or sell cloth or both.) Unlike the *Tale*-brothers, who exist outside the inherited sense of

31

language that most share, M.B. knows and appreciates the virtues of plain, traditionally defined words and thus is allied with the necessary orders of reason and civilization. Even though he disingenuously professes not to be book-learned (he makes numerous allusions to his reading), the Drapier is an incarnation of the humanist tradition, using rhetoric to change people's minds so that they act to improve their society.[11] Unlike the engulfing miasma of the *Tale*, the world of the Drapier is firm, its historical anteced-ents well understood, its common values clear, its continuity presumed, its progress a possibility.[12]

As opposed to the *Tale*-denizens, who insist on interpreting tropes in strange, self-serving ways, the Drapier straightforwardly uses the commonplace metaphor of cloth-as-discourse for the centerpiece of his at-tempt to rally the people of Ireland against the imposition of debased coin-age (Wood's Half Pence) on Ireland. In a letter to Lord Molesworth, for instance, the Drapier explains that

> it happened some Months ago, considering with my self, that the *lower and poorer Sort of People* wanted a *plain, strong, coarse Stuff, to defend them against the cold* Easterly *Winds; which then blew very fierce and blasting for a long Time together;* I contrived one on purpose, which sold very well all over the king-dom, and preserved many Thousands from *Agues.* I then made a *second* and a *third* Kind of *Stuffs* for the *Gentry,* with the same Success. . . .
>
> This incited me so far, that I ventured upon a *fourth* Piece, made of the best *Irish* Wool I could get; and I thought it grave and rich enough to be worn by the best *Lord* or *Judge* of the Land. I have now one Piece of stuff to be woven on purpose for your Lordships.
>
> (*PW* 10:82–83)

This passage creates a realm dominated by reason, order, causality, and memory. Language functions as it should: to communicate and reinforce shared values—in this case, the love of liberty. Just as the cloth he makes shields them from the "*cold* Easterly *Winds,*" the Drapier's discourse, if the Irish people heed it, will protect them from British economic oppression. The Drapier's language does explicitly what Swift believes all language ought to do: it improves human society. In the *Tale,* by contrast, language seems to lack any purpose. The narrator offers various reasons for his en-deavors but ends by saying that the real motivation for his discourse was to use the "Collection of Seven Hundred Thirty Eight *Flowers,* and *shining Hints* of the best *Modern* Authors" in his commonplace book that he had been unable "after five Years, to draw, hook, or force into Common Con-versation" (134). His book is for his benefit alone. He dismisses the idea that discourse could improve the world by saying that "there is not, through all Nature, another so callous and insensible a Member as the *World's Posteriors*" (29), and then contradicting himself by declaring that there is no need for improvement, since he is "so entirely satisfied with the whole Procedure of human Things" (32).

Whereas *things* are the *Tale*-teller's concern, the Drapier is an idealist who hates oppression and injustice. He fights to ensure that the Irish are treated with the common forms of fairness that prevail in England, that they are not perceived of, Swift writes in another place, as "one of their *Colonies* of *Out-Casts* in *America*" (*Proposal for the Universal Use of Irish Manufacture, PW* 9:21). Presuming the existence of a collective memory and conscience, the Drapier appeals to the commonly accepted, traditional understanding of the rights and privileges of a British citizen.

The Drapier calls for the unification of the Irish behind a just cause; he seeks to strengthen society, not disrupt it; "I will lay before you, how you ought to act in common Prudence, and according to the *Laws of your Country*" (*PW* 10:4). In contrast to antisocial recidivists like Peter and Jack, M.B. is a self-styled champion of law and order. Fearing that self-interest could fragment the Irish into babbling factions, the Drapier compels them to speak against Wood's tyranny with one voice and language: "I am confident that the most ignorant among you can safely swear from your own Knowledge, that [Wood] is a most notorious Lyar in every Article; the direct, contrary being so manifest in the whole Kingdom, that if the Occasion required, we might get it confirmed *under Five hundred thousand Hands*" (65). The Drapier, then, using mutually understood language, unites the citizens of Ireland for their common good, whereas Peter and Jack foment social disintegration with their eccentric and egocentric misuse of the will, or the (English) word.

Unlike the *Tale*-brothers and the Modern hack, the Drapier is guided by common sense in understanding words. His interpretations, not peculiar to him, are in agreement with others' opinions, a point he is at pains to make clear. In his citation of the law to prove his case against Wood's Half Pence, for example, M.B. gives his source, adding, "This Book is very Ancient, and of great Authority for the Time in which it was wrote." He then interprets a clause and concludes persuasively that "this is the True *Construction* of the *Act*, [which] appears not only from the plain Meaning of the Words, but from my Lord *Coke's* Observation upon it" (9). Unlike Peter, who declines to name the book in which he finds the bizarre information that fringe means broomstick (one suspects he himself is the author of this fact), the Drapier is very careful to acknowledge his references and allows his interpretations to be checked by those who would. Swift's rhetorical strategy is to create a persona who claims not to distort or contrive the meaning of the words he reads. Allying himself with the common man and common sense, he purports to react to words as any sane, native speaker might. To reinforce his ethos of a man with a cultural memory, Swift has the Drapier add the corroboration of "Ancient" authorities.

The Drapier is able to muster the Irish people to oppose Wood's Half Pence because he speaks a language accessible to all. The individual letters to the different social classes may vary in rhetorical appeal, yet basically all have the same direct, conversational style. Although he is modestly educated, the Drapier stresses that he has "endeavoured (. . . without the Help of Books) to improve that small Portion of Reason, which God hath pleased to give me; and when Reason plainly appears before me, I cannot turn away my Head from it" (28). Self-consciously a common man speaking to common men, the Drapier contrasts the ordinary language with which he converses with his fellows to the "Terms of Art" employed by Wood and his henchmen. He, for instance, decries as uncommon usage Wood's convenient designation of Ireland as a "depending Kingdom": "*A depending Kingdom* is a *modern Term of Art;* unknown, as I have heard to all antient *Civilians*, and *Writers upon Government;* . . . [thus the term] is now talked of, without any Ground of *Law, Reason, or common Sense*" (62). In the same manner, the Drapier shows how Wood has twisted the usual meaning of *prerogative*, saying that if the Irish people accept his definition, the world will conclude that "we have neither *common Sense*, nor *common Senses*" (55). Throughout the *Drapier's Letters*, Swift shows the radical divorce of Wood's ahistorical perceptions from common sense and common forms, which are grounded in a memory of the past.

To improve his arguments, the Drapier through conversation assimilates the combined wisdom of a variety of people in contrast to the *Tale*-brothers' ignorance-producing antisocial isolation. M.B. notes, "I have discoursed with several of my own, and also other Trades; with many Gentlemen of both City and Country; and also, with great numbers of Farmers, Cottagers, and Labourers" (16). Establishing the nature of the general consensus and sharpening his wits in this way prepares the Drapier for his battle against the bureaucratic Goliath, his only weapon being his clear, ordinary language: "How shall I, a poor ignorant Shopkeeper, utterly unskilled in Law, be able to answer so weighty an Objection? I will try what can be done by plain Reason, unassisted by Art, Cunning or Eloquence" (29). Implicit in this statement is Swift's equation of verbal articulation with the reasoning faculty, a concept derived from the classical rhetoricians, which is at the center of his idea of "Proper Words in proper Places" (to be discussed in Chapter 7). The Drapier writes to liberate the Irish people, whereas the Moderns in the *Tale* want to confine everyone else's ideas to the same narrow "Length, and Breadth, and Heighth of [their] own" (105). In short, through his proper use of language to foster social coherence by binding together those of common sense, M.B., Drapier, epitomizes the humane values that Swift wished to encourage.

The word machine at the Academy of Lagado in the third book of *Gulliver's Travels* can be seen as a caricature of the Drapier's loom. Like a loom, the word machine is called a "Frame" (*PW* 11 : 182), and the illustration in the text shows strands intersecting at right angles that look like warp and woof. Whether or not one agrees that the word machine is an anti-loom, it does symbolize the forces of linguistic fragmentation that Swift abhorred. Instead of promoting the weave of common language, the Lagadan word machine generates verbal entropy—completely mindless, contextless arrangements of words divorced from the "Pattern of Human Learning" represented by usual formations of the English language. Gulliver describes the word machine as follows:

> It was Twenty Foot square, placed in the Middle of the Room. The Superfices was composed of several Bits of Wood, about the Bigness of a Dye, but some larger than others. They were all linked together by slender Wires. These Bits of Wood were covered on every Square with Paper pasted on them; and on these Papers were written all the Words of their Language in their several Moods, Tenses, and Declensions, but without any Order. . . . The Pupils at [the projector's] Command took each of them hold of an Iron Handle, whereof there were Forty fixed round the Edges of the Frame; and giving them a sudden Turn, the whole Disposition of the Words was entirely changed.
> (184)

The pupils transcribe the words at every turn of the handles, resulting, Gulliver says, in "several Volumes in large Folio already collected, of broken Sentences, which [the projector] intended to Piece together" (184), much as the *Tale*-teller assembles the fragments in his commonplace book. Here, although spinning occurs, no weaving takes place. The Lagadan word machine reduces the production of discourse to a mechanical process; words are mere things to be manipulated like dice. No minds are necessary to create the "Volumes in large Folio," only strong arms to turn the cranks.

Swift believed that to foster any sweetness and light man must continually fight against anarchy on all sides. Writing to Stella in this vein,

Swift jots some hasty notes: "Method is good in all things. Order governs the world. The Devil is the author of confusion." He lists those who impose order: "a general of an army, a minister of state; to descend lower, a gardener, a weaver" (*JS* 1:72). In *A Tale of a Tub*, it is a weaver, in clear, bold language, who reminds the pushy slob who crowds in to hear the mountebank of the common forms of decent behavior to promote freedom for all: "At last, a Weaver . . . could hold not longer: A plague confound you (said he) for an over-grown Sloven. . . . Is not the Place as free for us as for you? Bring your own Guts to a reasonable Compass . . . and then I'll engage we shall have room enough for us all" (*PW* 1:28; italics omitted). On the loom, the weaver, through human agency and choice, produces fabric. The Lagadan word machine, however, generates verbal "Collections" (*PW* 11:184), a word that is invariably pejorative in Swift's lexicon and signifies to him an orderless, inhuman, and materialistic jumble, of which the Epicurean universe is a paradigm.

Using the Epicurean universe as a metaphor for Babel, Swift speaks in his early "Ode to the Athenian Society" of the peculiarity of Modern wit that is no more than "a *Crowd of Atoms* justling in a heap" (*P* 1:20, 127). Similarly he describes the noisy "rout" of female card players by saying that "The Jumbling Particles of Matter / In Chaos made not such a Clatter" ("Journal of a Modern Lady," *P* 2:450, 184–85). In the *Tritical Essay upon the Faculties of the Mind*, the speaker asks, "How can the *Epicureans* Opinion be true, that the Universe was formed by a fortuitous Concourse of Atoms[?]; which I will no more believe, than that the accidental Jumbling of the Letters in the Alphabet, could fall by chance into a most ingenious and learned Treatise of Philosophy" (*PW* 1:246–47).[13] "Accidental Jumbling" exactly describes the Lagadan word machine. Babel or Chaos results, Swift suggests, from a random, thought-free process in which words are removed from their ordinary connotative context and volleyed about like balls to create ephemeral patterns like the arrangement, at any given moment, of atoms in a void or the shape of clouds in the sky. Meaning can be found only within the common forms of culture, of which the English language is perhaps the most important, Swift implies, because it expresses all the rest.

3

Private Use of Language: The Conversational
Microcosm

> To discourse, and to attend,
> Is to *help* yourself, and Friend.
> Conversation is but *carving*,
> Carve for all, yourself is starving.
>
> . . . .
>
> And, that you may have your Due,
> Let your Neighbors *carve* for you.
> >> "Epistle to a Lady," *P* 2:633–34,
> >> 121–25, 131–32

The primary function of language, for Swift, was to bind people together, a process he generally described as conversation. Judging from the amount Swift wrote on the topic, conversation was of paramount importance to him, in part because he was an heir of the Renaissance courtesy tradition emphasizing practical improvement of the verbal and behavioral forms that made men more civilized, and in part because he saw conversation as an embodiment of utopian possibilities.[1] People talking together in a casual and congenial fashion represented to him a model of an ideal, albeit miniature, society. Swift had, as Herbert Davis characterizes it, an "almost extravagant notion of conversation,"[2] even in an age that valued conversation much more than our own.

Conversation is typically private, informal discourse, whose only requirement, in Swift's view, is that it "entertain and improve" the participants (*Hints towards an Essay on Conversation, PW* 4:92). In a mixed group, obviously, the common forms of language are necessary so that all can understand, but in an intimate relationship, conventional linguistic forms

37

may be abandoned in favor of an ersatz language the participants use only with one another.

Good Conversation

In *Hints towards an Essay on Conversation*, Swift states that in the neglect of conversation "we see how human Nature is most debased" (94). Conversation is a manifestation of two related, specifically human characteristics: sociability and rationality. To choose the proper words for discourse requires an act of discrimination Swift equates with human reason, a quality that allows man to see the benefits of social relationships with his fellows.

Good conversation, however, is not a natural occurrence. It must be carefully nurtured, yet it is an achievement within the reach of all, for although not everyone can be a brilliant wit, yet "Nature hath left every Man a Capacity of being agreeable." Unlike some other social ideals such as having a "true Friend, a good Marriage, a perfect Form of Government"—good conversation is easily attainable. Indeed, Swift notes that he was prompted to write his *Hints towards an Essay on Conversation* because of "mere Indignation, to reflect that so useful and innocent a Pleasure, so fitted for every Period and Condition of Life, and so much in all Men's Power, should be so much neglected and abused" (88).

Conversation is an organic process in which the participants give and take information and come to know others' thoughts in a way that produces the highest pleasure: "The two chief ends of conversation," Swift says, "are to entertain and improve those we are among, or to receive those Benefits ourselves" (29). This enjoyable and enlightening reciprocity also characterizes conversations with written words. According to the *Oxford English Dictionary*, *conversation* was used to signify "occupation or engagement with *things*, in the way of business or study," but Swift often uses the word more literally to imply an actual discourse with an author. He remarks, "When I am reading a Book, whether wise or silly, it seemeth to me to be alive and talking to me" (*Thoughts on Various Subjects, PW* 4:253). Not only do authors talk to him, he talks back. His extensive marginalia indicate that reading for him was an active conversational process, one he recommends to others. Specifically comparing conversation with reading, he tells a young clergyman, for instance, that he should not read "without entering into the Genius and Spirit of the Author" (*Holy Orders, PW* 9:76).

Good conversations are binding, not rending. Conversing to gain advantage or to injure and destroy others is a Hobbesian version that Swift rejects. Moreover, social discourse should be congenial and spontaneous, a

38

specific, engaged response to the words of others. Thus mechanical and bestial behavior, such as the inane repetition of stories, insertion of choice witticisms regardless of context, listening without talking, and talking without listening—all cited in *Hints towards an Essay on Conversation*—must be avoided. Quite simply, good conversation elicits the qualities that characterize human beings at their best.

Conversation is essential to human understanding because it exposes men to views beyond their own narrow perspectives. Perhaps influenced by the classical tradition that revered the idea of dialogue, Swift and his peers looked to social intercourse as the prime means of determining reality. As William Piper explains it, for them "truth [was] the product of spirited but lucid talk between plain, sensible men."[3] Good conversation demands that the participants constantly modify their outlooks as added information from other sources arrives. Among sociable, discriminating people, truth can be winnowed from error.

Since the range of individual inquiry is limited and divine revelation is infrequent, good conversation provides man with the fullest view of the world he can usually achieve. In the "Apology" to *A Tale of a Tub*, for instance, Swift claims, perhaps ironically, that "By the Assistance of some thinking, and much Conversation, he had endeavor'd to strip himself of as many real Prejudices as he could" (*PW* 1:1; italics omitted). As Swift notes in his sermon "On the Trinity," "*Reason* itself is true and just, but the *Reason* of every particular Man is weak and wavering, perpetually swayed and turned by his Interests, his Passions, and his Vices" (*PW* 9:166). A single man's view is necessarily incomplete; completeness can be approached only when several minds come together. One of the Modern's chief sins is pride in self-sufficiency that promotes the belief that the wisdom lodged in the great tradition of human learning is irrelevant.

Swift's writing is full of his conviction that conversation with books and people will bring men closer to truth, such as it can be known by mortals. This idea underlies his twitting of Stella when he tells her, "Your judgment is spoiled by ill company and want of reading" (*JS* 1:315). In a similar vein, he sarcastically praises the conversations of the October Club (a group of radical Tories) for their ability "very much [to] improve each others Understanding, correct and fix [their] Judgment, and prepare [themselves] against the Designs of the opposite Party" (*Some Advice to the October Club*, *PW* 6:71). As Swift's irony suggests, the self-reflexive members of the October Club were incapable of having enlightening discussions that might modify their crazy visions. In like manner, Gulliver's refusal at the end of his *Travels* to talk to his wife, family, or indeed any "English Yahoo" signals his distance from rationality. Swift continually stresses that an accurate picture of the world can be assembled only through collective effort, with each person's perspective providing a small piece of the whole.

Swift believed that to ensure the efficacy of conversation, one needs to expose oneself to a wide range of views. In this vein, he urges young preachers to study, not just the Christian fathers and the Bible, but heathen philosophers, "By the reading of which, you will soon discover your Mind and Thoughts to be enlarged, your Imagination extended and refined, your Judgment directed, your Admiration lessened, and your Fortitude increased" (*Holy Orders*, *PW* 9:74). Ideally, exposure to other people's thought helps uproot error, although Swift jokingly admits that when he reads an author he agrees with, he proclaims, "*That was excellently observed*," but "When we differ, there I pronounce him to be *mistaken*" (*Thoughts on Various Subjects*, *PW* 4:248). Even in this process, though, Swift is forced to evaluate his own thinking.

In *Hints towards an Essay on Conversation*, Swift encourages males and females to talk together for the betterment of both. The women will prevent the men from tending toward vulgarity, and the men will contribute their knowledge of the wide world to the women. Not to share in lively exchange with members of the opposite sex, Swift tells a young woman, would limit her intellectual horizons: "It is a shame for an *English* Lady not to relish such Discourses, not to improve by them, and endeavor by Reading and Information, to have her Share in those Entertainments; rather than turn aside, as it is the usual Custom, and consult with the Woman who sits next her, about a new Cargo of Fans" (*Advice to a Young Lady*, *PW* 4:91). Only by contact with a large number of other thinking minds, through eclectic reading and a varied acquaintanceship, can one come to understand ideas of lasting importance.

Although Swift did not agree with the aims of the Royal Society, its promotion of conversation among people of differing viewpoints as an approach to knowable truths was similar to his. Indeed, both were a reaction, to some extent, to the rampant "enthusiasm" perceived to be prevalent during the English Civil War. The society's historian, Thomas Sprat, advocated admitting all people of merit, regardless of rank, profession, national origin, party, or religion, to "make the *Royal Society* the general *Banck* and Free-port of the World," a veritable treasury of human experience.[4] Like Swift, Sprat admired the effect of active discussion among disparate individuals as a way to prevent the calcification of private (as opposed to common) sense. Swift allegorizes this concept in *The Battel of the Books* when he contrasts the spider, who spins webs out of his own excrement, with the bee, who gathers materials from various sources "to fill our Hives with Honey and Wax, thus furnishing Mankind with the two Noblest of Things, which are Sweetness and Light" (*PW* 1:151; italics omitted).

Mutual talk provides an opportunity for the members of a group to know themselves and each other better. The common forms of language combined with the common forms of decent behavior, or politeness, should shatter the facades and misunderstandings that breed dissension. In an arena where mutual respect is enforced, petty differences can be aired and eliminated. Thomas Sprat expresses this belief in the benefits of politeness when he brags about the efficacious debates of the Royal Society, which succeed, he says, because of the "decency, the gravity, the plainess [of language], and the calmness" by which they are conducted.[5] In a letter to Swift, Pope claims to have practiced such a balanced dialogue and acquired a dispassionate perspective through his "Life & Conversation . . . among all Sexes, Parties & Professions. . . . The Civilities I have met with from Opposite sets of People have hinder'd me from being either Violent or sowre to any Party" (*C* 2:459). Effective conversation creates an equilibrium that allows objective analysis.

The give and take of conversation forces recognition of the ideas of others and prevents self-absorption. Conversation, therefore, is antithetical to pride, which tends to isolate a person in his own mind, cutting him off from common sense and social obligations. In his sermon *On Mutual Subjection*, Swift expatiates on the humbling influence of mutual discourse:

> But this Subjection we all owe one another is no where more necessary, than in the common Conversations of Life; for without it there could be no Society among Men. If the Learned would not sometimes submit to the Ignorant, the Wise to the Simple, the Gentle to the Froward, the Old to the Weaknesses of the Young, there would be nothing but everlasting Variance in the World. This our Savior confirmed by his own Example; for he appeared in the Form of a Servant, and washed his Disciples Feet. . . . A thorough Practice of this Duty of subjecting ourselves to the Wants and Infirmities of each other, would extinguish in us the Vice of Pride.
> (*PW* 9:144–45)

Good conversation, the social use of language in private life, is to Swift a model of human harmony. Common sense and reason prevail to foster pleasant, informative reciprocity, which is a model for human organization in general. Swift's utopian hopes for conversation are expressed by a maxim in "Thoughts on Various Subjects" from the Swift–Pope *Miscellanies:* "There is nothing wanting to make all rational and disinterested

People in the World, of one Religion, but they should talk together every day."[6] Mutual subjection makes "us rest contented in the several Stations of Life wherein God hath thought fit to place us" and simultaneously erodes these hierarchies by bringing us eventually "back as it were to that early State of the Gospel when Christians had all things in common" (*On Mutual Subjection*, PW 9:147).

Swift hoped that the dynamic of conversation would level the differences between Bolingbroke and Oxford that were threatening to collapse the Tory administration in 1713–14. By backing out at the last moment, Swift tricked the two leaders into riding by themselves to Windsor, a trip the threesome usually made. He recalled thinking, decades after the incident took place, that if the two men just conversed with each other for the length of the journey, "they would come to some éclaircissement" (*C* 5:45–46). Unfortunately, the scheme did not work. Oxford and Bolingbroke emerged from the coach with their animosities intact. At the time, the Earl of Peterborough scoffed at Swift's idealistic stratagems to make peace between the two ministers, demanding, "How came you to frame a System (in the Times we Live in) to govern the world by Love" (*C* 1:235).

Swift saw talking things out as one way of moving toward political and social harmony. In *The Examiner* Swift states that "if two Men would argue on both Sides with Fairness, good Sense, and good Manners; it would be no ill Entertainment to the Town, and perhaps the most effectual Means to reconcile us" (*PW* 3:35–36). Making issues explicit in conversation allows men to establish common ground or to realize that their differences are groundless, a point illustrated by a parable Swift relates in *The Drapier's Letters:* "I have heard of a Quarrel in a Tavern, where all were at Daggers-drawing, till one of the Company cryed out, desiring to know the *Subject of the Quarrel;* which, when none of them could tell, they put up their Swords, sat down, and passed the rest of the Evening in *Quiet*" (*PW* 10:134).

Good conversation depends on a standard common language, a linguistic medium of exchange that ensures general access to ideas in books and people. Without a national standard, people from various parts of England might have difficulty communicating if regional linguistic differences deepened or if the products of the London presses became completely adulterated with cant. Moreover, if the language continued to change, the discourse of one age would be undecipherable by succeeding ones. The human waste and misery that would ensue are dramatized by the plight of the immortal Struldbruggs in *Gulliver's Travels*. Gulliver notes: "The Language of this Country being always upon the Flux, the

Struldbruggs of one Age do not understand those of another; neither are they able after two Hundred Years to hold any Conversation (farther than by a few general Words) with their Neighbors the Mortals; and thus they lye down under the Disadvantage of living like Foreigners in their own Country" (*PW* 11:213). Swift did what he could to correct, improve, and ascertain the English tongue so that all members of British society could converse with their fellows in the next shire or the next century and not feel "like Foreigners in their own Country."

Bad Conversation

Herbert Davis suggests that Swift's view of conversation "sharpens and intensifies his satire against all the things in society which at various levels threaten to ruin it."[7] The factors that "threaten to ruin" conversation are all corrigible because, as Swift notes, "The Reason . . . why Conversation runs so low . . . is not the Defect of Understanding; but Pride, Vanity, ill Nature, Affectation, Singularity, Positiveness; or some other Vice, the Effect of a wrong Education" (*Thoughts on Various Subjects, PW* 4:244). Many of Swift's satires, are forms of a "right education" to encourage good conversation by pointing out how antisocial, irrational behavior can destroy the possibilities of communication and thus create dystopias. A number of Swift's poems treat the theme of conversation, and I have chosen to discuss two in detail that dramatize particularly well the inimical effects of bad conversation. In the first, "The Dean's Reasons for Not Building at Drapier's Hill," the possibilities of a pleasant society are destroyed by one-sided silence. In the second poem, "Journal of a Modern Lady," talk abounds, but it does not "entertain and improve" the company. Instead of binding the people in this little world, the pseudo-conversation atomizes them.

"The Dean's Reasons for Not Building at Drapier's Hill" humorously explains in verse Swift's argument against erecting a house on land he had bought at Market Hill to be near his friends, Sir Arthur Acheson and his wife, Anne. Even though the land was situated in the Irish countryside, an unlikely locale in which to find truly civilized commerce, the rhetoric of the poem implies that Swift had entertained the hope of creating a personal utopia there. The hostility of the place did not frighten Swift because he imagined that the bulk of his time would be spent chatting with the erudite Sir Arthur, whom he dubbed "the Knight of Gosford."

> How could I form so wild a vision,
> To seek, in deserts, Fields Elysian?

> To live in fear, suspicion, variance,
> With Thieves, Fanatics, Barbarians?
>
> . . . .
>
> [But] With so conversible a friend,
> It would not signify a pin
> Whatever climate you were in.
> <div align="center">(<i>P</i> 3:899, 15–18, 24–26)</div>

Yet although Sir Arthur, like all human beings, is able to converse, he refuses to. Swift finds that he cannot elicit the most basic responses from his putative friend. Swift asks,

> . . . what advantage comes
> To me [. . .]
>
> . . . .
>
> Though I should see him twice a day,
> And am his neighbor cross the way;
> If all my rhetoric must fail
> To strike him for a pot of ale?
> (27–32)

It soon becomes clear that the "Thieves, Fanatics, and Barbarians" that Swift feared might inhabit the rural Irish "desert" are all embodied in Sir Arthur himself. Because Sir Arthur is a man of more than usual learning and taste, who nonetheless keeps his ideas selfishly to himself, Swift characterizes him first as a "us'rer" (28) and then as a "miser" (36): his "uncommunicative heart, / Will scarce one precious word impart" (42–43). He steals from Swift by denying him the conversation that would improve both their lives.

In addition to being a "Thief," Sir Arthur is a "Fanatic," wholly sucked into his own vortex, "rapt in speculations deep, / His outward senses fast asleep" (45–46). An extreme enthusiast, the Knight of Gosford completely insulates himself from everyday concerns. John Bullitt suggests that such people are less than human: "When the mind depends upon fanciful and therefore fictional associations for the facts upon which the reason must operate, the mind loses the flexibility of common sense and operates with an inhuman rigidity."[8] This mechanical behavior is evident in the knight. Swift gripes that while he talks Sir Arthur

44

> . . . a song will hum,
> Or, with his fingers, beat the drum;
> Beyond the skies transports his mind,
> And leaves a lifeless corpse behind.
> (47–50)

Sir Arthur's brain waves are flat; to outside appearances he is a "lifeless corpse." His self-reflexive philosophizing denies him communication with both nature and man. His preference for his own private visions transforms him into an automaton—humming and tapping like a well-oiled machine.

When Swift contemplated the threat of "Barbarians" in the countryside, he could not have foreseen that Sir Arthur would be chief among them. Neither cultivating human relationships nor his garden, Sir Arthur fails to nurture civilized values:

> His rural walks he ne'er adorns;
> Here poor Pomona sits on thorns:
> And there neglected Flora settles
> Her bum upon a bed of nettles.
> (91–94)

The images of decay reinforce the general suggestion that Sir Arthur's silence is dangerously antisocial, for the untended garden is an archetypal symbol of cultural desuetude.

In contrast to his portrait of Sir Arthur as aloof and lifeless, Swift presents himself as engaged and vital. He says he has no time for "high flying" philosophy and brags that his concerns are more down to earth: "[I] send my mind (as I believe) less / Than others do, on errands sleeveless" (53–54), such as trying "To understand Malebranch or Cambray" (52). He compares Sir Arthur to a "bust," an image that suggests his lifelessness and his incomplete nature—a head without a body. In contrast, Swift portrays himself as an integrated human being: "My spirits with my body progging, / Both hand in hand together jogging" (57–58). Unlike Sir Arthur, Swift feels the need to communicate—"I talk, as talk I must" (67)—and he knows the importance of listening, even when it is difficult at times, as for instance, when someone is telling "a tale humdrum" (55). While Sir Arthur prefers to keep to himself and study arcane tomes, Swift depicts himself as one who enjoys the conversation of his country neighbors and simple pleasures, like reading *Tom Thumb*.

The Knight of Gosford thinks he can exist without the ordinary communion that most find pleasant and beneficial. Although Swift cannot make Sir Arthur see the abstract value of friendly talk, he points out to him its practical implications. Having been rebuffed, Swift will not inform Sir Arthur when people cut down his hedges, steal his milk, pilfer his fruit, and let their pigs root up his meadow. Sir Arthur will begin to suffer not just spiritually but materially from a lack of commerce with Swift. In this way, silence generates silence, and the "Abyss of Things" lies gaping below. The integrity of the little society on Drapier's Hill is threatened because men will not join together against the forces of entropy.

Despite his efforts, Swift cannot attain an "intercourse of minds" (64) with the Knight of Gosford because of his silence. Swift also demonstrates that intellectual union can fail to occur when there is ample talking: utterance is not the same as conversation. Many conversations are merely pseudo-conversations. On the surface they may resemble social colloquies, but upon closer examination they prove to be completely antisocial. Although all men are born with a quintessentially human "Capacity of being *agreeable*" they often abdicate their human potential and become either animals or machines.

In "Journal of a Modern Lady" (*P* 2:444–53) pseudo-conversation resulting from animalism and mechanism is fully described. The poem records the words that fill the "Female Day" (35), yet none of the discourse bears any resemblance to the type of conversation Swift felt necessary for the fulfillment of the human spirit and the stability of society. The "modern Dame" (38) starts talking as soon as she awakens—at noon! Staring into the mirror, she barrages her maid:

> "*Betty*, pray
> "Don't I look frightfully to Day:
> "But, was it not confounded hard?
> "Well, if I ever touch a Card:
> "Four *Mattadores*, and lose *Codill!*
> "Depend upon't, I never will.
> "But run to *Tom*, and bid him fix
> "The Ladies here to Night by Six."
> (48–55)

Of course, the vanity that motivates the first question precludes an honest answer—and Betty would have a hard time reciprocating in this "conversation" anyway. Talking to her image in the mirror, the lady is the epitome of the arrogant Modern who does not know what she lacks. Nor will she ever find out. Yet her deficiencies are clearly evident in the confused and ungrammatical nature of her monologue. Since she jabbers only to please herself and never listens to others, the niceties of logic and form are superfluous to her.

In the next great event of the day, "Enter the Folks with Silks and Lace: / Fresh Matter for a World of Chat" (79–80). Here the word *matter* is key, for nothing is discussed in the Modern "World of Chat" but *things*. Although a verbal exchange of sorts does take place, it is not a mutual exploration of ideas, but rather a pro forma haggle over consumer goods. After "This Business of Importance [is] o'er" (90), the Footman approaches "in his usual Phrase" (92) saying that dinner is ready; she answers in "her usual Style" (94) that she is not prepared. After finally arriving at the table, the Modern lady "acts her Part, / Has all the Dinner-Cant by Heart" (99–100). No rational processes formulate her thoughts. Like a wind-up doll, she spews forth meaningless verbiage on cue. The poet-recorder quotes the mechanical dinner monologue at length and then notes that

> with all this paultry Stuff,
> She sits tormenting every Guest,
> Nor gives her Tongue one Moment's Rest,
> In Phrases battered, stale, and trite,
> Which Modern Ladies call polite. . . .
> (109–13)

The next opportunity for the "intercourse of minds"—the ladies gathering for evening tea—is characterized as such a babel that "the God of *silence* flew, / And fair *Discretion* left the Place" (119–20). This is another antisocial social event. The poet-recorder realizes that he is inadequate to his task: his discriminatory faculties are completely overwhelmed by the ladies' incoherent prolixity:

> Why should I ask of thee, my Muse,
> An hundred Tongues, as Poets use,
> When, to give ev'ry Dame her due,
> An hundred Thousand were too few!
> Or how should I, alas! relate
> The sum of all their senseless prate. . . .
> (136–41)

The "senseless prate" is vicious gossip to shred those both present and absent. Everyone talks at once; no one listens. Words are not used to connect the speakers to each other or to a knowledge of the world but to acquire domination over others. This is a Hobbesian world of continuous war; all talk for victory. Governed by behavior that "passes . . . for common Form" (271), the ladies have become predatory animals in a jungle, or worse yet, atoms whirling in the void.

The Modern lady probably acquired her conversational skills by reading one of the many books that purport to improve conversation but actually undermine all humanistic premises. Swift parodies these conversation "cookbooks" in *A Compleat Collection of Genteel and Ingenious Conversation . . . in Several Dialogues*, commonly known as *Polite Conversation*, yet his parody is hard to distinguish from some of the seriously-intended guidebooks to manners published at the time.[9] In the introduction to *Polite Conversation*, the Modern persona, Simon Wagstaff, demands that his readers completely memorize all the hackneyed expressions in the dialogues, the gestures to accompany them, and the appropriate places to laugh (these are supposed to be marked with asterisks). He touts the work as a "Collection," a term Swift associates with chaos.

Wagstaff's dialogues are almost unreadable. The text is a patchwork of time-worn aphorisms and repartee stitched together from Wagstaff's commonplace book. Commonplace, however, is not the same as common form, and indeed the talk in these dialogues is far from what is normally accepted, a fact of which Wagstaff is proud. Unlike ordinary conversation that requires no "great Study or Genius" (*Hints, PW* 4:87), Wagstaff's brand of polite conversation requires "much Time, Study, Practice, and Genius, before it arrives to Perfection," sufficient obstacles to prevent such a mode of discourse from "falling into common Hands" (*PW* 4:112).

Not only are the characters of *Polite Conversation* mindlessly mechanical in their relations with one another, they are also bestial. Their table manners, for example, are appalling, and the stage directions include such items as "Miss spits" and "Colonel hawks." Lewdness abounds. At one point, Miss Notable is forced to scream, "Can't you keep your filthy Hands to yourself?" (191). The final dialogue, with the women only, is filled with salacious innuendo. As Lady Smart says, "'Tis nothing what we say among ourselves" (196). Again, bad conversation creates a Hobbesian dystopia with "every man, [warring] against every man."[10] No information is exchanged, no pleasure is provided, no understanding emerges. Such talk rends the social fabric and may ultimately destroy it. *Polite Conversation* is an eschatological vision.

The analyses above demonstrate how the lack of good conversation generates chaos. Without rational, congenial talk, "all Society is lost" ("To Dr. Delany," *P* 1:217, 73). Good conversation, though, was not just an abstract ideal for Swift. It was one of his greatest personal pleasures.

Conversation in Swift's Life

When Swift thought of the joys he had shared with his friends, he thought of their talks together. Reminiscing the night of Stella's funeral, Swift wrote a memorial for her that primarily eulogized her as an excellent conversationalist. Truth and graciousness flourished in her presence: "If a good thing were spoken, but neglected, she would not let it fall, but set it in the best light to those who were present" (*On the Death of Mrs. Johnson, PW* 5 : 234). Stella guided the insecure to their points, for "she laught at no mistakes they made, but helped them out with modesty" (234). She was not only a good talker but a good listener, fully devoted to making the gathering profitable for all participants: "She never had the least absence of mind in conversation, nor given to interruption, or appeared eager to put in her word by waiting impatiently until another had done" (230). Thus she was free of the prime faults of conversation Swift cites in his *Hints towards an Essay on Conversation*. Writing to Sheridan of Stella's death, Swift laments, "I have long been weary of the World, and shall for my small remainder of Years be weary of Life, having forever lost that Conversation, which could only make it tolerable" (*C* 3 : 147).

Swift relished his own talent in creating lively conversation. While in London, he sent synopses of various discussions to Stella, at one point commenting, "Is it not silly to write all this? but it gives you an idea what our conversation is with mixt company" (*JS* 1 : 304). His ability to talk with all manner of people was a source of pride. He bragged of his success in the conversational clubs established by both Oxford and Bolingbroke and of his open-mindedness in conversing even with his Whig opponents such as Addison (*C* 2 : 370). Some of his friends did not understand his eclectic taste in talk. Lord Orrery, for example, disapprovingly writes of Swift's seeking out conversation "with waggoners, hostelers, and persons of that rank; and he used to lye at night in houses where he found written over the door, *Lodgings for a Penny*." [11] A predilection for the talk of common folk can be seen in his letter from Holyhead, where, stuck waiting for good weather so his ship could sail, Swift cast about for diversion: "I should be glad to converse with Farmers or shopkeepers, but none of them speak English. A Dog is better company than the Vicar [a fellow traveler], for I rememb[e]r him of old" (*Holyhead Journal, PW* 5 : 204). In Dublin he enjoyed chatting with the pin-sellers and gingerbread hawkers who plied the streets near St. Patrick's Cathedral. Swift refused to be bound by the limits of what others might consider "proper" discourse.

Swift succeeded in "entertaining and improving" his friends, as their comments on his conversation demonstrate—comments that go beyond

49

mere compliment. Bolingbroke, writing from France, told him that "if I could have half an hours conversation with you . . . I would barter whole hours of life" (*C* 2 : 219). Oxford experienced the same sense of deprivation when apart from Swift: "Two years retreat has made me taste the conversation of my Dearest Friend with greater relish, that even at the time my being charm'd with it in our frequent journeys to Windsor" (*C* 2 : 282). Arbuthnot aired similar feelings: "I am sure I can never forgett yow, till I meett with, (what is impossible) another whose conversation I can so much delight in. . . . god knows I write this with tears in my eyes" (*C* 2 : 122). And Pope recalled his colloquies with Swift as a foreshadowing of heaven: "The two summers we past together dwell always on my mind, like a vision which gave me a glympse of a better life and better company, than this world otherwise afforded" (*C* 4 : 278). The eighteenth century put a higher premium on conversation than we do in the present, but nonetheless these expressions of admiration seem to illustrate that Swift had an extraordinary effect on those with whom he discoursed.

Swift's exile to Ireland removed him from direct conversation with some of his most stimulating colleagues, although he maintained contact with them through writing. Once in Ireland he created a new circle of friends whose talk stirred his mind, albeit in different eddies. Toward the end of his life, however, deafness, which he called his "unconversable disorder" (*C* 3 : 35ff), removed him from everyday talk. He laments that the loss of the "sense of hearing . . . is the greatest loss of any, and more comfortless than even being blind; I mean in the article of company" (*C* 5 : 64).

Swift's deafness finally forced him to give up all hopes of returning to see his fellow Scriblerians. He recognized that "my common illness is of that kind which utterly disqualifies me for all conversation; I mean my Deafness; and indeed it is that only which quite discourageth me from all thoughts of coming to England" (*C* 4 : 476). Verbally isolated, Swift felt himself becoming progressively duller. To one friend he confided, "This disorder and my Monastick life takes off all invention" (*C* 3 : 322). Because he put such a high value on the benefits of conversation, his increased inability to participate in it profoundly depressed him.

Even though Swift was cut off at times from his friends because of distance or deafness, he could still "converse" with them through correspondence. He wrote in direct, powerful language that wove a firm relationship between himself and the addressee. In letters from Swift to his friends, the reader senses the active engagement of two minds.

Swift often explicitly compared letter-writing with talk, as did many writers in the eighteenth century.[12] In a letter to Mrs. Caesar he declares that "I am full of talk; But you are to blame, for I imagine myself in your company" (*C* 4:185); to Pope he avers, "You see how I like to talk to you (for this is not writing)" (254); to the Duchess of Queensberry, Swift even exalts letter-writing over live conversation: "I know you more by any one of your Letters, then I could by six months conversing, [for] your pen is always more naturall and sincere and unaffectd then you[r] tongue. In writing you are too lazy to give yourself the trouble of Acting a part" (59). Good correspondence, like conversation, should be characterized by true reciprocity and a lack of mechanical forms, qualities Swift praises in the letters of Pope's friend, Patty Blount: she "is one of the best Letter-writers I know; very good sense, civility and friendship, without any stiffness or constraint" (*C* 3:289).

Swift strove in letters for the sense of spontaneity so essential to live discourse. Contrasting himself to Voiture, Tully, and Pliny, who wrote "their letters for the publick view, more than for the sake of their correspondents," he tells Pope, "I believe my letters have escaped being published, because I writ nothing but Nature and Friendship" (*C* 4:408). To Pope he also observes, "I believe we neither of us ever leaned our Head upon our left hand to study what we should write next" (384). Letters are most effective and pleasurable, therefore, when they are least artificial; the writer should engage the unique personality of his addressee and not write to Prince Posterity. Swift believed that "particular incidents" (408), not abstract observation, make the most interesting discourse, be it in live or epistolary conversation. More than two hundred years after they were written, Swift's letters bristle with vitality.

With his very closest friends, Swift abandoned the common forms to communicate in special, private languages. His use of these languages instead of standard English symbolized the *uncommonness* of the relationships and removed them from the brutishness of the everyday world. The most famous of his private colloquies is recorded in the so-called *Journal to Stella*, in which Swift eschews the fabric of everyday life.[13] He writes *en déshabillé* literally and figuratively. At one point in the *Journal* Swift makes a particular contrast between the private language he and "the ladies" use and traditional English. He speaks of his plan "to make up this Academy for the Improvemt of our Language," and then adds, "Fais we nevr shall improve it as much as FW has done. Sall we? No fais, ourrichar Grangridge [our little language]" (*JS* 2:510 n. 14). In other words, their "little language" needs no improvement; their utopia has a perfect means of discourse. Swift implies that people in society at large, however, are not so ideally attuned to their fellows and need to communicate in a standard *lingua franca*, perhaps regulated by an academy.

The *Journal* provided an opportunity for Swift "always [to] be in con-

versation with MD [my dears?] and MD with Presto [himself]" (*JS*
1:8–9). Despite the physical distance between the correspondents, the
letters between Swift and the ladies create an overwhelming sense of immediacy—"I can hardly imagine you absent when I am reading your
letter, or writing to you. No, faith, you are just here upon this little paper,
and therefore I see and talk with you every evening constantly" (232).
Elsewhere he characterizes the interchange similarly, emphasizing its conversational dynamic: "It is just as if methinks you were here and I prating
to you, and telling you where I have been: Well, says you, Presto, come,
where have you been to-day? come, let's hear now. And so then I answer;
Ford and I were visiting Mr. Lewis, and Mr. Prior, and Prior has given me
a fine Plautus . . ." (167).[14]

Comfortable and secure, the private bubble of the *Journal* floats above
the quotidian. Nothing jarring or painful is allowed to break its perfect
conversational harmony. When Swift has the shingles, for instance, he
tells Stella that such a condition is not within the compass of the world
they create for each other in their correspondence: "I dont love to write
Journals while I am in pain, and above all, not Journalls to Md" (*JS*
2:534). Another time, he begins writing of an official who recently died,
but then he inks out the entry, not wanting fleshly *realpolitik* to intrude:
"Faith, I could hardly forbear our little language about a nasty dead chan-
cellor, as you may see by the blot" (*JS* 1:108).

Significantly, Swift wrote his letters to Stella from the womblike sanc-
tuary of his bed, without his wig and his street clothes, the accouterments
of public life. He abandoned his usual handwriting for a sloppy scrawl
that MD could decipher but that would prevent the rest of the world from
prying: "Methinks when I write plain, I do not know how, but we are not
alone, all the world can see us. A bad scrawl is so snug, it looks like PMD"
(79).[15] Deane Swift glosses "PMD" by saying that "this cypher stands for
Presto, Stella, and *Dingley;* so much as to say, it looks like us three quite
retired from all the rest of the world" (79, n. 7). The *Journal* and its intimate style shelter the correspondents in an Eden without snakes.

For standard English, Swift rejected sound as a basis for orthography.
His private language to MD, however, was determined by pronunciation—peculiar pronunciation at that. To the ladies Swift writes: "Do you
know what? when I am writing in our language, I make up my mouth just
as if I was speaking it. I caught myself at it just now" (210). The *Journal*'s
language violates other proscriptions that Swift laid down for standard
English; it is, for instance, full of strange abbreviations, some so private
they cannot now be interpreted with any certainty. Twice in the *Journal*
Swift writes to Stella in a consciously designed code, which she deciphers

and returns in kind (*JS* 1:208, 2:493): "Yes, I understand your cypher, and Stella guesses right, as she always does" (208). Indeed, like his other correspondence, Swift's *Journal* is a substitute for conversation, but in this case, the participants do not want to speak dull, sublunary English.

The "little language" violates not only the common forms of words' graphic representations but also the common forms of decorum. Swift and Stella do not converse in a refined, conventionally "polite" way but sustain a colloquy permeated by the most intimate innuendo. Swift professed a distaste for bawdy talk, especially from women, and his general attitude can be seen in his comment about a letter from Mrs. Anne Long: "[It] has quite turned my stomach against her; no less than two nasty jests in it with dashes to suppose them. She is corrupted in that country town [where she lives] with vile conversation" (*JS* 1:118–19). Ironically, however, Swift tolerated, nay, encouraged, such repartee from Stella and replied in turn. Right after he castigated Mrs. Long for her "nasty jests," he joshed with Stella, "Faith, if I was near you, I would whip your ———— to some tune, for your grave saucy answer" (124). A few other instances of Swift's use of dashes include "———— [fucking] like a stoat" (a proverbial expression) in quoting a poem relayed by St. John (164); "this son of a b———— Patrick" (66); and, of Stella, after reading a passage of a letter from her, "I sd aloud—Agreable B—tch—" (*JS* 2:672). By his use of indecorous language, Swift emphasizes to Stella that they exist outside the common forms needed by others to regulate their discourse.

In addition to bawdy language, the *Journal* contains numerous double entendres. Swift, for instance, tells MD how Harley "appointed me an hour on Saturday at four, afternoon, when I will open my business to him; which expression I would not use if I were a woman. I know you smoakt it; but I did not till I writ it" (*JS* 1:41). When Stella's mother gave Swift special medicinal water for her daughter, the messenger delayed with it, provoking Swift's anger because he was "so impatient, that Stella should have her water, (I mean decently, don't be rogues)" (174). Another time, he forwarded a box to Stella via various negligent people, one of whom was a "woman who married a fellow in her journey to Chester; so I believe she little thought of any body's box but her own" (271). Similar references pervade the *Journal*. Only once does Swift draw back, remarking near the end of one letter, "Mesinks I writt a little sawcy last night, I mean [the rest is obliterated]" (*JS* 2:624), but this disclaimer, in a way, heightens the titillation of the *Journal*.

With a playful relish of impropriety, Swift accentuates the idea that he was "conversing" with MD while undressed in bed. (The *Oxford English Dictionary* gives *conversation* as a synonym for "sexual intimacy" during the eighteenth century.) In a mock address he says, "Go, get you gone to your own chambers, and let Presto rise like a modest gentleman, and walk to town" (*JS* 1:227). On another occasion he remarks, "I walked home for exercise, and at eleven got to bed, and all the while I was undressing my self, there was I speaking monkey things in air, just as if MD had been by, and did not recollect myself until I got into bed" (154–55). On one frigid night, Swift wishes "my cold hand was in the warmest place about you, young women, I'd give ten guineas upon that account . . . oh, it starves my thigh" (181). He tells them that he likes to converse with them in the evening and "sometimes in the morning, but not always in the morning, because that is not so modest to young ladies" (142–43). As he depicts himself in bed, he sometimes imagines Stella the same way, "just now shewing a white leg, and putting it into the slipper" as she arises (*JS* 2:410). The liberty Swift has with Stella is not attributable to the distance the letters provide. If anything, he implies that he would be more salacious if directly conversing with her, for at one point he queries, "Have you got the whale-bone petticoats amongst you yet? I hate them; a woman here may hide a moderate gallant under them. Pshaw, what's all this I'm saying? methinks I am talking to MD face to face" (409).[16] Swift's uncommon openness with Stella illustrates the freedom granted them in their utopian society.

Esther Vanhomrigh (Hessy or Vanessa) as well as Stella received Swift's letters in intimate, private language. Generally more accessible than the *Journal to Stella*, Swift's letters to Hessy nevertheless often contain codes, the most famous example of which is the "coffee" metaphor, which Horace Walpole first noted. A few examples of the "coffee" talk will suffice to suggest its allusiveness. After telling Hessy that "the Sluttery . . . [is] the most agreeable Chamber in the World" (*C* 1:276) in an earlier letter, Swift then writes, "I long to drink a dish of Coffee in the Sluttery, and hear you dun me for Secrets, and—drink your Coffee—Why don't you drink your Coffee" (308–9). Hessy responds using the same trope: "It is impossible to tell you how often I have wished you a cupe of coffee and an orange at your Inn" (365). Facetiously projecting a book about their relationship, Swift says it will include events from the "Time of spilling the Coffee to drinking of Coffee" (*C* 2:356).[17] Whether "coffee" refers to sexual intercourse or to some other experience that Swift and Hessy shared, it is clearly not being used denotatively. In addition to "coffee," other private allusions and abbreviations abound, as they would in any series of letters between long-standing friends. Furthermore, Swift and Hessy frequently corresponded in French (although they did not tutoyer each other), another way to elevate the world of their relationship beyond the everyday. Again Swift illustrates that special friendships demand, or perhaps create, special languages. As long as the friends understand one another, nothing else is required. In society at large, where people do not enjoy such closeness, the common forms are needed to allow good conversation to flourish. Here the absence of common forms emphasizes the freedom the relationship allows.

Although not so private as the languages he developed to communicate with Stella and Hessy, Swift created another "special" language to celebrate his friendship with Thomas Sheridan. The two men were united by their delight in word play, and they corresponded with each other in a wonderful mixture of English and Latin that they devised for the purpose. Swift describes the language to Lord Orrery: "[Sheridan] writes me English latinized, and Latin Englyfyed, but neither of them equal to mine, as my very enemyes allow. It is true indeed, I am gone so far in this Science that I can hardly write common English, I am so apt to mingle it with Latin. For instance, instead of writing *my Enemyes*, I was going to spell it *mi en emis*" (*C* 4:396). Following is one of Swift's earliest letters to Sheridan in mock Latin:

Erudissime Domine,

Mi Sana, Telo me Flaccus; odioso ni mus rem. Tuba Dia pusillanimum: emit si erit mos minimo. Fecitne Latina Sal? I sub me? a robur os. Nantis potatis. Moto ima os illud a illuc? Ima os nega? I dama nam? Memoravi i nos; Ima eris nisi! sit parta.

Si paca eruc? voco Tite nemo! Emerit tono, sit sola ni emit, na edit. Ima ni sum & dum? Ima nil ne ni erim! Tuba nisi no os tegi en parare.

Humillimus, &c

(*C* 2:467)

Harold Williams provides Walter Scott's interpretation of the letter:

I am an ass; O let me suck calf; O so I do in summer; O but I had mum in all I supt; Minim o' time is tiresome; writes of any tall lass; I buss 'em? O soberer. Nan, sit, sit a top. O Tom am I so dull, I a cully? I so agen? I a madman? I've a memory son. I'm a sinner. 'Tis a part.

Is a cap a cure? O covet O'men, tire me not; 'tis a loss in time and tide. I'm in a musing mood; I am kneeling in mire. A, but I see none, so I never get a rap.

(467, n. 1)

In addition to Anglo-Latin communications, Sheridan and Swift enjoyed conversing in a form of mutilated English that replaced standard forms with punning equivalents, as can be seen, for instance, in the following letter, where *ling* (a type of fish) recurs several times in every sentence:

Sir,

I suppose you are now angle ling with your tack ling in a purr ling stream, or pad ling and say ling in a boat; or sad ling your stum ling horse with a sap ling in your hands, and snare ling at your groom, or set ling your affairs, or tick ling your cat, or tat ling with your neighbour Price; not always Toy ling at your school. [The letter continues with almost a thousand more words in this vein.]

(*C* 4:346)

In another letter, Swift makes rhymes on the days of the week ("Sunday's a Pun-day, Monday's a Dun-day"), the months ("January, Women vary"), and the years ("One Thousand seven Hundred Thirty-seven, / When the Whigs are so blind they mistake Hell for Heaven"). At the letter's end he says, "I will carry these Predictions no further than to the Year 2001, when the Learn'd think the World will be at End, or the fine-all-Cat-a-strow-fee" (388). With their shared ground already established in long years of talk, Swift felt at liberty to romp linguistically.[18] Thus although he publicly advocated a standard language for discourse, he privately enjoyed violating the common linguistic forms in the near-perfect little worlds he occupied with his special friends.

In the sixteenth century Steeven Guazzo writes in *Civil Conversation* that "Nature hath given speeche to man, not to the ende to speake to himselfe, which were to no purpose, but to the ende it might stande in steede towardes others . . . whereby men come to love one another, and to linke themselves together."[19] Like the classical and Renaissance humanists before him, Swift too thought that language above all should serve a social function. For the world at large he prescribed a standard based on traditional use; for expressing his personal vision, he sought whatever forms were most congenial. Both the Drapier and the *Tale*-teller coexisted within Swift.

4

Public Use of Language: The National Macrocosm

> And indeed, although there seems to be a close
> Resemblance between the two Words, *Politeness*,
> and *Politics*; yet no Ideas are more inconsistent
> in their Natures.
>> "Introduction," *Polite Conversation*,
>> *PW* 4:120

In private conversation, Swift required only that the participants "entertain and improve" each other; he stipulated nothing about the language they spoke except that it be mutually intelligible. Swift required more of public spokesmen. Their use of language should reinforce historical consensus. Swift shared the common assumption that verbal and political coherence were inextricably linked, and so Britain's continuance as a great nation was directly correlated to the improvement of public discourse. To this end, writers such as Daniel Defoe and Joseph Addison called for an English academy, and others such as Alexander Pope in *The Dunciad* and John Dryden in *MacFlecknoe* satirized the dangers of verbal pollution in national life. But of all his contemporaries, Jonathan Swift seems to have explored most fully the relationship between politics and the English language. Through his writing, Swift tried to edge people closer to the human possibilities he saw in good conversation. Because they serve as exemplars to the populace and because they have wide audiences, extended through print technology, Swift believed that public figures—courtiers, politicians, lawyers, writers, critics, philosophers, preachers—had a responsibility to purify the traditional language that allowed different segments of society to speak to one another and to the great minds of the past, whose wisdom is found in books. Indeed, Swift believed that society in general, not just the society of the parlor, would be lost without spirited and open discussion that moved toward a higher level of politeness, a word that in the eighteenth century meant, according to the *Oxford English Dictionary*, "mental or intellectual culture," not just good manners.

In the perfectly "polite" world of the *Journal to Stella*, removed from worldly power struggles, Swift remarks, "I believe never 3 People conversed so much with so little Politicks" (*JS* 2:634). Swift's communion with MD was a respite from the discourse of the real world, where conversations were not as harmonious but perhaps more necessary. The welfare of the nation itself depended on unity, which could be established only if the various interests of society talked freely to one another. Swift describes the ideal operation of this process:

> Let us suppose five Hundred Men, mixed, in Point of Sense and Honesty, as usually Assemblies are; and let us suppose these Men proposing, debating, resolving, voting, according to the meer natural Motions of their own little, or much Reason and Understanding; I do allow, that . . . many pernicious and foolish Overtures would arise, and float a few Minutes; but then they would die, and disappear. Because, this must be said in Behalf of human Kind; that common Sense, and plain Reason, while Men are disengaged from acquired Opinions, will ever have some general Influence upon their Minds.
>
> (*Contests and Dissentions in Rome and Athens, PW* 1:232)

This is an optimistic description of political discourse: it presumes that some common ground can be determined despite the deflection of many "pernicious and foolish Overtures." Swift expresses a faith in "common Sense, and plain Reason" and the impotence of an individual's irrationality to obscure consensus, for "the Species of Folly and Vice are infinite, and so different in every Individual, that they could never procure a Majority" *unless*—here Swift severely qualifies his optimism—"other Corruptions did not enter to pervert Mens Understandings, and misguide their Wills" (232). Corruption ripens when political opportunists, through clever rhetoric, seek to gratify "their Pride, their Malice, their Ambition, their Vanity, or their Avarice" (234) and when the general populace become too lazy, too ignorant, or too cowardly to challenge irrational arguments. In the case of Wood's Half Pence, the English heard only one side of the story, "and having neither Opportunity, nor Curiosity to examine the *other,* they *believe a Lye,* merely for their Ease; and conclude, because Mr. *Wood* pretends to have *Power,* he hath also *Reason* on his side" (*Drapier's Letters, PW* 10:64).

Having won control with artful words, the powerful no longer have to re-sort merely to language to achieve their means. They have force at their command and do not have to listen to arguments. Even though any ra-tional person would agree that "*Government* without the Consent of the *Governed*, is the *very Definition of Slavery* . . . in *Fact, eleven Men well armed, will certainly subdue one single Man in his Shirt*" (63). Redefining words at will, the oppressor rends the social fabric; the common forms of British culture—the importance of liberty, the primacy of the Established Church, the sanctity of the law, and the literary tradition—disappear with the com-mon forms of language used to express them. Factions—both the cause and effect of linguistic corruption—

> turn Religion into a Fable,
> And make the Government a *Babel:*
> Pervert the Law, disgrace the Gown,
> Corrupt the Senate, rob the Crown;
> To sacrifice old *England's* Glory,
> And make her infamous in Story.
> ("Verses on the Death of Dr. Swift,"
> *P* 2:568, 373–88)

Even the memory of "England's *Glory*" will be lost if the energetic am-nesiacs who populate the world of the *Tale* and who worship that "new Deity . . . by some called *Babel*, by others, *Chaos*" (*Tale, PW* 1:124), take over. When they finish imposing their various agendas, nothing of any value or meaning will be left.

In an immediate, practical way, politics threatens England's culture by dissipating the nation's genius in stupid internecine quarrels. All the hu-man energy penned up in garrets in Grubstreet could be put to better use. Thus Swift writes, "I am apt to think this schism in Politics has cloven our understandings, and left us just half the good sense that blazed in our ac-tions: And we see the effect it has had upon ou[r] wit and learning, which are crumbled into pamphlets and penny papers" (*C* 1:211). Politeness, or civilized behavior, fosters sweetness and light; politics crumbles things out to their atomies. Politeness binds; politics rends.

As Swift explains in *Contests and Dissentions*, the ideal state is a harmo-nious balance of interests. The civil equilibrium is an analogue to good conversation; all parties benefit and none suffers. When one of the three elements of society (the people, the nobility, the ruler) obtains too much power, however, the balance of the state is disturbed, resulting in linguistic corruption. Such was the case in Rome as the empire began to disintegrate:

There were many Reasons for the Corruptions [of Latin] . . . As the Change of their Government into a Tyranny, which ruined the Study of Eloquence; there being no further Use or Encouragement for popular Orators: Their giving not only the Freedom of the City, but Capacity for Employments, to [certain colonists] . . . which brought a great Number of foreign Pretenders into *Rome:* The slavish Disposition of the Senate and People; by which the Wit and Eloquence of the Age were wholly turned into Panegyrick, the most barren of all Subjects: The great Corruption of Manners, and Introduction of foreign Luxury.

> (*Proposal, PW* 4:8)

Swift does not provide an exact cause-and-effect analysis here, but he implies that political oppression (a result of the vigor of the power-hungry and the complaisance of the populace) goes hand in hand with linguistic corruption, a point that Swift inspired George Orwell to reiterate in the twentieth century. The lack of traditional equilibrium also promotes certain unwise (whiggish) policies, such as colonization and commercial expansionism, all of which have the effect of debasing the language.

Swift shared the common view that the English Civil War and its aftermath damaged the English language. In the *Proposal for Correcting, Improving, and Ascertaining the English Tongue*, Swift describes the Interregnum as a time when an "Infusion of Enthusiastick Jargon prevailed in every Writing, as was not shaken off in many Years after" (*PW* 4:10). At one point he specifically refers to this period as Babel: "Yet, clearly to shew what a Babel they had built, after twelve years trial, and twenty sorts of government; the nation, grown weary of their tyranny, was forced to call in the son of him whom those reformers had sacrificed" (*Upon the Martyrdom of Charles I, PW* 9:226).

In France, Louis XIII declared that one of the main purposes of the Académie Française (founded in 1635) was "to remedie those disorders which the Civil Wars . . . have brought into [the language]."[1] Similar linkages between civil war and linguistic corruption prevailed in England and spurred men to propose means to clearer discourse. In *Leviathan* Thomas Hobbes warns of the dangers of "hard words"; they "Distract the people," encouraging the state to fall under "Oppression or [to be] cast . . . into the Fire of a Civill Warre."[2] Similarly, at the beginning of *Hudibras*, Samuel Butler associates "hard words" and civil broils, speaking of a time

> When civil Fury first grew high,
> And men fell out they knew not why;
> When hard words, jealousies and Fears,
> Set Folks together by the ears.[3]

John Locke notes in his *Essay Concerning Human Understanding* that if "the imperfections of Language, as the Instrument of Knowledge, [were] more thoroughly weighed, a great many of the Controversies that make such a noise in the World, would of themselves cease; and the way to Knowledge, and, perhaps, Peace too, lie a good deal opener than it does."[4]

When society is divided against itself and the common forms are forgotten, words are created and redefined at will without cultural or historical guidelines. Because these coinages and redefinitions derive from individual passion, and are not the product of collective agreement, they are necessarily antisocial and irrational, contributing to the "lapse into Barbarity" that is so easily possible. (It is not surprising that *babel* and *barbarity* are related etymologically.) Tumultous times, Swift notes, spawn "Cant-words" and "conceited Appellations [like Whig and Tory]. . . . Of this kind were the *Prasini* and *Veneti*, the *Guelfs* and the *Gibelines*, *Huguenots* and *Papists*, *Round-heads* and *Cavaliers*" (*Examiner*, PW 3:162). Such words are Modern; they are not part of the traditional, generally understood lexicon that the nation had inherited from previous generations. Thus in the thirty years that *Whig* and *Tory* had existed, they had "been pressed to the Service of many Successions of Parties, with very different Idea's fastened to them" (163).[5] Indeed, considering the controversy today over Swift's political label, there still seems to be a great confusion about what *Whig* and *Tory* mean,[6] a general problem, Swift believed, with words not grounded in ancient cultural institutions. Political parties were, to Swift, the epitome of a Modern form.

Whether society is under particular stress or not, however, its language is continuously attacked by egotists whose purposes are served by speaking in new and uncommon terms.[7] Unfortunately, the people who have the most power to reinforce historical consensus are the ones who understand it least. Society's leaders tend, ironically, to be antisocial. And the consequences are potentially profound. If a private citizen fails to speak clearly, few are hurt. At most he might damage his own reputation or disrupt his immediate circle. But if those who articulate cultural norms are deliberately or unintentionally obscure, the fabric of both language and society could be rent.

Although Swift saw ordinary folk as bulwarks of common sense, naturally resistant to antitraditional forces, he feared that they might be misled by clever men who could dazzle them with new terminology. He tells his Irish congregation to beware of "cunning Men [who] take Advantage, by putting Words into your Mouths, which you do not understand; then they fix good or ill Characters to those Words, as it best serves their purposes" (*On Brotherly Love*, PW 9:173). On the whole, as Swift notes in another sermon to his flock, "the common people" have enough wisdom to see the benefits of traditional values unless they "are deluded by false preachers, to grow fond of new visions and fancies in religion, which, managed by dextrous men, for sinister ends of malice, envy or ambition, have often made whole nations run mad" (*Upon the Martyrdom of Charles I, PW* 9:229). In short, Swift admonished his listeners to adhere to the common forms in religion, government, and, by implication, language, telling them "to avoid all broachers and preachers of new-fangled doctrines . . . *to obey God and the King, and meddle not with those who are given to change*" (231).[8] Radical changes in doctrine are inevitably signaled by what Swift calls "*Cant* words . . . the most ruinous Corruption in any Language" (*Proposal, PW* 4:8). Swift, therefore, focused his ire on categories of public discoursers whose cant was particularly subversive.

Guardians of the Common Forms of State

Like most Britons, Swift believed the nation's leaders should be exemplary models of morality, justice, and learning. Resembling the *Tale*-brothers, though, contemporary courtiers and politicians seemed to Swift to value only what was new and different; the present moment was the alpha and omega. To correct the scandal that the court was "the worst School in *England*" Swift suggests that "better Care be taken in the Education of our young Nobility; that they may set out into the World with some Foundation of Literature" (10). To read and write within a historical tradition would prevent courtiers from construing what they wish in words, an activity Swift satirically dramatizes in the School of Political Projectors at Lagado where the students become "very dextrous in finding out the mysterious Meanings of Words, Syllables and Letters. For Instance, they can decypher a Close-stool to signify a Privy-Council; a Flock of Geese, a Senate; a lame Dog, an Invader . . . a Broom, a Revolution; a Mouse-trap, an Employment; a bottomless Pit, the Treasury . . . a running Sore, the Administration" (*PW* 11:191). These artists construct definitions that are not constrained by the dictates of usage, logic, or common sense (although their misreadings, of course, prove ironically accurate—Swift has it both ways). The danger of such a radically iconoclastic attitude toward words is evident; if the artists could not find the term *broom* to signify revolution in a suspect's correspondence, *cat* or *shoe* would do as well.

If words are too unwieldy for the virtuosi of Lagado, they can concentrate on the fragmented letters, each of which has a hidden meaning (to be determined by them at their convenience): the linguistic mandate during

Gulliver's visit is that "*N*, shall signify a Plot; *B*, a Regiment of Horse; *L*, a Fleet at Sea" (191). Since writing usually contains several N's, B's, and L's, almost any communication would be considered treasonous. An alternative Lagadan method of delving into (that is, ignoring) the meaning of words is to reveal their anagramatic structure: "So for Example if I should say in a letter to a friend, *Our Brother* Tom *has just got the Piles;* a Man of Skill in this Art would discover how the same Letters which compose that Sentence may be analysed into the following Words: *Resist*, ——— *a Plot is brought home* ——— *The Tour*" (191–92). Gulliver's experiences derive from Swift's observation that he "never yet knew one great Minister who made any scruple to mould the Alphabet into whatever words he pleased" (*C* 1:185).

Swift joked with Stella about how factional interests generate weird, unintelligible phrases. He earnestly writes her, "*I have desired* Apronia *to be always careful especially about the legs.* . . . Party carries every thing now-a-days, and what a splutter have I heard about the wit of that saying. . . . Pray read it over again this moment, and consider it." Then Swift reveals that he is putting her on: "Why—aye—You must know I dreamt [the sentence] just now, and waked with it in my mouth. Are you bit, or are you not, sirrahs?" (*JS* 1:182–83).

Yet politically inspired redefinition and coinage of cant words were no laughing matters to Swift, who, while in the role of Mr. Examiner, enforced the doctrine that Tory principles embodied and preserved the common forms and thus the common good.[9] In his attacks on the Whigs Swift repeatedly condemns what he suggests is their ignorance of accepted definitions. He complains about one author who takes the resolutions of Parliament and "explains their Meaning into Nonsense, in order to bring them off from reflecting upon his Party" (*A Letter to Seven Lords*, *PW* 3:192). At another point, Swift voices his resentment over the Whig tactic of associating with the definition of *Tory* such concepts as *Popery*, *Arbitrary Power*, and *The Pretender*, "those important Words having, by dextrous Management, been found of mighty Service to their Cause, although applied with little colour, either of Reason or Justice" (*Examiner*, *PW* 3:143). In *A Letter to a Whig Lord*, Swift asks, "And will you declare you cannot Serve your Queen unless you chuse her Ministry? Is this *Forsaking your Principles?* . . . This is a new Party-figure of Speech, which I cannot comprehend" (6:128–29).

As an example of the divisiveness of political semantics, Mr. Examiner cites the following episode: "A *Whig* asks, whether you hold *Passive Obedience.* You affirm it: he then immediately cries out you are a *Jacobite, a Friend of France and the Pretender;* because he makes you answerable for the Definition he hath formed of that Term, however different it be from what you understand" (*Examiner, PW* 3:111–12), or, Swift implies, from what the term normally means. In his role as Tory pamphleteer, Swift repeatedly implies that the Whigs are aliens, babbling in a strange tongue. While he spoke as Mr. Examiner, Swift, like Samuel Johnson, would not have defined *Tory* as "a faction." Tory ideas were British ideas; Tory discourse, an admirable standard for the language. Anything else was schismatic.

Swift assumes that ordinary citizens are unified in their understanding of basic historical concepts—concepts that the power hungry would like to obliterate. When Swift tried to convince Robert Walpole that the Irish were oppressed, the prime minister did not seem to understand the common, accepted use of the word *liberty*. "I saw, he had conceived opinions . . . which I could not reconcile to the notions I had of liberty, a possession always understood by the *British* nation to be the inheritance of a human creature. Sir *Robert Walpole* was pleased to enlarge very much upon the subject of Ireland, in a manner . . . alien from what I conceived to be the rights and privileges of a subject of *England*" (*C* 3:132). Walpole's ignorance of the meaning of *liberty* is a shibboleth that marks him as a hostile foreigner ignorant of the most elementary cultural forms.

For similar reasons, Swift instinctively distrusted the ability of George I, a non-English-speaker, to achieve an understanding of the people he was supposed to rule. Nostalgically, Swift compares King George to King William, who "was no Stranger to our Language or Manners. . . . I could heartily wish the like Disposition were in another Court . . . because it may be disagreeable to a Prince to take up new Doctrines on a sudden, or speak to His Subjects by an Interpreter" (*Some Free Thoughts on the Present State of Affairs, PW* 8:96). Not sharing the common language of the people, George could not comprehend the basic ideas that constitute English culture. In mock charity, the Drapier suggests that because "his Majesty is not Master of the *English* Tongue . . . it is necessary that some other Person should be employed to pen what he hath to say, or write in that Language," and so George did not realize the injustice of granting Wood's patent (*PW* 9:70). Swift and others suggested that James's grandson be brought over and educated in England so that "the Nation might one day hope to be governed by a Prince of English Manners and Language, as well as acquainted with the true Constitution of Church and State" (*An Enquiry . . . of the Queen's Last Ministry, PW* 8:179). No wonder Swift was so distraught at Queen Anne's death. At least she could speak English and, by implication, had an understanding of "the true Constitution of Church and State."

Laws are expressions of the will of the state. English law, resting on precedent, represents in microcosm a model of how national values accrue over time. The law, ideally, anchors society to the common forms of the past so that changes occur within a controlling context. Swift, however, shared the prevalent view (then and now) that lawyers, who ought to expound the meaning of the law, typically choose to pervert it to help their clients and themselves achieve their private ends. Their reading of language is not governed by tradition, but, as Gulliver explains to the Houyhnhnms, "according as they are paid" (*PW* 11 : 248). Seeing in words only the meanings they are hired to see has an enervating effect on language because the most obvious definitions are confused: "By Words multiplied for the Purpose [lawyers can prove] that *White* is *Black*, and *Black* is *White*" (248). The Examiner complains when he sees what he views as a legalistic perversion of an explicit statement: "Lawyers may explain this, or call them Words of Form, as they please. . . . But a plain Reader, who takes the Words in the natural meaning" (*PW* 3 : 18), would come to entirely different conclusions.

A dramatic example of lawyers' linguistic ingenuity is cited by the Drapier, who laughs at their attempt, through specious etymology,[10] to convince a jury that *villain* and *knave* are not pejoratives:

> At a Tryal in Kent, where Sir *George Rook* was indicted for calling a Gentle-man Knave and Villain; the Lawyer for the *Defendant* brought off his Client, by alledging, that the Words were not injurious; for, *Knave*, in the old and true Signification, imported only a servant; and Villain, in *Latin*, is *Villicus*; which is no more than a Man employed in Country Labour.
> (*PW* 10 : 109–10)

If *knave* and *villain* can be made to denote the opposite of what common sense would dictate, then *right* and *wrong* become purely nominal concepts, a point Gulliver makes to the Houyhnhnms when he complains that lawyers have "wholly confounded the very Essence of Truth and Falshood, of Right and Wrong; so that it will take Thirty Years to decide whether the Field, left to me by my Ancestors for six Generations, belong to me, or to a Stranger three Hundred Miles off" (*PW* 11 : 250). The claim of "six Generations," the legacy of the past, has nothing to do with the here-and-now business of lawyers. They, like the *Tale* denizens, want freedom from common forms, not realizing that without the common forms, nothing exists but the "Abyss of Things"—the anarchy of Epicurean atoms careening in a void.

Guardians of the Common Forms of the Church

Although he did not do it himself in any conventional, concerted manner, Swift believed that clergymen have a duty to lead people to an understanding of religious truth, that is, the teachings of the Established Church.[11] These truths are evident if one reads the Bible in a straightforward way, guided by the consensus of interpretation evolved through time. A priest should present these common-sense interpretations of biblical texts to unify his congregation in the faith of their fathers. In contrast, priests who insist on ahistorical, peculiar readings of the Bible foment a variousness of opinion that undermines the foundations of traditional English life. Swift humorously dramatizes this effect in his *Argument Against Abolishing Christianity*, when a person, upon hearing there were several textual interpretations of a certain point, "most logically concluded: Why, if it be as you say, I may safely whore and drink on, and defy the Parson" (*PW* 2 : 38). In the absence of some standard, all interpretations appear to have equal validity—a premise Swift attacked as much for its immorality as for its effect on social unity. Needless to say, Swift staunchly opposed religious toleration, believing that only within the confines of traditional institutions could true freedom be found. Denying or forgetting the legacy of the past, symbolized by the father's will in *A Tale of a Tub*, is tantamount to self-lobotomy.

Refuting those, like freethinker Anthony Collins, who might ask, "What Authority can a Book pretend to, where there are various Readings?" (*Mr. Collins' Discourse of Free-Thinking, PW* 4 : 33), Swift stresses that although the Bible is a complex and mysterious work, "the Words in their plain natural Meaning must import" (*On Mutual Subjection, PW* 9 : 142). That the Bible is liable to multiple interpretations should not be surprising, Swift says, because "Laws penned with the utmost Care and Exactness and in the vulgar Language, are often perverted to wrong Meanings; then why should we wonder that the Bible is so?" (*Thoughts on Various Subjects, PW* 4 : 248). The individualistic tendencies of some readers, who as a point of pride try to impose new interpretations on the Bible, create exegetical confusion. Common sense—the accumulated opinion of rational readers—is the best guide to understanding the Scriptures.

Because religious truth is fundamentally clear, Swift warns the novice priest not to use arcane language to explain the gospel to his parishioners. Swift attacks those who say that the Bible is "the most difficult Book in the World to be understood: [and that] it requires a thorow Knowledge in Natural, Civil, Ecclesiastical History, Law, Husbandry, Sailing, Physick, Pharmacy, Mathematics, Metaphysicks, Ethicks, and every thing else that can be named" (*Mr. Collins' Discourse of Free-Thinking, PW* 4:29). To illustrate the point that simple, common-sense biblical analysis is best, Swift, in *Examiner* No. 15, tells the story of a fanatically religious farmer, "who . . . had confuted the Bishop and all his Clergy," and an unsophisticated, Bible-reading footman, who counter each other in a public exegesis contest. The footman walks away with the victory because he "explained his Texts so full and clear, to the Capacity of his Audience, and shewed the Insignificancy of his Adversary's Cant, to the meanest Understanding; that he got the whole Country of his Side" (*PW* 3:15). Such straightforward interpretations of the Bible must be sufficient, Swift observes, "or else God requires from us more than we are able to perform" (*Holy Orders, PW* 4:66).

Peter's interpretation of the will in *A Tale of a Tub* satirizes those who wrest meanings from Divine Writ to authorize their egocentric visions. Peter, in fact, is specifically likened to those "Commentators on the *Revelations*, who proceed Prophets without understanding a Syllable of the Text" (*PW* 1:51). Swift may have had in mind someone like "the old B[isho]p of Worcester who pretends to be a Prophet. . . . [He] went to the Queen . . . to prove to Her Majesty out of Daniel and the Revelations, that 4 years hence there would be a War of Religion: that the K. of France would be a Protestant, and fight on their side, that the Popedom would be destroyed, &c, and declared he would be content to give up His Bishoprick if it were not true" (*JS* 2:544). That the bishop, whose eminence guaranteed him authority, should be espousing these views no doubt disgusted and worried Swift. What if the bishop had succeeded in persuading the queen of his cockamamy theories?

Unfortunately, the country's ruling coterie, isolated in London from the common sense of the countryside, seemed to Swift particularly susceptible to heretical religious ideas, although in fact these ideas never had a significant following. In particular he cites the influence of Thomas Woolston, a freethinker who read the Bible in an ahistorical, allegorical manner, leading him, if one believes Swift's satiric summary, to opinions, among others,

> That *Jesus* was a Grand Imposter:
> That all his Miracles were Cheats,
> Perform'd as Juglers do their Feats.
>> ("Verses on the Death of Dr. Swift,"
>> *P* 2:564, 295–96).

If Woolston had confined his thinking to himself, he would be considered a harmless lunatic, but embraced as an intellectual guide by many others, he becomes seditious. In a humorously exaggerated vision, Swift describes Woolston's influence spreading like cancer through the body politic:

> Here's *Wolston's* Tracts, the twelfth Edition;
> 'Tis read by ev'ry Politician:
> The Country Members, when in Town,
> To all their Boroughs send them down:
> You never met a Thing so smart;
> The Courtiers have them all by Heart:
> Those Maids of Honour (who can read)
> Are thought to use them for their Creed.
> (281–88)

The Bishop of Worcester, Thomas Woolston, and their freewheeling counterparts in the *Tale*, Peter and Jack, have "converting Imaginations" that allow them to give free reign to their "peculiar Talent . . . [of] fixing Tropes and Allegories to the *Letter*, and refining what is Literal into Figure and Mystery" (*PW* 1:121). In other words, they ignore completely the "plain natural Meaning" of the text and substitute their own semantic systems.

Swift was dedicated and at times single-minded in defending the rights and prerogatives of the Established Church, especially after he became Dean of St. Patrick's Cathedral. How much Swift actually believed certain aspects of Christian doctrine has always been a mystery, but his commitment to the institution of the church was explicit and absolute. The church was threatened most, he believed, by self-interested parties trying to gain power by redefining crucial concepts. Swift notes, for instance, that "it is plain, that all the Stir, which the Fanaticks have made with this Word Moderation, was only meant to encrease our Divisions, and widen them so far as to make Room for themselves to get in betwixt" (*On Brotherly Love, PW* 9:176). With division after division, the social fabric will be in shreds.

Guardians of the Literary Tradition

The body of English literature represents a treasury of the articulated myths, dreams, and resources of the British people. It is a monument to their genius, a repository of common memories and experiences. The books of the past could become merely detritus unless two conditions prevail: "Our Language, and our Tast admit no great Alterations" (*Tale, PW* 1:1). If, through linguistic pollution, the language continues to change, authors will be denied a major incentive, the "chance for Immortality" (*Proposal*, *PW* 4:9). Their medium corrupted, they will turn their genius elsewhere; otherwise it would be "like employing an excellent Statuary to work upon mouldring Stone" (18). Not only would a shifting language discourage contemporary writers, but it would cut Britons off from the literature written in the past, thus obliterating the cultural memory of the nation. Changing taste, or a shift in the consensus of what is good and valuable, could also imperil the literary tradition. If the common sense of the past falls victim to Modern reassessments, no masterpiece is safe. Writers, therefore, have an obligation to buttress traditional ideas and forms. Bad writing can produce Struldbrugglike isolation that endangers every thinking person. And so Swift is not really being hyperbolic when he characterizes Richard Daniel as "a damnable poet, and consequently a public enemy to mankind" (*C* 3:312).

In contrast, Swift believed that good writers strengthen the language by using it properly to preserve communal values and hence the nation itself. He believed satire was particularly effective in promoting social welfare. In describing political frauds, for instance, Swift observes, "I am apt to think, it was to supply such Defects as these, that Satyr was first introduced into the World. . . . Next to taming and binding a Savage-Animal, the best Service you can do the Neighborhood is to give them warning, either to arm themselves, or come not in its Way" (*Examiner*, *PW* 3:141). The satirist's establishment of common ground is more beneficial to the nation than the efforts of political and ecclesiastical leaders, an idea explicit in Swift's compliment to John Gay on the success of *The Beggar's Opera*—"writing two or three Such trifles every year to expose vice and make people laugh with innocency does more publick Service than all the Ministers of State from Adam to Walpol" (*C* 3:278). Complimenting Pope in a similar vein, Swift says, "God Almighty preserve you for contributing more to mend the world than the whole pack of (modern) Persons in a Lump" (*C* 4:336). Swift's own satire was praised in this vein by William Pulteney: "I cannot help wishing to see some papers writ by you, that may, if possible, shame them out of [their villainy]. This is the only thing that can recover our constitution, and restore honesty" (*C* 4:438). Satire revitalizes the memories of ideals that unite all Britons. It is no wonder that Swift believes "all men of wit should employ it in Satyr" (*C* 4:138). Whatever Swift wrote, satiric or not, did in some way force men to acknowledge the ties that bound them together.

History writing was another literary endeavor crucial to the perpetuation of cultural values. Swift invested much effort in his *History of the Four Last Years of the Queen*, by which he sought to ensure that posterity would have the "correct" view of the events that he believed he had helped shape. But despite his diligent promotion, Swift did not manage to get the manuscript published in his lifetime. Because history was so important to him for both abstract and personal reasons, he sought the post of historiographer royal in 1714 and wrote to John Arbuthnot as follows: "I would not give two Pence to have it for the Value of it; but I had been told . . . that the Qu—— had a Concern for her history &c: and I was ready to undertake it" (C 2:62). Throughout his writings, Swift attacked those who seemed to misrepresent, and therefore to destroy, the past, although he himself often distorted history for propaganda purposes. Swift's desires to preserve, at least in theory, both historical and linguistic legacies are linked, as J. A. Downie notes, because a corruption of either would be "politically subversive."[12] Bad writing in any genre constituted a clear and present danger in Swift's eyes.

Swift unhappily observed that many self-styled writers did not use words to emphasize common truths and to eradicate error. Some were fools and some were knaves. The knaves were hacks who prostituted their pens to serve some private interest. Like lawyers, hacks are inspired to see in words what money urges them to. They employ language not to communicate comfort and joy to their fellows but to satisfy some patron or boss who will pay them for distorting facts. In "On Poetry," the old hack gives his young protégé advice on how to survive in a world where words are a salable commodity and not an expression of the human spirit.

> From Party-Merit seek Support;
> The vilest Verse thrives best at Court.
> A Pamphlet in Sir Rob's Defence
> Will never fail to bring in Pence;
> Nor be concern'd about the Sale,
> [Walpole] pays his Workmen on the Nail.
> (P 2:646, 185–90)

The hack and his employers, who reward only the "vilest Verse," exist in an illiterate demimonde where "Patrons never pay so well, / As when they scarce have learn'd to spell" ("Directions for a Birthday-Song," P 2: 463, 95–96).

The hack's perversity is epitomized by his ability, if paid adequately, to call black white and white black, just as lawyers do, according to Gulliver. Rather than writing with black ink on white paper, the common practice, the aspiring Grubstreeter is ironically advised to do the reverse.

> But you some white-lead ink must get,
> And write on paper black as Jet:
> Your Int'rest lyes to learn the knack
> Of whitening what before was black.
>   Thus your Encomiums, to be strong
> Must be apply'd directly wrong:
> A Tyrant for his Mercy praise,
> And crown a Royal Dunce with Bays.
>   (463–64, 113–20)

Knavishly confounding basic values, hacks hasten the "lapse into Barbarity" that Swift feared would occur unless somehow "*Politeness*" dominated "*Politics.*"

Some writers are merely ignorant or foolish. Swift repeatedly put some philosophers in this camp. Philosophers should explore the implications of important ideas and communicate their findings to others, but too often, Swift observed, they mire themselves in trivia or express themselves in incomprehensible jargon. He parodied their turgidity in the *Tritical Essay upon the Faculties of the Mind* and sections of *A Tale of a Tub*. The pseudo-profundity of mysticism and other forms of philosophy that defy common sense are often couched in language that is truly extraordinary and, for that reason, potentially destructive of the everyday English, which Swift believed was entirely capable of conveying any knowable truth. In their ignorance, philosophers often indulge in arguments that are "but vain babbling, and a mere sound of words, to amuse others and themselves" (*A Sermon upon the Excellency of Christianity*, PW 9:244). In philosophy as in politics, "tedious disputes about words" occur as "the natural product of disputes and dissentions between several sects" (242). Philosophical jargon has the advantage, Swift sarcastically observes to the novice priest, of being "equally understood by the Wise, the Vulgar, and the Preacher himself" (*Holy Orders*, PW 9:77), which is to say, not at all.

Swift shared Pope's view of the importance of the critic, who, with his superior education, should guide readers in determining whether a work represents "What oft was thought, but ne'er so well express'd," that is, whether it fosters or subverts communal values. Ideally, the critic discriminates good writing from bad, making publicly explicit the common sense of the rational readership. Because they function as custodians of language and discourse in general, good critics are as important as good writers in preserving cultural vigor. To fill this office, of course, the good critic must have a firm idea of the "common Forms . . . and the Pattern of Human Learning" (*Tale*, PW 1:108). Conversely, the bad critic is an enthusiast

71

who interprets works in light of his private interests. Peter, in *A Tale of a Tub*, prides himself on his critical ingenuity. In constructing linguistic arguments to serve his needs he literally disintegrates words. Using his supposed erudition, for instance, to construct a specious rationale for accepting C as K to justify wearing shoulder knots, Peter "proved by a very good Argument, that K was a modern illegitimate Letter, unknown to the Learned Ages" (50). Swift also satirizes irresponsible critics in his depiction of the *Tale*-teller himself, who adopts the role of critic to prove that there is such a thing, in the Modern world, as "a *True Critick*, agreeable to the Definition laid down by [him]" (58). With this tautological framework, the narrator finds *True Criticks* everywhere he looks, each time in a different form: "The Applications [are] so necessary and natural, that it is not easy to conceive, how any Reader of a *Modern Eye* and *Taste* could over-look them" (59). Even a Modern reader, however, would probably fail to discern that critics are being discussed in one passage that to any ordinary mortal seems to be a description of Indian reptiles. The *Tale*-teller, though, sees something very different, declaring that the author's "Meaning is so near the Surface, that I wonder how it possibly came to be overlook'd by those who deny the Antiquity of *True Criticks*" (61). If an Indian serpent can denote critic, then nothing means anything.[13]

Swift was not alone in fearing loss of meaning. He, like others of his period, was disturbed by the imprecise and irrational nature of public discourse, which all agreed must be remedied so that English society could survive and, perhaps, even thrive. Linguistic schemes and theories flooded forth, and Swift was fundamentally suspicious of most of them.

5

How Not to Improve Discourse: Satires of Modern Linguistic Theory

Call my Lord C—— a *Salamander.*
'Tis well.—But since we live among
Detractors with an evil Tongue,
Who may object against the Term,
Pliny shall prove what we affirm:
Pliny shall prove, and we'll apply,
And I'll be judg'd by standers-by.
    "The Description of a Salamander,"
    P 1:83, 22–28

The seventeenth century perhaps was the heyday of linguistic theorizing in England. Even early in the 1600s, it was clear to William Camden that "it is a greater glory now to be a *Linguist* th[a]n a Realist."[1] Many linguistic schemes were based on premises that Swift considered dangerously Modern in that they implied that meaning was not embedded in the historical pattern of English usage but elsewhere—in the mind of the individual or in the structural relationship of word and thing. Some theorists proposed new systems of signification because they believed that the English language was a random, redundant accretion that lacked the capacity for precise expression. Others sought to find universal languages so that the effects of Babel could be eliminated. Swift satirized a wide range of linguistic premises, all of which deny that the English language is a national inheritance, a palimpsest of accumulated experience.[2]

Creation of New, More Perfect Languages

Many language theorists in the seventeenth century used as a model the supposedly perfect communication Adam possessed in the Garden of

Eden. They believed that since signs were originally revelatory, Adam understood the nature of ravens merely by knowing the word for them. Adam could talk to all other men because before the Fall there was a single, immediately apprehensible language. These linguists observed that after the Fall and the Confusion, language became relatively opaque. Knowing the word for something did not provide information about the thing itself or its relation to the rest of Creation. Groups were separated from one another by their diverse tongues. The flaws in language, it was thought, destroyed the possibility of a congenial relationship with God, Nature, and one's fellows. Frustrated with the realization of what had been lost, numerous seventeenth-century language theorists constructed languages that they hoped would, among other things, unite word and thing, provide an insight into Nature, and reestablish linguistic universality. Two interrelated goals in seventeenth-century linguistic reform were to devise a real character and a philosophical language.

Swift, of course, viewed these schemes as hopelessly Modern. Not only did he disdain the arrogant optimism of thinking that language could be reformed in a more nearly perfect way, he laughed at the naive belief that such a mechanical remedy would relieve society of the problems that had afflicted previous generations. More important, Swift thought that dispensing with the English language was tantamount to dispensing with English civilization.

Interest in a "real character," a sign that contains its own meaning, was first expressed in England by Francis Bacon, who was stimulated by reports of Chinese pictograms: he writes, "It is the use of China and the kingdoms of the high Levant to write in Characters Real, which express neither letters nor words in gross, but Things or Notions; insomuch as countries and provinces, which understand not one another's language, can nevertheless read one another's writings, because the characters are accepted more generally than the languages do extend; and therefore they have a vast multitude of characters; as many, I suppose, as radical words."[3] Bacon was not the only English philosopher who yearned for a real character. Later in the seventeenth century, John Locke dreamed of a dictionary in which "Words standing for Things, which are known and distinguished by their outward shapes, [would] be expressed by little Draughts and Prints."[4]

John Wilkins's *Mercury; or the Secret Messenger* (1641) was the first elaboration in print by an Englishman of Bacon's notion of a real character. In *Mercury*, Wilkins discusses nonverbal forms of communication such as bells, birds, bullets, and arrows, to be used as codes in times of war. In addition, he muses on the possibilities of developing an immediately apprehensible language, patterned on the seemingly universal modes of mu-sical notes, arabic numbers, and Chinese script. Acknowledging a debt to Bacon and Wilkins, Cave Beck published *The Universal Character* (1657), in which he constructs a real character modeled on logarithms, hieroglyphics, and Chinese pictograms. The results look like algebraic formulas, with letters and numbers assembled to represent the different qualities of the thing signified. Other systems used signs composed of various squiggles to signify aspects of what is represented. Among the many proposals were George Dalgarno's *Ars Signorum* (1661), Francis Lodwick's *A Common Writing* (1647), and John Wilkins's *An Essay towards a Real Character and a Philosophical Language* (1668).[5]

Gesture as a universal, real character was briefly mentioned by Francis Bacon, and the idea was later expanded in stupefying detail by John Bulwer. His twin tracts, *Chirlogia: or the Natural Language of the Hand* and *Chirnomia: or the Art of Manual Rhetoric* (1644), exalt gesture above the tra-ditional use of words because it "had the happiness to escape the curse at the confusion of Babel."[6] Using gesture, in effect, brings man back to the paradisal understanding that he had with God in Eden, for the "language of the hand . . . hath since been sanctified and made a holy language by the expressions of our Savior's hands. . . . And God speaks to us . . . when he works wonders which are the proper signs of his hand."[7] Going far beyond the classical rhetorical tradition that emphasizes gesture as an adjunct to discourse,[8] Bulwer implies that men can better understand God's Creation without the barrier of man-made words.

In addition to the complaint in the seventeenth century that word and thing were not necessarily linked, ordinary language was faulted because its organization did not reflect the organization of the universe. The idea emerged, both in England and on the Continent, that a language might be created so that its structure would reveal the structure of nature. In such a system, the symbol for a thing would disclose its attributes and its rela-tionship to other things. The rationale behind a logically ordered philo-sophic language is explained by Francis Lodwick in *The Ground-work, or Foundation Laid . . . for the Framing of a New Perfect Language* (1652):

> Languages themselves were not at first invented by artists but common people whose invention encreased with their need of expressions, and wherein they heeded not the perfection and shortness of a language, but only what served their present necessity. . . . But now when we shall not be limitted to this or that particular language as we find it, but shall be at liberty in our invention and choice, what shall hinder but that we may con-trive such a grammar as respecting no particular language, but the genus or

kind of language may truly expresse things and their affections [qualities] by certain, short and constant rules, rectifying all those deffects we complain of in ordinary languages. And for the dictionary . . . we shall have enumerated things and rationally subordinated them.[9]

Like other "language planners," Lodwick proposed a linguistic revolution and advocated that the old "ordinary" language ought to be overthrown because it was constructed haphazardly over time through the usage of "common people," not "artists." Traditional English is not rationally ordered nor is it strictly denotative, which some linguists believed made it unsuitable for intellectual inquiry. Since the Modern seizes on simple remedies for complex problems, it is no wonder that Lodwick and others could conceive of nothing to "limit" or "hinder" Englishmen from creating a new and better language, which would in turn usher in an age of perfect enlightenment.

The prospect of a philosophical language that could serve as an instrument of scientific investigation encouraged the Royal Society to sponsor John Wilkins's project to formulate a real character and a philosophic language. Like Lodwick's universal character, Wilkins's consists of a hierarchy of signs that ostensibly reflects the order of the natural world. Wilkins writes in the "Dedication" to his *Essay*, "The reducing of all things and notions, to such kind of Tables, as are here proposed . . . would prove the shortest and plainest way to the attainment of real knowledge, that hath been yet offered to the World. And I shall add further, that these very Tables . . . do seem to me a much better and readier course, for entring and training up of men in the knowledge of things, then any other way of Institution that I know of."[10] A similar proposal for restructuring language was made by Johan Comenius, a mystic whose thought may have had considerable impact on the English-language theorists.[11] He declares that "a universal language ought to be a universal antidote to the confusion of thought. And it can only be that if [language's] course is parallel with the course of things."[12] Both visionaries and virtuosi embraced new forms of signification that would remove the obstacles to clear perception.

Swift laughed at the ludicrous possibility that fallen mankind might create essentially an unfallen language, and, of course, he was disturbed by the antisocial implications of such a pursuit. But he also demonstrated in his satire how impractical these language alternatives would be.

Swift's opinion of substitutes for ordinary discourse is evident in *Gulliver's Travels*, where, for instance, he implicitly evaluates John Bulwer's claims for gesture as a real character and universal language.[13] Gulliver's first three adventures in foreign lands are initiated by a gesture of supplication: usually he kneels and seems to beg for mercy, which he receives. The pattern of communication following this induction is generally similar in all the lands Gulliver visits. He uses gestures to signal his biological needs; his hosts comply. Understanding and harmony temporarily prevail. The generally halcyon period during which Gulliver communicates only in gesture is brief, and gradually he moves into a mixture of gestures and words. Finally he becomes master of the hosts' language, at which point unpleasant schisms develop. Once fluent in the Lilliputian tongue, for instance, he is threatened with blindness because he "plainly protested, that [he] would never be an Instrument of bringing a free and brave People [the Blefescudians] into Slavery" (*PW* 11:53).

The gesturing period in Gulliver's travels may seem Edenic, but Swift shows its limitations. Without speech, Gulliver is able only to indicate his most basic urges (to eat, to excrete, to sleep). Indeed, any lap dog could do as much, yet this primal level of communication is seen as an advantage by John Bulwer because it brings man into closer intimacy with animals, a "kind of knowledge that Adam partly lost with his innocency." [14] Thus if Gulliver appears human during his gesturing period, it is only as a baby. Indeed, in Brobdingnag, Gulliver is treated like a baby doll by Glumdalclitch, the farmer's daughter who initially discovers him: "Her Mother and she contrived to fit up the Baby's Cradle for me against the Night" (95), he reports.

By acquiring language, Gulliver in essence enters adulthood with its world of consequences, most of them painful. Swift implies, though, that unless one undergoes this maturation, one is not fully human. An absence of language denotes an absence of developed humanity, as Gulliver's inarticulate period demonstrates. The intellectual and spiritual abstractions that give life meaning cannot be communicated with mere body language.

The idea of a real character, which John Wilkins and others popularized, is specifically satirized when Gulliver visits the School of Languages at Lagado (185). There two projects are explained to Gulliver: "The first Project was to shorten Discourse by cutting Polysyllables into one, and leaving out Verbs and Participles; because in Reality all things imaginable are but Nouns" (185). This Lagadan linguistic innovation reflects several assumptions prevalent in contemporary schemes to replace standard language with new forms of signification, among them, that reducing the number of words will eliminate obscurity; that the purest and most effective languages are really concatenations of monosyllables; and that radicals, or monosyllabic units, ought to express observable things. The idea that the noun (or an "imaginable" thing) should be the linguistic building block derived from a variety of sources, including new theories of perception and current understandings about the nature of Chinese and Hebrew, languages whose clarity, it was believed, resulted from their use of discrete units of meaning to create signs.[15] In varying degrees, some of these ideas underlie Thomas Sprat's hope that "so many *things* [be delivered] almost in an equal number of words"[16] and Francis Lodwick's desire that his real character might "truly expresse things and their affections by certain, short, and constant rules . . . thereby much diminish[ing] the number of needful carracters."[17] When language planners complain about multiple terms for the same thing, they tend to ignore the connotative dimension of words and the importance of nuance.

In Wilkins's system of real characters, for instance, metaphoric associations are virtually eliminated. The gloss that Wilkins supplies on the symbol for *bread* [‹Ջ›] in his transcription of the first line of the Lord's Prayer is an illustration:

> This Character [‑Ջ‑] is appointed to signifie the Genus of *Oeconomical Provisions*, of which the first Difference denoted by the affix on the left hand, [‹] doth refer to *Sustenation ordinary* and the first Species at the other end [⌐] doth refer to such kind of ordinary food as is of a more solid consistence, made of Grain, or some other Vegetable baked, without any considerable mixture, being all other kinds of Food most Necessary and common which is *Bread*.[18]

Aside from the other problems inherent in Wilkins's real character—its ambiguity (couldn't biscuits as well as bread fit the description above?) and its unintelligibility to anyone who has not memorized his pages of tables—the notation presumes a literalness that removes the real meaning of the phrase *our daily bread*, which, of course, implies all man's temporal necessities, not just sandwich fixings.

The first of the Lagadan schemes satirizes some of the theoretical underpinnings of real characters; the second dramatizes what Swift believed was their profoundly materialistic nature by requiring that words be entirely abolished and things used instead: "Since Words are only Names for *Things*, it would be more convenient for all Men to carry about them, such *Things* as were necessary to express the particular Business they are to discourse on" (*PW* 11:185). Schemes of real characters also abolish words, replacing them not with the things themselves but with new and strange symbols. In both cases, the systems are unwieldy, whether one is thumbing through Wilkins's numerous tables or whether one, like the Lagadans using objects to communicate, is forced "to carry a [great] Bundle of *Things* upon his Back, unless he can afford one or two strong Servants to attend him" (185). The cumbersome nature of these real characters belies their creators' claims for their "convenience." They oppress rather than liberate.

Gulliver learns at Lagado that, "another great Advantage proposed by [replacing words with things] was, that it would serve as an universal Language to be understood in all civilized Nations, whose Goods and Utensils are generally of the same Kind" (186). Universality is a commonly cited benefit of real characters. A close look at the Lagadans, however, shows that they completely lack any understanding about the nature of either civilization or communication. Even if they were sincere in their aims to promote universal discourse in "all civilized Nations," what could be transmitted with their system—or any other system of real characters? [19] Since the fruits of rational thought are usually abstractions, nothing of any intellectual importance could be conveyed. Moreover, the character is more ambiguous, not less, than everyday language. If a Lagadan pulls a handkerchief and a tomato out of his backpack, what would he mean?

In *The Argument against Abolishing Christianity*, Swift facetiously criticizes the idea, inherent in the thinking of the language planners, that the faulty composition of language is to blame for man's folly and ignorance. At one point the Anti-Abolisher discusses the proposed advantages of removing the word *Christianity* from the lexicon; it will, proponents say, "utterly extinguish Parties among us, by removing those factious Distinctions of High and Low Church, of *Whig* and *Tory*, *Presbyterian* and *Church-of-England*" (PW 2:31). After consideration, the speaker rejects the idea for its impracticality, asking,

> Will any Man say, that if the Words *Whoring, Drinking, Cheating, Lying, Stealing*, were ejected . . . out of the *English* Tongue and Dictionaries; we should awake next Morning chaste and temperate, honest and just, and Lovers of Truth? Is this a fair consequence? Or if the Physicians would forbid us to pronounce the Words *Pox, Gout, Rheumatism*, and *Stone;* would that Expedient serve like so many *Talismans* to destroy the Diseases themselves? Are Party and Faction in Mens Hearts no deeper than Phrases borrowed from Religion; or founded upon no firmer Principles? And is our Language so poor, that we cannot find other Terms to express them?
>
> (32)

Although the *Argument* is laden with irony, this particular passage accurately reflects Swift's belief that modifying language cannot modify the nature of man or of things.

This idea is also illustrated in *Gulliver's Travels*. In every country

Gulliver visits, certain words are notably absent from the national vocabulary. The omissions are always ironic and betray the language users' lack of perception. In Lilliput, for instance, language includes the names of two countries only (*PW* 11:49), yet the absence of other place names, of course, does not mean they do not exist, for certainly Gulliver himself is proof of England's reality. The limitation of the Lilliputian tongue is a symptom of the extreme parochialism that constricts the country. In Brobdingnag, the dearth of political terms is specifically remarked, but even without the appropriate vocabulary to name it, politics is rife. Gulliver learns that the country has been beset with civil wars, attempted revolutions, and factious bickering. While in Laputa, Gulliver notes that the ideas of "Imagination, Fancy, and Invention, they are wholly Strangers to, nor have [they] any Words in their Language by which those Ideas can be expressed" (163), yet everything the airy Laputans think is either imagined, fancied, or invented. In the last voyage, Gulliver is told by the Houyhnhnms that they have no word for *"false Representation"* (241), but this does not prevent the horse master from concealing Gulliver's true nature.[20]

In all the cases above, reality is distorted by its lack of representation in language. Although many contemporary language theorists condemned what Bacon called the "Idols of the Marketplace"—errors of perception embedded in linguistic structure—for misleading men about the nature of things, Swift, hearkening to the classical tradition, put the blame for misconceptions squarely on men themselves. Throughout his canon, directly and indirectly, Swift stresses that language is an artifact created over time, which by gradual additions has gathered the means to express all the concepts men need. When new concepts arise, new words must be added to the lexicon, a process that extends, not rends, the weave of the language. If Latin had continued to be a living language, technological and political innovations would have generated new vocabulary, "yet the Antients would still have been read, and understood with Pleasure and Ease" (*Proposal, PW* 4:16). Swift would thus condemn the Houyhnhnms' need to alter reality (by expelling Gulliver) rather than to enlarge their lexicon with a word to describe him.[21] Although the horse master devised a workable label for Gulliver—"wonderful *Yahoo*" (*PW* 11:272)—the rest of the Houyhnhnms rejected it because "it was not agreeable to Reason or Nature, nor a thing ever heard of before among them. The Assembly did therefore *exhort* [the horse master], either to employ [Gulliver] like the rest of [his] Species, or command [him] to swim back to the Place from whence" he had come (279).

Many language planners hoped that if the flaws of everyday language were corrected, Englishmen could join together in peace.[22] In the Preface to his *Essay*, John Wilkins predicts that his plan will evaporate "some of our Modern differences in Religion, by unmasking many wild errors, that shelter themselves under the disguise of affected phrases."[23] George Dalgarno also promises that the system of signification he presents in *Ars Signorum* (1661) can bring back Edenic solidarity by remedying "the difficulties and absurdities which all languages are clogg'd with ever since the confusion, or rather since the fall."[24] Describing a world with an improved language, Johan Comenius sees all men becoming "as it were one race, one people, one household, one School of God."[25]

The relation of peace to linguistic perfection is a theme in *Gulliver's Travels*. The Lilliputians' language is full of circumlocution and redundancy, and indeed they are engaged in a particularly moronic civil war, which pits the low heels against the high heels. The commonplace seventeenth-century association of corrupt language with internal dissension seems validated there. In Brobdingnag, however, an opposite language prevails. Gulliver notes that "they avoid nothing more than multiplying unnecessary Words, or using various Expressions" (137) and that "as well as the *Chinese*," the Brobdingnagians have been masters of printing a long time, but because of their inability "to discover above one Interpretation" to laws and other doctrines, their literary output "doth not amount to above a thousand Volumes" (136). Judged by the criteria of many language planners, Brobdingnagian language, because of its succinctness and literalness, is close to ideal. Thus one would expect domestic harmony: not so. The king has to maintain peace with a militia of 208,000 persons, whom he has "kept in the strictest Duty" for two generations since the last civil war (138). The same lack of political and verbal coherence can be seen in Laputa. Although the School of Languages has developed the ultimate real character, the use of things themselves, the Lagadans are at war with their sister island.

The Houyhnhnm language is compared with Chinese (226) and Teutonic (234), two languages that had been associated with the Adamic language by various theorists. And as it was in the Garden, life in Houyhnhnmland is printless, presumably because the Book of Nature is fully accessible. The horses do not allow multiple definitions of words, nor do they perceive any ambiguities in their lexicon. Regardless of the seemingly ideal nature of their language, though, they are unable to live in peace with their compatriots, the Yahoos, or to accept Gulliver within their fold.[26] Their language restricts their ability to see virtues in any but their own kind or to analyze new situations. Thus in every country Gulliver visits some civil turmoil exists, whether or not the country's language approaches the language planners' ideals. In Swift's view, then, people, not language, cause obscurity.

Semantic Theories

How words convey meaning was of continuing interest to the linguists of the seventeenth and early eighteenth centuries. Schemes such as Wilkins's were devised to make the order of signs more congruent with the order of things. Then, according to Murray Cohen,

> By the beginning of the eighteenth century, the idea of language study had shifted from the taxonomic representation of words and things to the establishment of the relationship between speech and thought. Seventeenth-century linguists sought to establish an isomorphic relationship between language and nature; in the early eighteenth century, linguists assumed that language reflects the structure of the mind.[27]

Swift was opposed, on one hand, to the "scientific," empirical definition advocated by Bacon and others in the seventeenth century because he believed that it conflated words with things, and he was also disturbed by the contemporary notion that meaning was related somehow to the particular operations of the human mind. Rejecting both of these ideas, Swift believed language was a historical entity that transcended both materialism and individualism.[28]

Among seventeenth-century philosophers and language planners, according to Cohen, the "basic strategies common to all their linguistic taxonomies [were] . . . systematization, sequentiality, division into elements, and visualization."[29] Such an approach reduces language to a collection of empirical phenomena. Bacon, for instance, suggests that *heat* could be more precisely defined by breaking it down into concrete components, "fixed and exhibited in due order" in "tables and co-ordinations of instances."[30] He stresses the importance of bringing "men to particulars, and their regular series and order, and [that] they must for a while renounce their notions and begin to form an acquaintance with things."[31] Swift would reject the taxonomic systems of the seventeenth century as ad hoc, artificial constructs at variance with his idea of language as a fabric continually woven through time.

Swift emphasized satirically that in their attempts to link *res* and *verba* more firmly, language theorists reduce the traditional range of a word and confuse its commonly accepted meanings. The persona's discussion of *spirit* in *A Tale of a Tub* is a case in point. Explicating a text from Lucretius, the *Tale*-teller notes that one passage "is what the *Adepti* understand by their *Anima Mundi;* that is to say, the *Spirit,* or *Breath,* or *Wind* of the World. . . . Examine the whole System by the Particulars of Nature, and you will find it not to be disputed" (*PW* 1 : 95). Spirit is reduced to wind in "Abyss of Things"—the atomistic world Swift depicts in *A Tale of a Tub,* where literalization strips the common forms of any meaning. The *Tale*-teller's advice to "Examine the whole System by the Particulars of Nature" reminds one of the empiricists' goal, as stated by Bacon, to "bring men to particulars." By defining *spirit* so physically, the *Tale*-teller eliminates the range of metaphoric meanings the word usually has. His narrow materialism reveals his failings and those of "scientific" systems of definition.[32]

The recurrent strategies of definition used during this period—systematization, sequentiality, visualization, and division into elements—are further mocked by the *Tale*-teller's attempts to determine the meaning of *Humane Nature,* a concept obviously alien to him. He describes how he "dissected the Carcass of *Humane Nature . . .* till at last it *smelt* so strong, I could preserve it no longer. Upon which, I have been at great Expence to fit up all the Bones with Exact Contexture, and in due Symmetry; so that I am ready to shew a very compleat Anatomy thereof to all curious *Gentlemen and others*" (*PW* 1 : 77). The *Tale*-teller's misunderstanding of language is profound. Taking *anatomy* and *dissection* literally, he fails entirely to see the connotative or metaphoric aspects of words. The result of his surgical rather than intellectual operation is not a clearer idea of *Humane nature* but a collection of bones arranged in "due Symmetry," perhaps a parody of Bacon's statement that "it is better to dissect than abstract nature. . . . It is best to consider matter."[33]

Implicit in Swift's satire is the idea that words are social conventions, not physical things. By pushing them into things, one kills off their vital transcendence over circumstance and time. They lose their organic flexibility and their historical resonances. They become static, dead objects—like the corpse of *Humane Nature.* This materialistic process is mocked in the *Tale*-teller's discussion of *zeal* in which he shows "how it first proceeded from a *Notion* into a *Word,* and from thence in a hot Summer, ripned into a *tangible Substance*" (*PW* 1 : 86). Words reduced to things no longer operate as language.

John Locke's popularization of the argument that words refer to ideas in the mind rather than to things themselves forced linguists to consider the way in which the mind endowed words with meaning.[34] In his *Essay Concerning Human Understanding,* Locke says that most individuals do not assign meaning in any logical or objective way but allow words to become tinged with associations peculiar to themselves. Thus men's thoughts do not follow "natural correspondences" but rather "*Ideas* that in themselves are not at all of kin, come to be so united in some Mens Minds," causing definitions of words to vary from speaker to speaker.[35] Each person's singularity is so pronounced, Locke suggests, that all will forgive his calling the ordinary operations of the mind

> by so harsh a name as *Madness*, when it is considered, that opposition to Reason deserves that Name, and is really Madness; and there is scarce a man so free from it, but that if he should always on all occasions, argue or do in some cases as he constantly does, would not be thought fitter for Bedlam, than Civil Conversation. I do not here mean when he is under the power of an unruly Passion, but in the steady calm course of his Life.[36]

In a mad world where definitions are generated from individuals' unique associations with a word, communication is impossible. Swift's *Tale*-teller, seemingly mindful of the assumptions Locke makes about definition by association, blithely advises the reader to recreate exactly the particular events surrounding the authorship of his text:

> Whatever Reader desires to have a thorow Comprehension of an Author's Thoughts, cannot take a better Method, than by putting himself into the Circumstances and Postures of Life, that the Writer was in, upon every important Passage as it flow'd from his Pen; For this will introduce a Parity and strict Correspondence of Idea's between the Reader and the Author. Now, to assist the diligent Reader in so delicate an Affair, as far as brevity will permit, I have recollected, that the shrewdest Pieces of this Treatise, were conceived in Bed, in a Garret: At other times (for a Reason best known to myself) I thought fit to sharpen my Invention with Hunger; and in general, the whole Work was begun, continued, and ended, under a long Course of Physick.
> (*PW* 1:26–27)

In other words, to appreciate fully the wit "calculated for this present Month of *August*, 1697," one should rent a garret identical to the narrator's and use the same kind of laxative. The *Tale*-teller epitomizes the condition of human understanding as Locke conceives it. Without some remedy, meaning is ephemeral and singular rather than permanent and general. But, as Matthew Prior points out, "If this were so, then Locke's essay on human understanding could only be read by Locke himself."[37]

Locke hoped that exposing the irrational operations of the mind would bring men to embrace a new type of definition that would eliminate subjective ambiguity. Locke suggests that terms be broken down into discrete sense impressions, or "simple ideas," that, in combination, form all ideas. Thus his solution, unacceptable to Swift, was to have abstract words "defined, and reduced in their Signification . . . to determined collections of the simple *Ideas* they do or should stand for."[38] In Swift's view, Locke's method obscures, rather than reveals, meaning. When Matthew Tindal writes, "*It will be necessary to shew what is contained in the Idea of Government,*" Swift denounces "this refined Way of Speaking [that] was introduced by Mr. *Locke:* After whom the Author limpeth as fast as he was able." Swift then continues by contrasting the Modern method of definition, proposed by Locke, with the traditional one:

> All the former Philosophers in the World, from the Age of *Socrates* to ours, would have ignorantly put the Question, *Quid est Imperium?* But now it seemeth we must vary our Phrase; and since our modern Improvement of Human Understanding, instead of desiring of a Philosopher to describe or define a Mousetrap, or tell me what it is; I must gravely ask, what is contained in the Idea of a Mouse-trap?
>
> (*Remarks upon Tindall's Rights, PW* 2:80)

Instead of seeking definitions in the operation of the mind, Swift would appeal to common sense—traditional, generally accepted notions. Sarcastically he asks the reader "to observe how deeply this new Way of putting Questions to a Man's self, maketh him enter into the Nature of Things" (80) and then quotes Tindal's impenetrable discussion of the "*Idea of Government.*" After a lengthy quotation, Swift hoots, "What mighty Truths are here discovered; And how clearly conveyed to our Understandings? and therefore let us melt this refined Jargon into the *Old Style*, for the Improvement of such, who are not enough conversant in the *New.* . . . If the Author were one that used to talk like one of us, he would have spoke in this Manner" (80), and what follows is homespun wisdom in homespun words that the most uneducated person could understand. Inherent in the Old Style of definition is the tradition of strength and straightforwardness that made England great; inherent in the New Style is the threat of cultural annihilation.[39]

Investigation to Determine the Original Language

Unhappiness with existing language prompted various seventeenth-century thinkers to search for the original, Adamic language, which might have survived the Fall and the Confusion and thus be largely free from the linguistic pollution ensuing from those events. One popular candidate for the original language was Hebrew because of its conciseness (multiplication of terms was seen as a by-product of Babel), because of the belief that children in isolation naturally begin to speak Hebrew (an experiment King James is said to have tried),[40] and because of the perception that the structure of Hebrew mirrors the perfection of the cosmos, thus manifesting "that Primitive and Divine, or purely rational Sematology taught by Almighty God, or invented by *Adam* before the Fall."[41] Other existing languages, both ancient and contemporary, were also suggested as the *lingua adamica*. The proposal of Chinese as a language that escaped the ravages of Babel can be found, for example, in John Webb's *Historical Essay Endeavoring the Probability That the Language of China Is the Primitive Language* (1669).[42] In *Origines Antveripiae*, Goropius Becanus, a Dutchman, suggested it was Dutch.

Chauvinism frequently affected perceptions of what the original or primitive language might be. A Swede, Andreas Kemke, humorously speculated that "God spoke Swedish, Adam Danish, and the serpent French."[43] Nationalistic arguments were usually bolstered by etymologies that validated the antiquity of the language's culture. To "prove" his case, a language theorist might atomize Hebrew, Greek, or Latin words into "roots" that resembled words or syllables in his native language, thus demonstrating that it antedated the so-called ancient or original languages. These linguists "discovered" whatever patterns they sought and used that "evidence" to establish a close relationship of their culture with that of the biblical patriarchs and the heroes of classical civilizations.[44] Samuel Butler comments on this trend in *Hudibras* when he laughs at one scholar who

> For *Hebrew* Roots, although th' are found
> To flourish most in barren ground,
> He had such plenty, as suffic'd,
> To make some think him circumcis'd.

As for speculation about the languages spoken in the Garden of Eden, Butler marvels at those who ponder how Eve was seduced and "Whether the Devil tempted her / By a *high Dutch* Interpreter."[45]

By creating a ridiculous persona who believes that "the Greeks, the Romans, and the Jews, spoke the language we now do in England" (*PW* 4:239), Swift, in *The Discourse to Prove the Antiquity of the English Tongue*, mocks both the methods and the aspirations of those who seek to show that their particular language is original or primitive. The speaker proves his thesis by showing that classical names have English roots, which, like a real character, contain the name's meaning. For instance, "*Aristophanes* was a Greek comedian, full of levity, and gave himself too much freedom; which made a graver people not scruple to say, that he had a great deal of *airy stuff in his* writings: And these words, often repeated, made succeeding ages denominate him *Aristophanes*" (236). The biblical heroes also really have English names, Moses, for example, being so called "because he *mowed* the *seas* down in the middle, to make a path for the Israelites" (239).

Swift singles out four language theorists for special mention in the *Discourse* when the persona claims, "I shall use my readers much fairer than Pezron, Skinner, Vorstigan [Verstegan], Camden, and many other superficial pretenders have done" (231). Paul Pezron, a Frenchman, proved the ancient nature of the "Gaulish" language by constructing "large Alphabetical Tables"[46] to illustrate that men "who in *Ancient Times* were so *Famous* and *Renowned*, and by the Greeks and Romans *even worshipped* for Gods, nay more, for the Almighty Gods of Heaven and Earth, were of the same Race or People, from whom the Gauls afterwards came; and this is so manifest, that I shall make it out . . . from the Names of these supposed Divinities."[47] Pezron discounts national pride as the motivation for his research: "It may be thought I have undertaken this Subject with a Design to aggrandize my own Nation, by making it appear beyond Contradiction, to be one of the Ancientest in the World: I dare be bold here to affirm, that such Suggestions are utterly false."[48]

Whereas Pezron uses etymology to prove that "Gaulish" was the original language, Richard Verstegan (a.k.a. Richard Rowlands) proceeded with a similarly misguided method in *A Restitution of Decayed Intelligence* (first published in 1605; seven editions by 1673) to show that it was "Teutonic," or proto-English. Verstegan believes that biblical names make more sense if one searches for their Teutonic roots rather than assuming they have Hebrew roots. *Adam*, for instance, means "red clay" in Hebrew, but Verstegan contrives a series of Teutonic words that sound like *Adam* and mean "living breath," a likelier etymology, he contends. Verstegan argues that Teutonic, like Hebrew, displays aspects of a real character (he notes the links between *Babel* and *babble*, *devil* and *evil*, *Abel* and *able*, *God* and *good*) and that, like Hebrew, Teutonic consists of monosyllabic roots, "each having [its] own proper signification, as by instinct of God and nature they were first received and understood."[49] Thus one can, Verstegan says, look at an English word with Teutonic roots, such as *woman* and see its original meaning: *womb-man*.[50]

Swift rather unfairly includes William Camden and Stephen Skinner among the Modern etymologists. Although Camden is guilty of linking Gomer of the Old Testament with a Welshman named Kumero[51] and proposing some outlandish word origins ("*Sayle* as the *Sea-haile, Windor* and *Windowe*, as a door against the winde"), he heartily denounces false etymologizing.[52] Stephen Skinner, the last of the linguists Swift mentions in the *Discourse*, makes no particularly extravagant claims for the ancestry of the English language, although he cites rather farfetched etymologies in his *Etymologicon Linguae Anglicanae* (London, 1669). Moreover, Skinner speculated about relationships between languages in what Swift would consider to be a very Modern manner: in his arguments, "any letter, and presumably any sound [could] . . . become any other, without regard to time, place, or linguistic relationship."[53] Although the *Discourse* is a very minor and quite silly literary production, it reveals Swift's wide reading on linguistic matters and reflects his concern, albeit humorous, with illegitimate etymology.

Swift, therefore, satirizes solutions to verbal obscurity that would radically alter the traditional forms of the English language with Modern innovations. In contrast to some of his contemporaries who believed the Royal Society's motto, *Nullius in Verba*, Swift trusted the language's capacity to transmit the important truths that people needed. Language as it was prevalently used, however, often did not serve that function, and so, like others of his age, Swift pondered ways to improve communication. His *Proposal for Correcting, Improving, and Ascertaining the English Tongue* is the most doctrinaire expression of his ideas.

6

How Possibly to Improve Discourse: The Proposal for an Academy

> I hope, when this Treatise of mine shall be translated into Foreign Languages . . . that the worthy Members of the several *Academies* abroad, especially those of *France* and *Italy*, will favorably accept these humble Offers, for the Advancement of Universal Knowledge.
> *A Tale of a Tub, PW* 1:65

In the mid- to late seventeenth century, the desirability of creating an academy to regulate language was generally accepted in England and on the Continent, where the French and Italians had already founded institutions for this purpose. Although Swift's *Proposal for Correcting, Improving, and Ascertaining the English Tongue* ostensibly argues that England ought to remedy her linguistic problems through the work of an academy, the document is confusing because it subverts its own arguments. The text and the subtext of the *Proposal* are at odds, reflecting Swift's own dualism, his wish on one hand for some regulation of language and on the other, his suspicion of instant (as opposed to ancient) institutions, such as an academy. Contradicting each other also are the national and personal goals that Swift simultaneously promotes in the essay.

The Text

Swift's *Proposal*, contrived as an epistle to Robert Harley, articulates the need for a national institution to guide the development of the English language and to provide some method of standardizing it. Because Swift believed that preserving the common forms of language was necessary for national well-being, he urged the immediate implementation of plans for an academy. He refutes the idea that "*all such Thoughts must be deferred to a Time of Peace:* a Topick which some have carried so far, that they would not have us by any Means think of preserving our Civil or Religious Constitution, because we are engaged in a War abroad" (*Proposal, PW* 4:5–6). Here Swift argues against statements such as Dryden's that England not form an academy until "the quiet of the Nation . . . be secur'd; and a mutuall trust, betwixt Prince and people be renew'd."[1] Dryden may be echoing the sentiments of the French, who delayed the establishment of their academy until "publick tranquility" and "good order" were restored after civil and foreign wars, because they felt that the polishing of their language should occur only in a time of peace.[2] In contrast, Swift believed that the "Civil [and] Religious Constitution" and the English language expressing it must be maintained regardless of political distractions.

To this end, Swift advocated a bipartisan, nonpolitical academy, whose members would be selected without regard to "Quality, Party, or Profession" (14). To Stella he explains, "tis no Politicks, but a harmless Proposall about the Improvemt of the Engl. Tongue" (*JS* 2:535). At one point he wrote Archbishop William King that he and Harley had chosen ten men from each party for the academy (*C* 1:295). And as a conciliatory gesture toward the Whigs, Swift praises Steele in the *Proposal*, later telling him "that, in the only thing I ever published with my name, I took care to celebrate you as much as I could" (*C* 1:360). Although he would be insulted at the comparison, Swift's linguistic society is similar in concept to the Royal Society, which admitted people without consideration of religion, occupation, or nationality, so that, as Sprat says, "there will no one particular of them overweigh the other, or make the *Oracle* onely speak their *private* sence."[3] On one level, then, Swift saw the academy as a national conversation, ideally drawing all parts of society together in a matter of mutual concern. On another level Swift used the *Proposal* to establish certain partisan and personal stances that were at odds with the theme of unity.

The major functions of the academy, suggested by the *Proposal*'s title page, would be "Correcting, Improving, and Ascertaining the English Tongue." These actions are necessary, Swift implies, because increased publication had solidified into print many "Alterations" that violated traditional norms. In the past, when the world was less book-ridden, linguistic change was impeded by such works as the Bible and the *Book of Common Prayer*, which, because they were "perpetually read in Churches, have proved a Kind of Standard for Language, especially to the common People" (*Proposal, PW* 4:15). In recent times, however, all sorts of solecisms were committed to print, a complaint of a purported letter-writer in one of Swift's *Tatlers:* "I would engage to furnish you with a Catalogue of English Books published within the Compass of seven Years past, which at first hand would cost you an hundred Pounds; wherein you shall not be able to find ten Lines together of common Grammar, or common Sense. . . . Without some timely Remedy," he warns, the English language "will suffer more by the false Refinements of Twenty years past, than it hath been improved in the foregoing Hundred" (*Tatler, PW* 2 : 174; italics omitted). Swift expresses this opinion directly in the *Proposal* when he wonders whether "from that great Rebellion to this present Time [1712] . . . the Corruptions in our Language have not, at least, equalled the Refinements of it" (*PW* 4:9–10). Swift seemed to believe that an academy could slow the rate of linguistic corruption.

Abbreviation and faddish invention are two types of linguistic disintegration an academy might control. These are the vices allegorized in Peter's elaboration of his coat and Jack's shredding of his. In either case, the traditional fabric of language is rent by Moderns, like the men about town, "who had Credit enough to give Rise to some new Word, and propagate it in most Conversations; although it had neither Humour nor Significancy"; or poets, who create "Manglings and Abbreviations" to "fit [words] to the Measure of their Verses"; or university men, who "reckon all their Errors for Accomplishments, borrow the newest Set of Phrases; and if they take a Pen in their Hands, all the odd Words they have picked up in a Coffee-House, or a Gaming-ordinary, are produced as Flowers of Style; and the Orthography refined to the utmost" (10–12). Swift cites the self-styled elite as the source of linguistic pollution that will inevitably filter into that wellspring of pure language, the speech of common people.

In *An Argument against Abolishing Christianity,* Swift humorously describes the process by which fads emanate from the top of the social hierarchy, gradually trickle down, and ultimately disappear. The speaker here notes that abolishing Christianity may be a waste of time because no one believes in it anymore anyway:

> I freely own, that all Appearances are against me. The System of the Gospel, after the Fate of other Systems is generally antiquated and exploded; and the Mass or Body of the common People, among whom it seems to have had its latest Credit, are now grown as much ashamed of it as their Betters: Opinions, like Fashions, always descending from those of Quality to the Middle Sort, and thence to the Vulgar, where at length they are dropt and vanish.
>
> (*PW* 2:27)

In this apocalyptic vision, all common forms of religion are forgotten, but the common people are the last to let go of their memories.

To prevent the meaning of words from being "dropt" and vanishing, Swift, sharing the position of many early eighteenth-century linguists,[4] sees etymology as the anchor that stabilizes the language by linking it to its historical origins. He opposed concocted or mangled words because their etymologies were either illegitimate or indiscernible. The Modern, though, has so little concern for traditional forms that he sees the shortening of words as a step toward "Perfection," the ultimate "Perfection" being total annihilation: Swift satirizes this idea when he ironically declares, "Some Words are hitherto but fairly split; and therefore only in their Way to Perfection; as *Incog.* [for incognito] and *Plenipo's* [for plenipotentiaries]: But in a short Time, it is to be hoped, they will be further docked to *Inc* and *Plen*" (*Tatler, PW* 2:175–76). Equally vitiating are linguistic inventions, "such as *Banter, Bamboozle, Country Put, and Kidney* . . . some of which are now struggling for the Vogue, and others are in Possession of it" (176). Here is the process of verbal "uncreating" that horrified both Swift and Pope.

Swift, like most people, did not necessarily expect people to talk strictly in standard English, but he believed that those who committed their thoughts to print had an obligation to reinforce traditional linguistic practice. (Swift's requirements for spoken and written discourse are discussed in Chapter 7.) Swift was not alone in fearing that casual alterations of the language in conversation might find their way into print. John Dryden, for instance, worried that "so long as some affect to Speak them, there will not want others who will have the boldness to Write them."[5] When the *Tale*-teller fails to impress people with his conversation, he is inspired to set himself up as an author because print gives a certain cachet to his utterances, "For, I have remarked many a *towardly Word*, to be wholly neglected or despised in *Discourse*, which hath passed very smoothly, with some Consideration and Esteem, after its Preferment and Sanction in *Print*" (*PW* 1:134–35). Swift realized that an army of Moderns with easy access to printing presses could shortly destroy the language. Swift did not seem to agree with Samuel Johnson's opinion, expressed later in the century, that linguistic variations "will always be observed to grow fewer, and less different, as books are multiplied."[6] If all authors are as energetic and as entropic as the *Tale*-teller, who even as he is finishing one collection of fragments threatens an immediate sequel, the language is in great peril.

Although Swift is not explicit in the *Proposal*, one presumes Modern manglings and abbreviations are some of the "many Words that deserve to be utterly thrown out . . . [and] to be corrected." In addition, he notes that "the Grammar-part" of the language is "very defective" and that there are numerous other "gross Improprieties" to be remedied by the academy (*PW* 4 : 14).

To improve the language, Swift suggests that certain words be added. Indeed, incorporating new vocabulary to reflect new ideas is a feature of enduring cultures.

> Had the *Roman* Tongue continued vulgar in that City till this Time; it would have been absolutely necessary, from the mighty Changes that have been made in Law and Religion; from the many Terms of Art required in Trade and in War; from the new Inventions that have happened in the World; from the vast spreading of Navigation and Commerce; with many other obvious Circumstances, to have made great Additions to that Language; yet the Antients would still have been read, and understood with Pleasure and Ease. The *Greek* Tongue received many Enlargements between the Time of *Homer*, and that of *Plutarch;* yet the former Author was probably as well understood in *Trajan's* Time, as the latter. What *Horace* says of *Words going off, and perishing like Leaves, and new ones coming in their Place*, is a Misfortune he laments, rather than a Thing he approves: But I cannot see why this should be absolutely necessary, or if it were, what would have become of his *Monumentum ære perennius*.
>
> (15 – 16)

Swift emphasizes here that amplification of a language is a natural process, one that in no way lessens the intelligibility of literature to future generations. Exactly how he thinks words should be added to the lexicon is vague, but, judging from his stress on etymology, one would suppose he advocates the creation of words from recognizable roots. To maintain the currency of all works written in English, Swift asserts that no words should be dropped from the national lexicon because they are obsolete, an opinion that Samuel Johnson found ridiculous.

Improvements and corrections to the language, however, are not what Swift had "most at Heart" in the *Proposal*. His paramount interest was "in *Ascertaining* and *Fixing* our Language for ever, after such Alterations are made in it as shall be thought requisite" (14). The bulk of the epistle argues this point. Swift laments that the readership of English writers is "confined to these two Islands; and it is hard it should be limited in *Time* as much as *Place* by the perpetual Variations of our Speech" (14). Authors, particularly historians, will lose their incentive to write: "How . . . shall any Man . . . be able to undertake . . . a Work with Spirit and Cheerfulness, when he considers, that he will be read with Pleasure but a very few Years, and in an Age or two shall hardly be understood without an Interpreter?" (18). Without some standard, the literary relics of the past will be lost and future productions aborted by the fear of impermanence. The memoryless void the Struldbruggs or the *Tale*-brothers inhabit would soon be home for everyone.

How did Swift propose fixing and ascertaining the language? Perhaps he had in mind a dictionary such as the Académie Française sought to compile, but he does not suggest this, either in his *Proposal* or elsewhere. He is adamant, though, that English be "refined to a certain Standard" (9)—not a theoretical standard but one that could be effectively realized, for, he says, "it is better a Language should not be wholly perfect, than that it should be perpetually changing" (14). Samuel Johnson agreed that the anomalies of language cannot be eradicated but "require only to be registered, that they may not be increased, and ascertained, that they may not be confounded" and that "for the law to be *known*, is of more importance than to be right. . . . There is in constancy and stability a general and lasting advantage, which will always overbalance the slow improvements of gradual correction."[7]

Although he provides no details, one assumes that Swift would have the academy standardize the spelling of words. Otherwise basic aspects of language, corrupted by the vagaries of pronunciation, would slowly change from generation to generation. As a case in point, Swift notes that "the rude *Latin* of the Monks is still very intelligible; whereas, had their Records been delivered down only in the vulgar Tongue . . . so subject to continual succeeding Changes; they could not now be understood" (18). To guarantee a language's persistence over time and geography, Swift believed that consistency in graphic forms must be maintained. In this sense he wished to "fix and ascertain" English.

Swift told Harley that the events of Queen Anne's reign "ought to be recorded in Words more durable than Brass, and such as our Posterity may read a thousand Years hence" (17). He cites Chinese as an example of a language resistant to linguistic change; its characters are understood by all China's inhabitants, regardless of their regional speech differences, and have survived thousands of years. Swift argues that not only will a language with set graphic forms assure cultural continuity, but it will foster national unity by eliminating barriers of dialect. For this reason Swift opposes suggestions that spelling ought to conform to pronunciation: "Not only the several Towns and Counties of *England*, have a different Way of pronouncing, but even here in *London*, they clip Words after one Manner about the Court, another in the City, and a third in the Suburbs; and in a

94

few Years, it is Probable, will all differ from themselves, as Fancy or Fashion shall direct" (11). London will crumble out to atomies, and the rest of the country will follow, unless a uniform spelling standard is enforced. Swift's conviction that a standard written language would preserve the political and cultural unity of England explains his almost fanatic emphasis on proper spelling.

One of the first persons to focus on the uncertainties of English spelling was William Camden. He noted, as did most writers on this subject, that English spelling has a bewildering inconsistency. To illustrate the point, Camden cited the experiment of Sir John Price, who "reporteth that a sentence spoken by him in English, & penned out of his mouth by foure good Secretaries, severally, for trial of our Orthography, was so set downe by them, that they all differed one from the other in many letters."[8] For those who sought to ascertain the spelling of doubtful words two choices existed: they could establish spelling to reflect either pronunciation or etymology. Some of the most radical proposals for spelling reform came from theorists who sought to make the graphic representations of words mirror current pronunciation. One of the first of these innovators was Sir Thomas Smith, Queen Elizabeth's secretary, who proposed resurrecting certain letters from Anglo-Saxon to express English sounds not adequately designated by Roman letters,[9] an idea that Ben Jonson and others supported.[10] Charles Butler suggested even more sweeping spelling revisions; a brief example is his expression of his belief that the language would be most easily fixed "if wee writ' [his system involves the use of apostrophes to signify certain sounds] altogether according to the sound nou generally received."[11]

In the first decades of the eighteenth century, spelling books were commonplace, the most popular being Thomas Dyche's *A Guide to the English Tongue* (1707); Dyche and other spelling book compilers wanted words to reflect their historical origin and thus grounded orthography in etymology,[12] a movement Swift supported. Decrying those who "spell as they speak," Swift sarcastically denounced pronunciation as a basis for written forms—"A noble Standard for Language!" (*Tatler, PW* 2:176). Swift elaborates this idea in *Proposal* when he condemns the "foolish Opinion . . . that we ought to spell exactly as we speak; which beside the obvious Inconvenience of utterly destroying our Etymology, would be a Thing we should never see the End of. . . . All which reduced to Writing, would entirely confound Orthography. [It would be just as wise to shape our Bodies to our Cloathes and not our Cloathes to our bodyes]" (*PW* 4:11, brackets in the text). The sound of words is subject to the vagaries of time and place, but etymology is a historical constant. Samuel Johnson accepted this as a guiding principle in publishing his *Dictionary* (1755), which, more than anything else, standardized English spelling.

If spelling is to be regulated by etymology, how should definitions be determined? Again, Swift does not specify this in the *Proposal*. In his passing remarks on the subject elsewhere, Swift implies that meanings of words derive from a historical consensus. But what discourse should be the standard—that of the "best" or most educated speakers, as Quintilian, Ben Jonson, and John Dryden argued, or that of the "ordinary" speaker, as Cicero, Thomas Wilson, and Thomas Sprat argued? This debate about whose discourse should be the basis for a standard began in ancient times and continues to the present day.[13] Swift's satires against erudite definition as a means of obfuscation and his suspicion that the educated elite are an active force in shredding the language suggest that he would seek meaning among the common speakers of the language rather than the "best" speakers.

The following examples, multiplied for effect, show the pervasiveness in Swift's thought of the idea that the average, modestly rational English-speaker knows exactly what a certain word means in a certain context and that in ordinary discourse, words do not need definition: "Politicks, as the Word is *commonly understood,* are nothing but Corruptions" (*Thoughts on Various Subjects, PW* 4:246); "If those two Rivals were really no more than Parties, *according to the common Acceptation* of the Word" (*Examiner, PW* 3:122); "what we call *Whigs* in the Sense which by that Word is *generally understood*" (*Drapier's Letters, PW* 10:132); "we are a free People, in the *Common Acceptation of that Word*" (100); "Liberty and Property are words of *known Use and Signification in this Kingdom;* and that the very Lawyers pretend to understand" (87); "and a man may be very loyal, in the *common sense* of the word, without one grain of public good at his heart" (*On Doing Good, PW* 9:233); "I believe him to be an honest Gentleman, as the Word *Honest* is *generally understood*" (*Advice to the Freemen of Dublin, PW* 13:84); "there is no Word more frequently in the Mouths of Men, than that of *Conscience,* and the Meaning of it is in some measure *generally understood*" (*Testimony of Conscience, PW* 9:150); "But that is not what in *common speech* we usually mean by Church" (*References to Tindall's Rights, PW* 2:87); "The whole Kingdom had given the same Interpretation that I had done. . . . Friends and Enemies agreed in applying the word *Faction*" (*Some Remarks upon a Pamphlet, PW* 3:192) (some italics added; others deleted). One would suppose, therefore, that the members of Swift's proposed academy would not determine the definitions of words in the abstract but, rather, would somehow gather the particulars of everyday speech to establish meaning, although this operation, like most others, is not elaborated in the *Proposal*.

The Subtext

The *Proposal for Correcting, Improving, and Ascertaining the English Tongue* is a strange document because its factional rhetoric is at odds with Swift's vision of a bipartisan academy. Although no theory satisfactorily explains the odd combination of assertions in the *Proposal*, one might conclude that the creation of an English academy was not his main object in publishing the piece. Indeed, the academy and its methods are barely mentioned. If the academy is not the focus of the *Proposal*, what is?

Louis Landa suggests that the "red flags" in the document—the insults to the Whigs, the fulsome praise of Harley, and Swift's signature—indicate that he wanted to accentuate its Tory bias so as to "provoke opposition and to avoid any leaven of Whiggism in the . . . Academy." In other words, Swift "wished the Whigs to dissociate themselves from the project [so that] entire credit for the founding of the Academy should rest with Harley and Harley's supporters."[14] This interpretation of Swift's motives is also offered by Irvin Ehrenpreis, who believes that Swift wanted to cast a "permanent lustre on his friends' political administration" by making sure all knew that this was a Tory idea.[15] Yet Swift seems to acknowledge that without general support, the British academy could not function because he praises Steele, a Whig spokesman, and asserts their agreement on matters linguistic. At the same time, though, Swift pointedly offends the Whigs in his praise of Harley as a man who saved England from ruin "by a *foreign War*, and a *domestick Faction*" (18).

Creation of an academy in the *Proposal* may be secondary to Swift's interest in using it as a means to patch up the quarrel between the Lord Treasurer, Harley, and the Secretary of State, Bolingbroke, that threatened the stability of the Tory ministry. Swift could argue to himself that if the Tories lost power, England's cultural integrity would be imperiled by the rapacious moneyed class with its latitudinarian prejudices. Knowing that both Harley and Bolingbroke would concur on the importance of correcting, improving, and ascertaining the English language, Swift seems to have used the proposal for an academy as an excuse to involve them in an issue he hoped was bigger than their petty feud, all the while reminding them of their common enemy, the Whigs. Swift describes the process to Archbishop King:

I have been engaging my Lord Treasurer and the other great Men in a Project of my own, which they tell me they will embrace, especially his Lordship. He is to erect some kind of Society or Academy under the Patronage of the Ministers, and Protection of the Queen, for correcting, enlarging, polishing, and fixing our Language. The Methods must be left to the Society . . . I am writing . . . some general Hints, which I design to publish. . . . All this may come to nothing, although, I find, the ingenious and learned Men of all my Acquaintance fall readily in with it.
(*C* 1:239)

Unfortunately, the two men he was most concerned to enlist in his project, Harley and Bolingbroke, did not "fall readily in with it." Yet during this period Swift repeatedly refers to the general support for his plan, hoping against hope, perhaps, that it will save the ministry: "My Lord Treasurer," Swift writes King again, "hath often promised he will advance my Design of an Academy; so have my Lord Keeper and all the Ministers; but they are now too busy to think of any Thing beside what they have upon the Anvil" (*C* 1:301).

Swift's political motives, whatever they might be, do not wholly explain the unfocused nature of the *Proposal* or his signature on the document, although it was not one of his better literary efforts. Perhaps the oddness of the *Proposal* can be partially illuminated by looking at events in Swift's life at the time he conceived the idea of the academy, for in many ways it was designed to answer certain implicit and explicit criticisms of his conduct. The rhetoric of the *Proposal* seems to counter accusations that Swift was a low menial in Harley's circle, in general, a follower rather than an initiator; that he was a writer of trifles and propaganda, rather than a serious literary figure; and that he was motivated more by self-interest than idealism. Swift's presentation of himself in a way that modifies these views seems to supersede his concern with the particulars of an academy. The document may have been more important to him as autobiography than as an agent of linguistic reform.

The genre of the *Proposal* and its tone—an epistle to Harley that begins on a note of cozy intimacy—emphasizes Swift's familiarity with the power elite. This approach seems calculated to answer public critics who viewed him merely as a Tory hack and an employee of the state. And the *Proposal* may have been fashioned to quash not just his public critics but his private fears, which were exacerbated by an incident that seems of crucial importance in explaining why Swift proposed the idea of an academy at the time he did. On February 5, 1710/11, Swift's putative friend and mentor, Harley, offered him fifty pounds for his work on the *Examiner*. Swift, who cherished the illusion that he was on equal ground with the nation's leaders, was stung by Harley's action, which instantly branded him as "hired help."

How deeply Harley wounded Swift can be seen in the mode of his reaction, his repeated allusions to the event, and the length of time it took his anger to fade. The first notation of the insult appears in the entry for February 6 in the *Journal to Stella*, when, after describing how Patrick, his servant, had lodged a noisy, dirty bird in their rooms, he tells Stella that he is slow to show annoyance: "I say nothing: I am tame as a clout." Immediately following, however, is the icy statement: "Mr. Harley desired I would dine with him again to-day; but I refused him, for I fell out with him yesterday, and will not see him again till he makes me amends" (*JS* 1:181–82). Significantly, here and throughout the duration of Swift's pique, he was too bruised to name the event directly.

Swift was still furious the next day when writing to Stella:

> I was this morning early with Mr. Lewis of the secretary's office, and saw a letter Mr. Harley had sent to him, desiring to be reconciled; but I was deaf to all intreaties. . . . I expect further satisfaction. If we let these great ministers pretend too much, there will be no governing them. He promises to make me easy, if I will but come and see him; but I won't, and he shall do it by message, or I will cast him off.
> (182)

Nine days later, in his February 16 letter to Stella, Swift notes, "We made up our quarrel" (193). On March 7, he writes, "Stella guesses right as she always does. [Harley] gave me"; the rest is a coded message that says "A bankbill for fifty pounds" (208, 208n).

Throughout his life, Swift sought a permanent place in The Great Tradition—he always wanted literary fame—but about the same time as Harley's insult, Swift suffered several other assaults that damaged his concept of himself as a great writer. He was miffed by a review of the *Examiner* in *The Present State of Wit* that implied his hireling status and only tepidly praised his style.[16] In addition, the publication of his *Miscellanies* (1711), which he arranged by stealth, was remarked on by Archbishop King as follows: "You see how malicious some are towards you, in printing a parcel of trifles, falsely, as your works. This makes it necessary that you should shame those varlets, by something that may enlighten the world, which I am sure your genius will reach, if you set yourself to it" (*C* 1:268). A parcel of trifles!

Against this background, Swift started to formulate the idea of a British academy. Perhaps worried about the flukiness of literary fame, he sought to create, not a subjective work of art but a permanent cultural edifice, "something," as Archbishop King said, "that will enlighten the world." Charles Kerby-Miller notes that "it does not in any way derogate from Swift's sincerity and high motives in pursuing his plan for an academy to realize that he had a very high personal stake in the matter."[17] This "high personal stake" explains some of the peculiar elements of the *Proposal*. Its pretentious and turgid style can be seen as Swift's self-conscious attempt to counteract the perception that he was a writer of "trifles"; his appeal to Harley in the "Name of all the learned and polite Persons of the Nation" (*PW* 4:6), a stance at which his enemies hooted, was designed to show him as a leader among writers, not as a hack. In the *Proposal*, then, Swift sought to correct, improve, and ascertain his image in his own eyes and in the eyes of others. In this context, he would care little about the actual composition of the academy, only that he be remembered as the promoter of the idea. For that reason he signed his name.[18]

Political and personal concerns, therefore, eclipse Swift's idea of an academy, yet another explanation for his vagueness in the *Proposal* is his fundamental suspicion of institutional solutions. "Methods" come under attack in his writing as do "academies," both of which he associates in other places with enthusiasm and madness. The crazy Lagadans, of course, have a School of Languages in their academy, and in *A Tale of a Tub*, the schools of pederasty, hobbyhorses, looking glasses, salivation, and spelling are components of the academy that the Modern speaker proposes to protect the commonwealth against the "Wits of the present Age" (*PW* 1:24–25).

In the *Proposal* Swift revealingly characterizes himself as a projector, a pejorative term in his vocabulary. At the beginning of the epistle, he calls himself a "visionary Projector . . . [with] his Schemes" (*PW* 4:6) and at the end says, "But I forget my Province: and find my self turning Projector before I am aware" (20). These passages indicate that Swift was uneasy with his *Proposal* because it smacks of the systematization and regimentation that he typically abhorred. Even though the process of creating an academy could involve the country and his party in a useful colloquy that would encourage their unity and at the same time demonstrate his leadership ability, Swift was not wholeheartedly in favor of the institution he was suggesting.

Swift recognizes that he is being vague and offers an overabundance of excuses for it: "Writing by Memory only, as I do at present, I would gladly keep within my Depth; and therefore shall not enter into further Particulars. Neither do I pretend more than to shew the Usefulness of this Design, and to make some general Observations; leaving the rest to that Society." He concludes, furthermore, that any spelling out of details would be unnecessary because "such a Society would be pretty unanimous in the main Points" (16). As to who should constitute it, he tautologically suggests "such Persons, as are generally allowed to be best qualified for such a Work" (13–14). Swift then helpfully notes that these people ought to meet "at some appointed Time and Place," but how they should proceed beyond that, he says, "is not for me to prescribe" (14). Swift says that the English academy should follow the model of the Académie Française "to imitate where [they] have proceeded right, and to avoid their Mistakes" (14), but he does not indicate what these are.

The vagueness of Swift's *Proposal* can be seen when it is contrasted with others of his proposals, such as *A Proposal for Giving Badges to Beggars*, *Some Reasons against the Bill for Settling the Tyth of Hemp, Flax, &c by a Modus*, and the famous *Modest Proposal*. All of these are extremely concrete and detailed. Moreover, Swift's plan seems quite general when compared with a similar proposal for an academy by Daniel Defoe, who itemizes the membership of the proposed academy, saying that there ought to be thirty-six people—twelve nobility, twelve private gentlemen, and "a Class of Twelve to be left open for meer Merit, let it be found in who or what sort it would." [19] In addition, Defoe states who should *not* be members of the academy, except on some "some extraordinary Occasion"—lawyers, clergymen, physicians, or those whose "Business or Trade was Learning"—because they all tend to use one sort of jargon or another. Defoe also points out definite activities the academy might initiate, which include censoring the stage, establishing a program to stop swearing, publishing essays on style, and creating a lecture series on language. [20] In short, Defoe's proposal is more of a blueprint for action than Swift's.

Regardless of his motives, Swift persistently struggled to get the powers-that-be interested in his idea of an academy. He writes Stella on June 22, 1711, that Harley "enters mightily into it, so does the dean of Carlisle; and I design to write a letter to [the] lord treasurer with the proposals of it, and publish it" (*JS* 1 : 295–96), but Swift's colleagues were too preoccupied to devote much attention to his proposal. When Swift finished the manuscript, he gave it to Harley, who merely passed it along to Prior, who subsequently forgot about it and placed Swift in the embarrassing position of having to retrieve the paper from Prior so that he could give it to the printer. [21]

The *Proposal* finally appeared on May 17, 1712, but no progress on the academy ever resulted. Many years later, when it was republished in 1735 by Faulkner, a headnote (probably written by Swift and certainly approved by him)[22] recounts the reasons Swift's British academy was never established:

> It is well known, that if the Queen had lived a Year or two longer, the following Proposal would in all Probability have taken Effect. For the Lord Treasurer had already nominated several Persons without Distinction of Quality or Party, who were to compose a Society for the Purposes mentioned by the Author; and resolved to use his Credit with Her Majesty, that a Fund should be applyed to support the Expence of a large Room, where the Society should meet, and for other Incidents. But this Scheme fell to the Ground, partly by the Dissentions among the great Men at Court; but chiefly by the lamented Death of that glorious Princess.
> (*Textual Notes, PW* 4:285)

Here Swift mourns what might have been: the continuation of the Tory regime with himself as the English Richelieu—leader of the church, confidant of princes, and founder of the national linguistic academy. Yet one wonders how Swift thought the academy would be realized when his *Proposal* is at once vague and divisive. Throughout, the rhetoric seems at cross-purposes.

Swift felt comfortable about traditional institutions—the Established Church, the common law, and the constitutional monarchy—because they are inextricably intertwined with Britain's history. The order they impose on society gives all men the freedom to develop their talents. A Modern institution, on the other hand, could pose a threat. Unrestrained by traditional ballast, it might disrupt rather than preserve English culture. Swift, of course, does not grant the academy any far-reaching mandate, and particularly not censorship powers such as those possessed by Defoe's proposed academy and the Académie Française. Indeed, the functions of the academy are hardly specified because Swift seems to be avoiding the subject. Instead he praises Harley, recounts the history of the English language, analyzes the causes of linguistic corruption, and argues the importance of a verbal standard. The essay is written in very un-Swiftian prose. The awkward, contradictory, and diffuse style may have been generated by Swift's fundamental uneasiness about what he was saying.

Swift clearly lamented the slow evolution of the language that made Chaucer less accessible than Dryden, yet he might have feared that the academy, isolated in a room in London from the linguistic consensus of the countryside, would change the language more by fiat than linguistic accidents had changed it in three hundred years. In the end, the English academy might become like the Laputan academy in trying to extinguish the discourse "of their Forefathers" (*PW* 11:185). No doubt Swift feared the elitism that characterized the Académie Française. Paul Pellisson-Fontanier, who wrote its history, characterizes the Académie as follows: "As much as wisdom is above the multitude, the soul above the body, and the desire of knowledge above that of living: so much is the Academy above the Common-wealth."[23] Such a separation of *wisdom* from the *multitude* and the *Academy* from the *Common-wealth* would have been anathema to Swift.[24]

Swift's ambivalence about the academy may have grown out of the fundamental rifts in his personality. But although he had mixed feelings about an institutional effort to improve language, as a moralist he was consistently firm about the individual's responsibility to discourse in the common forms or "Proper Words." Regardless of the linguistic pollution around them, people have the ability to speak clearly and the social duty to do so. This is illustrated by Gulliver in Lilliput. Although the Lilliputian language is circumlocutory and redundant, Gulliver uses it to be brutally blunt about the plight of the Blefescudians: "I plainly protested, that I would never be an Instrument of bringing a free and brave People into Slavery" (*PW* 11:53). Only by personal acts of will can chaos be abated and society preserved. "Style," or "Putting Proper Words in proper Places" was no minor issue for Swift.

7

How to Improve Discourse: Put Proper Words in Proper Places

To morrow We our *Mystick Feast* prepare,
Where Thou, our latest *Proselyte*, shalt share:
When We, by proper Signs and Symbols tell,
How, by *Brave Hands*, the *Royal TRAYTOR* fell.
. . . .
At Monarchy we nobly shew our Spight,
And talk *what Fools call Treason* all the Night.
"Toland's Invitation to Dismal,"
P 1:162–63, 7–10, 15–16

Chary of institutional solutions in general, Swift placed responsibility for improving discourse on the individual. Indeed, Swift
gauged an individual's character by the degree to which he could
formulate socially appropriate language, a concept Swift subsumed in the
term *style*. Swift defines *style* in a letter to a young clergyman to whom he
says that "Proper Words in proper Places, makes the true Definition of a
Stile: But this would require too ample a Disquisition to be now dwelt on"
(*Holy Orders, PW* 9:65). At first glance the injunction to put "Proper
Words in proper Places" seems almost tautological, yet upon reflection, by
constructing from his premises the "too ample . . . Disquisition" that
Swift lacked time to develop, one sees that the concept had wide-reaching
implications for him. Not only is it a "true Definition of Stile," but "Proper
words in proper Places" is also a "true Definition" of reason. Quite simply,
to discriminate ideas, words, and sentences—to determine the verbal requirements of a particular social context—represents the triumph of man's
mind over barbarism. Swift's attention to style was generated by his belief
that style is not a superfluous quality but an embodiment of whatever rea-

son man is capable. And that reason informs man of his social nature and the need for proper language.

In *Language in Wycherley's Plays*, James Thompson points out that *propriety* had gathered a range of meanings by the late seventeenth century. The "proper" use of language could mean uniting ethical and aesthetic concerns by considering the relation of discourse to some ideal of harmony, adapting discourse to a particular audience, weighing the effect of discourse on the culture as a whole, and conforming discourse to accepted or expected standards.[1] Swift used "proper" almost exclusively in the last three senses, which stress the social-cultural implications of discourse and the individual's obligation to reinforce the common forms.

Creating proper words is an act of will that defies the entropy that governs the universe at large and the mind of man in particular. Accepting contemporary models of the mind as a jumble of random impulses,[2] Swift observes in *Some Thoughts on Free Thinking* that "if the wisest man would at any time utter his thoughts, in the crude indigested manner, as they come into his head, he would be looked upon as raving mad" (*PW* 4:49). These assumptions may have been influenced by the work of Port-Royal linguists in France, who emphasized the importance of judgment to create syntactical structures capable of conveying the mind's ideas.[3] For Swift, the idea of "propriety," however, did not refer to grammatical or logical relationships but to social relationships.

Swift believed that every man, even with his inner roil of thoughts, can present ideas clearly for others' scrutiny. Not to do so is antisocial and hence irrational. To be rational, though, requires a considerable effort. It is not an easy task to subdue one's mental anarchy into "Proper Words," for "in the great multiplicity of ideas, which ones mind is apt to form, there is nothing more difficult than to select those, which are most proper for the conduct of life [that is, those that are socially appropriate]" (49). Because men do not properly articulate their thoughts without conscious effort, which some people cannot or do not make, Swift was convinced that the human species is not rational but merely capable of reason—a crucial distinction (*C* 3:118).[4]

To combat chaos by reason is man's unique responsibility. It elicits his higher faculties and gives his life meaning. Swift observes that "wherever God hath left Man the Power of interposing a Remedy by Thought or Labour, there he hath placed Things in a State of Imperfection, on purpose to stir up human Industry; without which Life would stagnate, or indeed rather could not subsist at all" (*Thoughts on Various Subjects, PW* 4:245). God gave man speech to communicate to his fellows but left it in a "State of Imperfection" that requires human agency—"Thought or Labour"—to remedy. To articulate thoughts into language that creates understanding or reinforces common forms and common sense, therefore, is a test of man's mettle, an existential necessity.

All men think incoherently, but only insane or antisocial men write or talk that way, among them the narrator of the *Tale*, who, far from keeping his mind "under the strictest Regulation," wants to give an "uncontroulable Demonstration" of his thoughts in print (*PW* 1:21). Although society itself is so insane that babblers are often undetected, or even exalted, Swift places them where they belong: in Bedlam. Specifically identifying the inmates in "The Digression on Madness" by their deviation from normal discourse, Swift condemns them to whips and straw. Swift's Bedlamites include one who is "Swearing and Blaspheming . . . [and] foaming at the Mouth" (soldier); one who is "talking, sputtering, gaping, bawling in a Sound without Period or Article" (politician); one who natters irrationally of "hard Times, and Taxes, and the *Whore of Babylon*" (puritan merchant); one who is in "Conversation with himself. . . . [and] has forgot the common Meaning of Words, but an admirable Retainer of the *Sound*" (courtier) (111–12).[5]

Not only does one have an obligation to himself, his community, and his nation to put proper words in proper places when he is speaking or writing, but he must also do the same when interpreting the words of others. It does no good for one man rationally to choose his words if another man willfully distorts them. John Locke suggested that imperfect interpretation is inevitable because each man ascribes peculiar, personal meanings to words in a truly mad manner, so that, without some reform in definition, the words of one person can never be fully intelligible to another. Swift, on the other hand, is more sanguine than Locke about the ability of men to interpret words clearly. Free from "Pride, Vanity, ill Nature, Affectation, Singularity, Positiveness; or some other Vice, the Effect of a wrong Education" (*Thoughts on Various Subjects*, *PW* 4:244), they will naturally accept the common meanings of words. The ability to reason— to put proper words in proper places in discourse or interpretation—is innate and not the product of education. In fact, education too often is a "wrong Education," which interferes with the communication of clear meaning.

What Is Proper?

A word of warning should be issued at the beginning of this discussion: although in his explicit statements on style Swift emphasizes the importance of general intelligibility, he nonetheless savored the rich and strange realm of verbal enthusiasm. His sallies into bizarre frames of reference can be read ironically as examples of what not to do. But often norms in Swiftian works are elusive, as reams of scholarly prose demonstrate. Ambiguities are inherent in Swift's work because he derived great enjoyment in exploring the tremulous juncture of propriety and impropriety, an idea developed at length in Chapter 1. What follows here are Swift's stylistic dicta for the world at large, some of which he noticeably violated at various times for ironic effect or because he believed that "Common Forms were not design'd / Directors to a noble Mind" ("Cadenus and Vanessa," *P* 2:706, 12–13). Moreover, Swift's stated theory may conflict with his literary practice because many of his injunctions on style concern the content and delivery of sermons, whose ideas should be immediately discernible. These caveats aside, certain principles strongly assert themselves.

What is proper, regardless of the type of discourse, depends on the social context. In conversation, few stylistic decorums need be imposed. But more is demanded of written discourse. Because publication sanctions usage, printed discourse must reinforce traditional linguistic forms that will unify the English people across time and geography. "Proper Words in proper Places" link men with the minds of others, living and dead, through live conversation and reading. Swift judges style, then, by its *social effect*—the relationship it establishes among people.

Too often words are used to deceive or betray. Some people pervert the meaning of words cynically for private gain, like the hack in "On Poetry: A Rapsody," who is paid "on the Nail" for prostituting his pen. Some use words to inflate their egos, pretending, like Wagstaff or the *Tale*-teller, that they write as a public service, when all they desire is to see their names in print. Others aggrandize themselves by flaunting their erudition, using "hard words" and peculiar jargons that no one else can understand in an effort to raise themselves above the common herd. All of these people are primarily concerned with how their use of language will promote not general understanding but their own personal stock.

In his own theory and practice, Swift consistently stressed the importance of gauging the beneficial effect of words on others. Of course, in sermon delivery, the auditors' comprehension is a key desideratum, but one to which priests are frequently oblivious. Swift speculates that if some divines would look out of their pulpits they might see "one Part of their Congregation out of Countenance, and the other asleep; except, perhaps, [for] an old Female Beggar or two in the Isles" (*Holy Orders, PW* 9:69). To develop an awareness of others in discourse, Swift advises the novice priest to "prevail upon some intimate and judicious Friend to be your constant Hearer, and allow him with the utmost Freedom to give you Notice of whatever he shall find amiss" (64), a policy Swift himself followed by reading his works aloud to his publisher and his servants. In speaking or writing, an individual should be sensitive to the response of the addressee because language should be used to create a reciprocal relationship.

If the prime function of language is to communicate thoughts and feelings to one's fellows, then clarity is a touchstone of "Proper Words in proper Places." To Swift, an idea expressed clearly is an idea expressed simply, for simplicity is the norm of natural expression. Swift makes an "appeal to any Man of Letters, whether at least nineteen in twenty of those perplexing Words [he uses], might not be changed into easy ones, such as naturally first occur to ordinary men, and probably did so at first to those very Gentlemen, who are so fond of the former" (66). Later reiterating the same point, Swift condemns periphrastic rhetoric as "nauseous to the rational Hearers. . . . [it] will seldom express your Meaning as well as your own natural Words" (68). Throughout his canon, Swift exhorts men to "that *Simplicity*, which is one of the greatest Perfections in any Language" (*Proposal, PW* 4 : 15). Indeed, simplicity is the requisite for "Perfection" in any "human Performance," he tells the young priest (*Holy Orders, PW* 9 : 68).

With his insistence on simplicity, Swift rejects the idea that there are different levels of discourse. He thinks that the simplest communication is the easiest to understand, and more basically, that style ought to reflect the nature of truth, which itself is fundamentally clear and simple. Such an attitude prompts Swift to admonish the young priest that a "Divine hath nothing to say to the wisest Congregation of any Parish in this Kingdom, which he may not express in a Manner to be understood by the meanest among them" (66). Thus the divine should employ "A PLAIN, convincing Reason [which] may possibly operate upon the Mind both of a learned and ignorant Hearer, as long as they live" (70). This "PLAIN, convincing Reason" should be expressed in a simple language; "otherwise, I, and many Thousand others, will never be able to retain . . . a Syllable of [the] Sermon" (71). In this regard, Samuel Johnson's assessment of Swift's style would please him (although it is not clear Johnson meant it as praise): "He always understands himself, and his reader always understands him: the peruser of Swift wants little previous knowledge; it will be sufficient he is acquainted with common words and common things."[6] A preponderance of words with Anglo-Saxon roots is certainly noticeable in Swift's poetry, but many of his prose satires are characterized by unusual words borrowed from some high-flying jargon or coined for the occasion. The question of Swift's style is more complicated than Johnson suggests because Swift enjoyed ventriloquizing; one cannot tell when he is speaking *in propria persona* or what "his" voice is.[7]

Communicating in simple, traditional language does not limit what can be said, and in fact, "When a Man's Thoughts are clear, the properest Words will generally offer themselves first; and his own Judgment will direct him in what Order to place them, so they may be best understood" (68). The words that "naturally first occur" are "easy ones" (66). One can see Swift's own commitment to the universality of a simple style in his boast that he would preach no differently to the court than to the Irish peasantry; in imagining his maiden sermon in front of the queen, he predicts that "all the puppies" who "throng to hear me, and expect something wonderful [will be] plaguily baulkt; for I shall preach plain honest stuff" (*JS* 1:126).

Simplicity is violated by those who use an out-of-the-ordinary vocabulary that they have invented or have derived from some arcane lexicon. People who use uncommon language do so knowingly. They are knaves rather than fools. Their motive is pride—"To shew their Learning, their Oratory, their Politeness, or their Knowledge of the World" (*Holy Orders, PW* 9:68), not to communicate information and pleasure to others. When Swift wants to show how antisocial his enemies are, he frequently points out their affected styles, abnormal definitions, and self-serving coinages. It is no wonder that he finds these vices rampant among Whigs, freethinkers, Presbyterians, lawyers, hacks, bad critics, projectors, and other subversives.

Swift often characterizes murky, egocentric, antisocial discourse and interpretation as *occult*, a term which to him suggested a private system of language claimed to be superior to everyday English, but which, in fact, is enthusiastic babel. The *Tale*-teller, for instance, is an occultist, who quotes Thomas Vaughan, Jacob Boehme, and other mystics and who advises his readers to take "the Number of O's multiply'd by *Seven*, and divided by *Nine*" to discover the text's "very profound Mystery" (*Tale, PW* 1:118–19). If that does not suffice, he suggests that one "transpose certain Letters and Syllables according to Prescription, in the second and fifth Section; they will certainly reveal into a full Receit of the *Opus Magnum*" (119). In these occult schemes, words are not seen as integral units of meaning but as assemblages of symbols with hidden significance. Freed from traditional definitions, words are at the mercy of any fanatic who wishes to impose "profound," "mystical," or "divine" meaning on them.

With the Duchess of Queensberry, Swift jokes about mystic communications (an oxymoron in his view) when she sends him the following "message":

> Poll manu sub linus darque dds
> Sive Nig tig gnipite gnaros[.]
> (*C* 3:504)

He responds: "Madam,—I have consulted all the learned in occult Sciences, of my acquaintance, and have Sate up eleven nights to discover the meaning of those two hieroglyphicall lines in your Graces hand . . . but all in vain Onely tis agreed, that the language is Coptick, and a very profound *Behmist* [Boehmist] Assures me the Style is poetic" (*C* 3:507). No doubt, too, Swift had a good laugh when William Wotton earnestly tried to decipher the gibberish on the title page of *A Tale of a Tub* ("Basma eacabasa eanaa irraurista, diarba da ceatotaba sobor camelanthi"), identifying it as "a Form of Initiation used antiently by the *Marcosian* Hereticks."[8] In the absence of a clear style, diverse interpretations, which destroy any possibility of consensus, are encouraged and legitimized. Indeed, Swift blames one of the most cataclysmic events of his life, the fall of the Tory administration, on the leaders' "Mysticall manner" of proceeding that allowed them to infer assumptions that betrayed them in deepest consequence (*Some Free Thoughts on the Present State of Affairs, PW* 8:86). Swift suggests that if the ministers had talked in a plain, easy, natural manner, perhaps the tragic dissolution could have been averted.[9]

In social intercourse, Swift detested any behavior that prevented the participants from moving closer to an understanding. "Good-Manners," Swift notes succinctly," is the Art of making those people easy with whom we converse" (*On Good-Manners, PW* 4:213). In "conversation" between an author and a reader, a sense of easiness or accessibility ought to prevail. A style that militates against the "intercourse of minds" is improper. Of course, occasions exist, especially in satire, when improprieties are used to shock an audience into a new realization. In general discourse, however, the two most common violations of decorum are stiffness and looseness.

Stiffness, or overformality, interferes with the natural flow of language that Swift thought should characterize not only speech but writing. Although ceremony and formality are demanded in public addresses and elevated poetry, an unnaturally stiff style is a fault in other circumstances. For example, Swift criticizes Lord Somers (the addressee of *A Tale of a Tub*) for his "extreme Civility [that] is universal and undistinguished; and in private Conversation, where he observeth it as inviolably as if he were in the greatest Assembly, it is sometimes censured as formal" (*The History of the*

Four Last Years of the Queen, *PW* 7 : 5). Writing to an aspiring poet seeking his advice, Swift recommends the replacement of *whilst*, which seemed artificial and affected, with plain, old *while*, yet he notes that "*Noll* is too much a cant word for a grave poem" (*C* 4 : 321). Criticism of stiffness, or indecorousness, in other people's writing can also be seen in Swift's grumbles about one "letter from Ned Synge this Post . . . in a most silly starched affected Style" (*C* 2 : 250).

Bawdiness or vulgarity—forms of verbal looseness—are as indecorous and improper in Swift's mind as excessive stiffness. In his treatises on conversation and manners, he condemns such impropriety because it also freezes out possible participants in discourse and thereby limits its effectiveness. Particularly proud of his reputation for being intolerant of looseness, he complains to Stella at one point that "Mr. secretary had too much company with him today; so I came away soon after dinner. I give no man liberty to swear or talk b——dy, and I found some of them in constraint, and so I left them to themselves" (*JS* 1 : 273).

In his satire, of course, Swift uses ungenteel terms freely; he purposefully associates his enemies with filth, lowness, and obscenity. He has the Irish Parliament dabble in its dung; he graces the king of France with an anal fistula; he attributes prurience to puritan enthusiasts by describing their religious experiences in sexual imagery. When characterizing people he wants the reader to reject, Swift often puts offensive dialogue in their mouths. In "The Intended Speech," for example, Swift endows the Earl of Nottingham with language that bespeaks his vulgarity, his lack of principles, and his lack of intelligence:

> I talk'd of a *Peace*, and they both gave a start,
> His G—— swore by ——, and her
>   G—— let a F——t;
> My *long old-fashion'd Pocket*, was presently
>   cramm'd;
> And sooner than Vote for a Peace I'll be
>   d——nd.
>   (*P* 1 : 143, 15–20)

Verbal crudeness is used here by Swift to characterize the new barbarians who threaten British civilization, although many of Swift's critics, past and present, are convinced that he enjoyed wallowing in nastiness.

Looseness also includes the use of a style not appropriate to the occasion, a breach of linguistic decorum that betokens a distressing ignorance of normal social and moral values. One example is the *Tale*-teller's coolly declaring "how much [flaying] altered [a woman's] Person for the worse"

(*Tale*, *PW* 1 : 109). Or the rude insensitivity of the queen in "Verses on the Death of Dr. Swift," who, when hearing that the dean has died, remarks, "Why let him rot" (*P* 2 : 559, 184). Or the reductionist crassness of the "old experienc'd Sinner," who advises young writers how to market "The Product of your Toil and Sweating; / A Bastard of your own begetting" ("On Poetry: A Rapsody," *P* 2 : 644, 115 – 16). Or Cassinus, who finding out that his ethereal goddess excretes like other animals, shrieks out in horror, "Nor wonder how I lost my Wits; / Oh! *Cælia, Cælia Cælia* sh——" ("Cassinus and Peter," *P* 2 : 596, 117 – 18). These inappropriate utterances reveal an ignorance or a flouting of the decent understandings that unite civilized people. Comfortable, congenial talk is the norm against which Swift asks one to measure the wild array of discourse that he presents.

Special Proprieties in Written Discourse

Swift believed that proper language was not the exclusive province of the literate. In fact, he was convinced that the often illiterate common folk, especially those in rural areas, naturally speak with propriety because they are innocent of the affectations in language created by the pseudo-sophisticated metropolitans. Those who are literate, however, and particularly those who venture into print, have, in Swift's view, a special obligation to enshrine the purity and strength of the language in a permanent form. Thus in addition to the general requirement for spoken discourse to "entertain and improve" others, Swift applied other particular criteria to written or published material: he demanded correct spelling, correct grammar, and a mellifluous and varied style.

All rational people should put proper words in proper places, but those who have had the benefits of education and know how to write have another charge: to put proper letters in proper places, that is, to spell correctly. If varieties of spelling were allowed to flourish, Swift feared that the written standard could not be maintained and English would degenerate rapidly. Because Swift viewed misspelling as a crime that threatened the continuity of British culture, he heartily satirized erring orthographers. Simon Wagstaff, "author" of the Introduction to *Polite Conversation*, reveals dangerously antisocial tendencies in his desire to alter spelling; for him, "it is a true Mark of Politeness in both Writing and Reading, to vary the Orthography as well as the Sound [of words]" (*PW* 4 : 104). When slamming the feckless John Partridge (the butt of Swift's famous April Fool's joke who was figuratively buried alive), Swift remarks on astrologers' inability to "spell any Word out of the usual Road" (*Predictions for the Year 1708*, *PW* 2 : 142). In another case, to demonstrate the worthlessness of a certain clergyman, Swift encloses a letter from him which will, he says to Mrs. Whiteway, "shew you the goodness, the wisdom, the gratitude, the truth, the civility of that excellent divine, adorned with an orthography (spelling) fit for himself" (C 5:176). These are but a few of the times Swift links misspelling with general personality defects.

Because women did not have the benefits of education available to many men, Swift was more tolerant of their misspellings. Misspelling, in fact, was seen as stereotypically feminine. Richard Steele, in *The Guardian* (March 28, 1713), for instance, pretends to find some verses— "at first sight, I could not guess whether they came from a Beau or a Lady; but having put on my Spectacles. . . . I found by some peculiar Modes in spelling . . . that it was a Female Sonnet." [10] Similarly, Swift jests with a woman friend who can spell, saying that her "way of *spelling* would *not be intelligible*" to other women (C 4:258).

Swift took it upon himself to educate the women of his acquaintance about spelling. One of his female correspondents, for instance, asks him to "make [her] amends by chiding [her] for every word that is false spelt" (C 4:180). In his *Letter to a Young Lady*, Swift tells Deborah Staunton that she should teach herself to spell by daily making "Collections [of new words] from the Books you read" (PW 9:92).

Swift's most famous student, though, was Stella. Throughout the *Journal to Stella* Swift twits her for her errors: "Pray, Stella, explain those two words of yours to me, what do you mean by *Villian* and *Dainger* . . . ?" (JS 1:234); "But who are those *Wiggs* that think I am turned Tory? Do you mean Whigs? Which *Wiggs* and *wat* do you mean?" (JS 85); "Stella has made twenty false spellings in her writing; I'll send them to you all back again on the other side of this letter, to mend them; I won't miss one" (JS 2:388); "Tell me truly, sirrah, how many of these [on the list he has made] are mistakes of the pen, and how many are you to answer for as real ill spelling? There are but fourteen; I said twenty by guess. You must not be angry, for I will have you spell right, let the world go how it will. . . . I allow you henceforth but six false spellings in every letter you send me" (392–93). Later Swift reports to Stella on her progress—in her last letter, just "four false spellings in all. Shall I send them to you? I am glad you did not take my correction ill" (418).

Despite Swift's self-appointed role as spelling police, he himself spelled variously. In jest, he admits this to Stella in the process of correcting her errors:

> Pray let us have no more *Bussiness*, but *Busyness;* The deuse take me if I know how to spell it . . . it does not look right; let me see, *Bussiness, Busyness, Business, Bisyniss, Bisness, Bysness;* faith, I know not which is right, I think

the second; I believe I never writ the word in my life before; yes, sure I must though; *Business, Busyness, Bisyness*—I have perplexed myself, and can't do it . . . *Business*, I fancy that's right. Yes it is. . . . Oh, now I see it as plain as can be; so yours is only an s too much.
(426)

Although Swift was punctilious about spelling in formal letters and published manuscripts, he was more casual in his letters to friends, often spelling by sound, although he denounced the practice publicly. In Swift's manuscripts, the shortened forms of words, particularly verbs, often came naturally to him, but upon revision he invariably opted for the fuller, longer versions, ever with an eye to preserving the etymology and morphology of a word.[11]

Although Swift did not emphasize proper grammar as much as spelling, he was naturally attentive to it in written or printed documents. While reading Gilbert Burnet's *History of His Own Times*, Swift constantly commented on Burnet's style in the margins of the book, noting that one phrase "wants grammar" (*Marginalia, PW* 5:269), pointing out shifts in tense ("*Who was—who is*, pure nonsense" [281]), and commenting on vague antecedents—when Burnet writes "Lord Halifax and he (Lord Hyde) fell to be in ill terms: for he hated Lord Sunderland beyond expression, though he had married his sister," Swift questions in the margin, "Who married whose sister?" (280). At one point in the *History*, Burnet ungrammatically describes *Paradise Lost* as "the beautifullest and perfectest poem that ever was writ, at least in OUR language." Taking offense at Burnet's phrase, "OUR language," Swift observes in the margin: "A mistake, for it is *in English*" (270).

Another propriety that Swift demanded in written discourse was euphony. He had George Faulkner, his Dublin printer, "attend to him early every Morning . . . to read to him [his works], that the Sounds might strike the Ear, as well as the Sense the Understanding" (*Faulkner's Preface, PW* 13:202–3). To Swift and other writers of the period, the Teutonic nature of English seemed an obstacle to creating the smoothness one might desire in literary works.[12] Swift explores this theme in several places, but most particularly in the *Proposal for Correcting . . . the English Tongue*, where he laments the "perpetual Disposition to shorten our Words, by retrenching the Vowels, [which] is nothing else but a Tendency to lapse into the Barbarity of those *Northern* nations from whom we are descended, and whose Languages labour all under the same Defect"—the "Roughness and Frequency of Consonants" (*PW* 4:12–13).

As one might expect, Swift's most specific statements on sound patterning are found primarily in reference to poetry. Swift twits his friend Pope by criticizing the "many unjustifiable Rhymes to *war* and *gods*" (*C* 2:176) in his translation of Homer. Elision, another poetic convention, was opposed by Swift because it accentuated the harsh, Teutonic aspects of English. He condemns poets who, "although they could not be insensible how much our Language was already overstocked with Monosyllables, yet to save Time and Pains, introduced that barbarous Custom of abbreviating Words, to fit them to the Measure of their Verses . . . to form such harsh unharmonious Sounds, that none but a *Northern* Ear could endure. They have joined the most obdurate Consonants, without one intervening Vowel" (*Proposal*, *PW* 4:11).[13] Knowing Swift's opinion, Sheridan, as a joke, sent him a poem that is almost entirely full of elided words, with lines like "Think n't your 'p'stle put m'in a Meagrim" ("A Copy of Verses," *P* 3:1020, 8). Swift responded with mock praise for "that Circumcision, / By modern Poets, call'd *Elision*," which he says creates verse "Smoother than *Pegasus'* old Shoe, / 'Ere *Vulcan* comes to make him new" ("George Nim-Dan Dean, Esq.; to Mr Sheridan," *P* 3:1021, 11–12, 7–8).

To Swift, the senseless repetition of words and sounds in both poetry and prose betrays a callousness toward the audience, who naturally find this stylistic flaw distracting. Swift parodies William Fleetwood's annoying repetition of the word *such:* "Never was such Strength of Thought, such Beauty of Expression, so happily joined together. Heavens! Such Force, such Energy in each pregnant Word! Such Fire, Such Fervour, in each glowing Line! . . . O! the irresistible Charm of the word *Such!*" (*A Letter of Thanks from my Lord Wharton to the Lord Bishop of Asaph*, *PW* 6:153). Swift's sensitivity to repetition is especially evident in his marginalia. Jotting notes in his copy of Bishop Burnet's *History of His Own Times*, Swift snipes at Burnet's persistent infelicity. Where Burnet writes, "The King . . . communicated *that* to them; and with *that* signified, *that* it was his pleasure *that* the army should be disbanded," Swift gibes in the margin, "Four *thats* in one line" (*Marginalia*, *PW* 5:272). In another place, Burnet's prose contains the clause "that which *was* most particular *was*, that he *was* to have a son by a widow, and *was*. . . ." Swift remarks glumly, "Was, was, was, was" (275). Swift concludes that Burnet "is in most particulars the worst qualified for an historian. . . . He discovers a great scarcity of words and phrases, by repeating the same several hundred times, for want of capacity to vary them" (*Short Remarks on Bishop Burnet's History*, *PW* 5:183). Such a lack of variety signals a lack of intellectual "capacity." Burnet's stylistic inadequacy, moreover, reveals his distance from the values of English society: thus Burnet "is very unhappy in the Choice and Disposition of his Words, and, for want of Variety, repeating them . . . in a Manner very grating to an *English* Ear" (*A Preface to . . . Dr. Burnet's Introduction, PW* 4:82). As author and churchman Gilbert Burnet had a duty to serve as an exemplar in language and thought. Swift believed that the failure of Fleetwood and Burnet to observe certain obvious proprieties in written discourse confirmed their subversive natures, for indeed, he disagreed with them on fundamental issues concerning the church and state.

Self-Appointed Arbiter of Style

Swift saw style as "his" subject. He instructs Stella how to tell which anonymously published essays were written by him by telling her, "In general you may be sometimes sure of things, as that about style, because it is what I have frequently spoken of" (*JS* 1:86). Style, of course, was not merely a rhetorical matter to Swift but a reflection of attitudes toward personal, social, and national integrity. In devoting much of his life to the promotion of better style, Swift felt he was engaged in an issue of paramount importance. It gave him a focus for his energies and an authority he valued. In all of his roles—churchman, adviser to politicians, essayist, satirist, poet, friend—he stressed the necessity of choosing the appropriate discourse to suit the social situation.

Swift made himself known to his friends as a linguistic stickler, who often corrected the oral and written discourse of those in his immediate circle. For instance, Lady Howth writes him, "I don't know whether you will be as free in writing as you are in speaking; but I am sure, were I at your elbow when you read this, you would bid me go to a writing school and a spelling book" (*C* 4:246). Proud of his insistence on certain standards of expression, Swift relates to Lord Orrery how he was supposed to sign a document "but would not do it till the words *Mobb* and *behave* were alter'd to *Rabble* and *behaved themselves*. Curse on your new-fangled London wits . . . [my style] is corrupted, and you out of spite will in your next letter torment me with sho'dnt, wodn't, [etc.]" (*C* 4:396). The use of the word *behaved* in speech would prompt a similar response. Deane Swift recalls how "Dr. Swift never could endure to hear any one say, Such a one *behaved* well, &c. *Behaved? Behaved what?* he used to ask with some kind of emotion. I remember his giving me an account, how he rebuked my Lord *Carteret* for this, and that my Lord promised him not to be guilty of the like for the future" (*C* 4:160n).

Swift publicly identified himself with the position that correct style was requisite for those whose duty it was to explain religion to others. Writing to Henry Clarke, then a Fellow and later Vice-Provost of Dublin's

Trinity College, Swift charges him with the responsibility of better educating future priests: "I quarrel . . . with all writers and many of your Preachers, for their careless incorrect, and improper Style, which they contract by reading the Scribblers from England, where an abominable Taste is every day prevayling. It is your business who are coming into the World to put a stop to these Corruptions; and recover that simplicity which in every thing of value ought chiefly to be followed" (*C* 4:274). Swift's own attempt to educate a novice preacher is contained in his *Letter to a Young Gentleman, Lately Enter'd into Holy Orders*, where in addition to giving detailed instructions on the composition and delivery of sermons, Swift includes his famous definition of style as "Proper Words in proper Places" (*PW* 9:65).

In affairs of state as well as church, Swift consciously enforced proper words in proper places. As Mr. Examiner and author of many other political tracts, he self-righteously exposed what he construed to be the semantic shadings of the opposition; his attacks on dangerous philosophies frequently take the form of almost line-by-line literary criticism, style and political morality being condemned simultaneously. This technique is used in, among others, *The Drapier's Letters*, *The Importance of the Guardian Consider'd*, and *Remarks on the Barrier Treaty*, where, for example, in close exegesis he points out that the allies "have put a different Meaning upon the word *Barrier*, "from what it formerly used to bear" (*PW* 6:88); that in contrast to previous agreements "the Style is wholly changed" (89); that the allies vaguely stipulate that "the Queen is obliged, whenever a Peace is treated, to procure for them *whatever shall be thought necessary* besides; and where their *Necessity* will terminate, is not very easie to foresee" (91). In the *Remarks*, Swift quotes extensively from the Barrier Treaty and then glosses these excerpts to illustrate that the stylistic obscurities of the treaty cloaked its unfairness to England. Swift calls his exegesis a "*Translation*" (85) to imply that the Barrier Treaty was foreign to English interests. Here and in other political tracts, Swift depicts himself as a soldier on the front lines, guarding the nation from enemy onslaughts of deceptive language.

Swift felt that his style distinguished him as a historian. At the very beginning of *The History of the Four Last Years of the Queen*, a work to which he devoted considerable energy, he announces that he will proceed in a different manner from what one usually expects of a chronicler of contemporary events. Instead of addressing a London audience, he will produce a "generally intelligible and useful" document, for "Most People, who frequent this Town, acquire a sort of Smattering (such as it is) which qualifies them for reading a Pamphlet, and finding out what is meant by Innuendo's or Hints at Facts or Persons, or initial Letters of Names; wherein Gentlemen at distance, although perhaps of better Understandings, are wholly in the dark" (*PW* 7:2). In another place, Swift distances himself from such unintelligible historians as Gilbert Burnet and offers to "translate" Burnet's book "into vulgar Language for the Use of the Poor" (*Preface to Dr. Burnet's Introduction, PW* 4:69).

In the world of literature, of course, Swift perceived of himself as one of "three or four Cotemporaries . . . [who] if they could be united would drive the world before them" (*C* 2:464). From his vantage on Parnassas, he excoriated the bad writers of his generation in such satires as "On Poetry: A Rapsody" and *A Tale of a Tub*. In a playful exchange of poems with Patrick Delaney, Swift imagines himself in league with Apollo, god of poetic creation, who addresses him with easy familiarity in, for instance, "Apollo to Dean Swift, by Himself." No doubt relishing the bonhomie that reinforced his self-image as dean of letters (as well as Dean of St. Patrick's), Swift acted as a literary adviser both to minor poets, who desired the great man's blessing, and to coequals, who valued his candor. For instance, he twits Pope for his lack of euphony—"I checkt a little at the article *the* twice used in the second line. . . . The beginning of the last line, *striking their aking* bosoms. Those two participles come so near, and sounding so alike, I could wish altered" (*C* 4:133). As for triplets (which he hated), Swift claims to have prevailed "with Mr. Pope, and Gay, and Dr. Young, and one or two more, to reject them" (*C* 4:321), a self-portrayal that reflects the power and influence he liked to think he possessed in matters stylistic. Perhaps the most calculated attempt Swift made to establish himself as *the* man of letters was in *The Proposal for Correcting . . . the English Tongue*, in which he creates a magisterial persona, who, "in the Name of all the learned and polite Persons of the Nation [complains] . . . that our Language is extremely imperfect" (*PW* 4:6). As architect of the English academy, Swift would institutionalize his concept of himself as arbiter of style.

Because Swift publicly and privately set himself up as a literary authority, he was extremely conscious of his own style. He contrasts himself with Steele, a man, Swift implies, who was incapable of verbal discrimination: "The Author of the *Conduct of the Allies* [himself] writes Sense and English, neither of which the Author of the *Crisis* [Steele] understands" (*Publick Spirit of the Whigs, PW* 8:52). Swift, therefore, was outraged when Steele, whom he cast as an epitome of impropriety, accused him of writing an *Examiner* in which he had no part: "Is he so ignorant of my temper, and of my style?" (*C* 1:348). Swift was also insulted when a letter to the queen with his falsified signature was accepted as his own—"is it not wonderfull, that I should be suspected of writing to her in such a style" (*C* 3:484), Swift snorts with disgust.

Swift presumed that antisocial, uncommon, ahistorical discourse would be soundly rejected by the average reader with common sense, who, by virtue of his social instincts, would be able to tell improper words from proper words. Little did he suspect the lack of discrimination among some in high places, who, for instance, failed to see the irony in *A Tale of a Tub*. He found himself contending with "the ignorant, the unnatural, and uncharitable Applications of those who have neither Candor to suppose good Meanings, nor Palate to distinguish true Ones" (*PW* 1 : 2; italics omitted). Swift had to answer a charge of heresy for his facetious representations in the *Tale*. In a somewhat defensive "Apology," which attacks more than it apologizes, he painfully explains the possible sources of confusion in the *Tale*, much as someone might condescendingly explain an obvious joke. He clearly holds in contempt those who missed his point: "There is one Thing which the judicious Reader cannot but have observed, that some of those Passages in this Discourse, which appear most liable to Objection are what they call Parodies, where the Author personates the Style and Manner of other Writers, whom he has a mind to expose" (3; italics omitted).

That linguistic usage exposes basic existential decisions—in particular, whether to preserve the common forms or to subvert them, in other words, whether to be a render or a weaver—governed Swift's judgment of others and himself.

8

Judgment of Others

The most effectual Way to baulk
Their Malice, is—to let them talk.
"On Censure," *P* 2:414, 29–30

Since classical times, the idea that a man's speech reveals his character has been axiomatic. "Speech is the picture (index) of the mind" and "As the man is so is his talk" were common proverbs in the Renaissance,[1] and they lie behind Ben Jonson's statement, "Language most shewes a man: speake that I may see thee. It springs out of the most retired, and inmost part of us, and is the image of the Parent of it, the mind."[2] Later, all of these are succinctly summarized in Comte Georges Louis Leclerc de Buffon's epigram, "Le style est l'homme même." What does style reveal about a person? To Swift, style signaled whether one had an allegiance to the values and institutions that constitute British culture. "Proper Words" reinforce and extend the inherited fabric of civilization, whereas improper words hasten the "lapse into Barbarity" that Swift thought might be imminent. A person's style, in Swift's view, is not an isolated, individual act, but one that affects all Britons, past, present, and future. For this reason, Swift habitually assessed people's styles and judged whether they were weavers, who advance the human enterprise by strengthening social ties, or renders, who would, if unchecked, consign English-speakers to the fate of the Struldbruggs, or worse, the Yahoos.

Nowhere in his canon does Swift mention a bad man who writes well.[3] In his schema, a bad man—an enemy, for instance, to church or state—would also disrespect the simple and direct style that characterizes "Proper Words in proper Places." Swift repeatedly emphasized that education and study are not necessary to determine what is proper in ordinary, everyday discourse, that all men are capable of achieving the simple goal of entertaining and improving their fellows in conversation. More is required in written discourse, but a good man, one who is instinctively social, would have little trouble formulating his ideas within the context of accepted decorums.

Most normal individuals put "Proper Words in proper Places," and "When Men err against this Method, it is usually on Purpose" (*Holy Orders, PW* 9:68). Swift argued that those who are deficient in propriety, a concept with both verbal and moral dimensions, either lack the natural urge to be sociable or the usual complement of human intelligence. The former is far more common than the latter; the inability to communicate or interpret properly is "nine [times] in ten owing to Affectation and not to the want of Understanding" (68). Thus, as Martin Price puts it, a failure of propriety can result only from "willful neglect or brutal stupidity."[4] No matter what the cause, improper words reflect the absence the basic human(e) qualities needed for the maintenance of society in microcosm (private conversation) or macrocosm (public discourse).

Since the common forms of the Established Church, the English constitutional monarchy, and the English language were intertwined in Swift's mind, it is not surprising that his attacks on persons whom he considered threats to the social order come in the form of stylistic analyses. Swift's examinations of the prose of Richard Steele and Matthew Tindal are extended examples that illustrate the extraordinary degree to which Swift judged discourse, especially printed discourse, by its social effect.

Both Tindal and Steele are characterized as shredders or renders of language, not weavers or binders. Swift observes that Steele's work is "made up of a half-dozen Shreds" (*Publick Spirit of the Whigs, PW* 8:46) and that Tindal's "whole Discourse seemeth to be a motly, inconsistant Composition, made up of various Shreds of Equal Fineness, although of different Colours" (*Remarks on Tindall's Rights, PW* 2:68). Swift demonstrates how both Tindal's and Steele's stylistic defects are symptoms of seditious urges that allow them to espouse freethinking, on one hand, and whiggery, on the other.

Those Who Lack Propriety

Matthew Tindal's *Rights of the Christian Church Asserted* (1706) angered Swift because it questioned the supremacy of the Established Church by arguing that it was subject to civil authority. To prepare an answer to Tindal, Swift took notes which reveal his stylistic desiderata and his conviction that improper discourse is inevitable if one has improper or antisocial ideas. (The initial italicized words in the selections below are Tindal's.)

Page. 8. *Damned all the Canons.* What doeth he mean? A grave Divine could not answer all his Play-house and *Alsatia* Cant, &c. He hath read *Hudibras*, and many Plays.

(*References to Tindall's Book, PW* 2:85)

Page. 87. *Misapplying the Word Church, &c* This is cavilling. No doubt his Project is for exempting of the People: But that is not what in common Speech we usually mean by the Church. Besides, who doth not know that Distinction?

(87)

Ibid. *Constantly apply the same Ideas to them.* This is, in old *English*, meaning the same Thing.

(87)

Page 258. *Play the Devil for God's Sake.* If this meant for Wit; I would be glad to observe it, but in such Cases I first look whether there be common sense, &c.

(99)

Page 364. *Can any have a Right to an Office without having a Right to do those Things in which the Office consists?* I answer, the Ordination is valid. But a Man may prudentially forbid to do some Things.

(104)

Page 368. *A choice may be made by Persons who have no Right to chuse, is an Error of the first Concoction.* That battered simile again: this is hard. I wish the Physicians had kept that a Secret, it lieth so ready for him to be witty with.

(104)

Page 370. *If Prescription can make mere Nullities to become good and valid, &c.* There is a Difference; for here the same Way is kept, although there might be Breaches; but it is quite otherwise if you alter the whole Method from what it was at first. We see Bishops. There were always Bishops. It is the old Way still. So a Family is still held the same, although we are not sure of the Purity of every one of the Race.

(104)

Here Swift is talking to Tindal, answering him point for point, as he advised others to do as they read. He calls attention to inappropriate diction, skewed definitions, semantic confusion, clichés, and other stylistic flaws signalling that Tindal is beyond the pale of common sense. Because Tindal had the advantages of education, he knew better, but had made a conscious choice to be at war, Swift believes, with the majority who support traditional ideas and who speak traditional language. Tindal is more familiar with "*Alsatia* Cant," the slang of the criminal underworld, than he is with the writings of the church fathers (a charge often leveled at Swift himself).

After jotting these notes in his *References to Tindal's Book*, Swift digested them into an essay entitled *Remarks upon Tindall's Rights of the Christian Church*, whose focus is primarily Tindal's style. At the beginning of the essay, Swift reports that some think *Rights* was written by a "Club of Free-Thinkers" (*PW* 2 : 68), but he rejects this thesis because the work shows no evidence of collective thought. Tindal seems deprived of conversation with books and other men. His essay is too "confined and limited" (68) to be the product of several minds.

Tindal's writing is consistent—not a virtue when throughout "there is the same Flatness of Thought and Style: the same weak advances toward Wit and Raillery; the same Petulancy and Pertness of Spirit; the same . . . superficial Reading; the same . . . threadbare Quotations" (68). Swift professes amazement at the stylistic poverty of the *Rights* in light of the author's academic education. How could Tindal "with so many Advantages, and upon so unlimited a Subject, come out with so poor, so jejune a Production"? Tindal, however, has a totally Modern disdain for the past. Instead of writing "What oft was thought / But ne'er so well express'd," he has the "perverse . . . Talent" of talking "in an old beaten trivial Manner upon Topicks wholey new." To condemn Tindal, Swift says, one does not have to seek out his faults, but to do "little more than to rank his Perfections in such an Order, and place them in such a Light, that the commonest Reader may form a Judgment of them" (69). The effectiveness with which style communicates meaning to the "commonest Reader" is the measure Swift consistently applied to himself and others. Tindal's prose fails utterly on this account.

To illustrate, Swift provides an extended example of Tindal's style by quoting his definition of *government:*

> It would be in vain for one intelligent Being to pretend to set Rules to the Actions of another, if he had it not in his Power to reward the Compliance with, or punish the Deviations from his Rules by some Good, or Evil, which is not the natural Consequence of those Actions; since the forbidding Men to do or forbear an Action on the Account of that Convenience or Inconvenience which attendeth it, whether he who forbids it will or no, can be no more than Advice.
> (80; italics omitted)

Swift apologizes for the length of the citation but says that he could not "forbear to offer [it] as a Specimen of the Propriety and Perspicuity of this Author's Style" (80). Finding the passage too "refined" for common understanding, Swift recasts Tindal's paragraph as "If the Author were one that used to talk like one of us," that is, Britons who understand the common forms. In everyday language, Tindal's idea is that

> One Man will never cure another of stealing Horses, merely by minding him of the Pains he hath taken, the Cold he hath got, and the Shoe-Leather he hath lost in stealing that Horse; nay, to warn him, that the Horse may kick or fling him, or cost him more than he is worth in Hay and Oats, can be no more than Advice. For the Gallows is not the natural Effect of robbing on the High-Way, as Heat is of Fire: And therefore, if you will govern a Man, you must find out some other Way of Punishment, than what he will inflict upon himself.
> (80–81)

Swift's homely, concrete style makes the triviality of Tindal's point completely clear.

Not only does Tindal use convoluted jargon, he seems unaware of the usual meanings of words. Swift notes the "Strength of his Arguments is equal to the Clearness of his Definitions." Swift cites an example (in italics) and then comments on it:

> p. 7 *As to a legislative Power, if that belongs to the Clergy by Divine Right, it must be when they are assembled in Convocation: But the 25 Hen. 8. c. 19. is a Bar to such Divine Right.* . . . So the Force of his Argument lieth here; if the Clergy had a Divine Right, it is taken by the 25th of *Henry* the 8th. And as Ridiculous as this Argument is, the Preface and Book are founded upon it.
> (81)

To support his views in this case, Tindal cites a Mr. Washington, whom Swift characterizes as "an Author fit to be quoted by *Beaux*." Such is Tindal's conversation with books.

Semantics are irrelevant to Tindal. According to Swift, Tindal values the sound of words much more than their sense; he "affecteth to form a few Words into the Shape and Size of a Maxim, then trieth it by his Ear, and according as he likes the Sound or Cadence, pronounceth it true" (75). Tindal "hath a Talent of rattling out Phrases, which seem to have Sense, but have none at all." The result is a style that despite its cadence is "naturally harsh and ungrateful to the Ear." To disguise this failure, Tindal attempts to euphonize his expression, but, jabs Swift, "whenever he goeth about to polish a Period, you may be certain of some gross Defect in Propriety or Meaning" (78).

Swift believed that if discourse were conducted for the proper reasons—either to entertain or to improve—stylistic propriety would follow naturally. Conversely, improper motives beget improper style, as Swift demonstrated with Tindal. Swift believes that "When Books are written with ill Intentions to advance dangerous Opinions, or destroy Foundations; it may be then of real Use to know from what Quarter they come" (67). Swift then reveals that the "Principal" motive for publishing *Rights* is "a Sum of Money." Next is Tindal's desire for revenge against those who had impugned him—"To this Passion he has thought fit to sacrifice Order, Propriety, Discretion and Common-Sense, as may be seen in every Page of his Book." Swift then suggests a third possible motive, "as powerful as the other two; and that is, Vanity" (70). None of these impulses, needless to say, emanates from the higher reaches of the human character.

Instead of accepting, as most traditionally have done, the "very fair Consequences deduced from the Words of our Saviour and his Apostles," which have been woven permanently into the social fabric and which are no more alterable than the "common Laws of Nature" (77), Tindal stands arrogantly apart. He is like a man who will "take a Turnip, then tye a String to it, and call it a Watch, and turn away . . . Servants, if they refuse to call it so too" (76). Tindal cannot single-handedly redefine the historical relationship of civil and ecclesiastical power, but Swift is fearful enough of the powers of "Newthink" (Orwell's term) to point out what he considers the obvious.[5]

Although Swift and Steele were friends at one time, their partisan loyalties eventually pulled them into antagonistic camps. Steele came to represent in Swift's mind all that was wrong with contemporary whiggery, and whiggery's impropriety was evident to him in Steele's style. In two of his most virulent attacks on Steele, published within months of each other in 1713–14, Swift, in the manner of a literary critic, performs a particular analysis of Steele's language. To condemn Steele's *The Crisis . . . with Some Seasonable Remarks on the Danger of a Popish Succession*, Swift responded with *The Publick Spirit of the Whigs . . . with Some Observations on the Seasonableness, Candor, Erudition, and Style of [the Crisis]*. Using a similar method, Swift destroyed Steele's *Importance of Dunkirk Consider'd* in *The Importance of the* Guardian *Considered*. There he scrutinizes the text "partly as a Critick, and partly as a Commentator, which, I think, is to treat [Steele] only as my Brother-Scribler, according to the Permission he has graciously allowed me" (*PW* 8:4; italics omitted).

In *The Importance of the* Guardian *Considered*, Swift links Steele's ignorance of common forms and common sense to his isolation in London. Swift's essay is a letter to the bailiff and people of Stockbridge, whom Steele represented in Parliament, in imitation of Steele's *Importance of Dunkirk Consider'd*, which was similarly addressed. Swift declares, "I find several Passages . . . which want Explanation, especially to You in the Country. . . . I have therefore made bold to send you here a second Letter, by way of Comment upon the former" (5). He begins by explaining that "*London*-Writers" put titles on their works that bear little relation to the contents. Thus "*The Importance of Dunkirk*, is chiefly taken up in shewing you the *Importance* of Mr. *Steele*" (5). Steele's insulation from ordinary converse ("he never follows the Advice of His Friends") led to failures in all aspects of his life; he is "hurried away by his own Caprice; by which he hath committed more Absurdities in Oeconomy, Friendship, Love, Duty, good Manners, Politicks, Religion and Writing, than ever fell to one Man's share" (6). If one cannot discriminate "Proper Words in proper Places," Swift implies, then one is unable to make any of the choices that promote a useful and happy life. Ignorance of the common linguistic forms reveals that Steele understands little about the concepts that organize civilized life: "Oeconomy, Friendship, Love, Duty, good Manners, Politicks, Religion."

Swift applied the same standard to Steele's writing that he applied to Tindal's. Indeed, he used the same standard to measure the effectiveness of all styles, his own included: the touchstone of "Proper Words" was their intelligibility to the ordinary person. Like Tindal's style, Steele's failed the test; Swift pretends that it is necessary to provide "Annotations" that will "render this Matter clear to the very meanest Capacities" (8). Swift argues that Steele's overblown cant masks the explicit foolishness and knavery of his ideas. Swift believed it his duty to "translate" Steele's writing into accessible terms.

As a corrective to Steele's self-inflation, Swift shows that Steele's affected town jargon is merely part of his delusion that he is a man of consequence—or as Steele puts it, that "*he is no small Man*" (8). When Steele claims, for instance, that he is going to lay the matter of Dunkirk before the ministry, Swift annotates the line with a question: "Did you not, Mr. Bailiff . . . presently imagine he had drawn up a sort of Counter-Memorial . . . and presented it in form to my Lord *Treasurer*, or a Secretary of State? I am confident you did; but this comes by not understanding the Town." Swift then explains that Steele was using the phrase "*laying Things before the Ministry*" as a "Figure of Speech." In fact, all Steele means, Swift insinuates, is that he will publish his ideas in a "Peny-paper to be read in Coffee-houses." The ministry, Swift notes sarcastically, "never saw his Paper, unless he sent it [to] them by the Peny-Post" (12). As he does consistently throughout his canon, Swift contrasts the evanescent and self-involved ways of the town with the steadfastness and directness of the countryside.

Swift suggests that Steele does not understand syntax well enough to control his meaning by gleefully turning Steele's style into a weapon against him. When Steele says that "*he cannot offer against the* Examiner *and his other Adversary, Reason and Argument without appearing void of both,*" Swift hoots, "What a singular Situation of the Mind is this! How glad should I be to hear a man *offer Reasons and Argument, and yet at the same time appear void of both!* But this whole paragraph is of a peculiar strain; the Consequences so Just and Natural, and such a Propriety in Thinking, as few Authors ever arrived to" (12). Through his word choice—*singular, peculiar, few*—Swift depicts Steele outside the mainstream of ordinary thought, indeed, perilously near madness.

Steele illustrates that self-imposed exile from the common forms does not bring freedom but limitation. Swift implies that this limitation is evident in Steele's style, particularly in his repetition of words and phrases, which is a practice most individuals would avoid because it grates on the ear. Steele's initiation of a series of ten paragraphs in virtually the same way prompts Swift's gibes:

> In answer to the Sieur's *First.*
> As to the Sieur's *Second.*
> As to his *Third.*
> As to the Sieur's *Fourth.*
> As to Mr. Deputy's *Fifth.*
> [Etc. up to the Tenth]

> You see every Second Expression is more or less diversified to avoid . . . Repetition . . . I could heartily wish Monsieur . . . had been able to find Ten Arguments more, and thereby given Mr. *Steele* an Opportunity of shewing the utmost Variations our Language would bear in so momentous a Tryal.
>
> (10–11)

Swift also delights in demonstrating Steele's ignorance of simple rules of grammar. He quotes, for instance, a line from Steele and adds a sniping parenthesis: "*he thinks his Queen and Country is,* (or as a Grammarian would express it, *are) ill treated*" (19). Steele, like Tindal, does not see words as units of meaning but as patterns of sound: Swift, fending off those who might say that he is not interpreting Steele's words with any charity, rejoins, "If I have ill interpreted him, it is his own Fault, for studying Cadence instead of Propriety, and filling up Nitches with Words before he has adjusted his conceptions to them" (22). One case in point is Steele's thoughtless braggadocio about being *"spoken of more than once in Print,"* which elicits Swift's observation, "It is indeed a great Thing to be *spoken of in Print,* and must needs make a mighty Sound at *Stockbridge* among the Electors" (8).

Swift suggests that Steele's inappropriate discourse reflects his inability to comprehend the other basic features of British society. When Steele informs the queen that *"the British Nation EXPECTS the IMMEDIATE Demolition of Dunkirk,"* Swift seizes on Steele's lack of proper deference and constructs a letter with which the queen might reply: "Mr. Richard Steele . . . I do not conceive that any of your Titles empower you to be my Director, or to report to me the Expectations of my People" (18–19; italics omitted). Steele understands English expression as well as he does the natural respect he owes the monarch.

In *The Publick Spirit of the Whigs,* Swift also harps on Steele's impropriety—in all senses. He begins by establishing that Steele's motives for writing were not to improve or entertain his audience; he sought personal, materialistic gain. Tongue in cheek, Swift praises the Whigs for their charity in paying writers, such as Steele, with "no Question offered about the Wit, the Style, the Argument" of what they produce (*PW* 8 : 31). He then commends notorious hacks and speculates that Steele might rise to their level "provided he would a little regard the Propriety and Disposition of his Words, consult the grammatical part, and get some Information in the Subject he intends to handle" (32). Since the Whigs who ordered *The Crisis* be written never will read it, they make ideal employers of needy writers: they "will pay us before-hand, take off as much of our Ware as we please to our own Rates, and trouble not themselves to examine [it] either before or after they have bought it." No discrimination exists here: books are not expressions of thought but inanimate "Wares" to be bought and sold in bulk. In contrast, Swift feels an obligation to "examin[e] the Production itself." What he finds is worthless, a testimony to "the implicit Munificence of these noble [Whig] Patrons" (33).

Swift characterizes the ideas in *The Crisis* as a collection, "a Heap of Extracts" (35), whose components have little or no relation. The words in Steele's sentences are also collections which contain a number of *things*, for he uses words not as signifiers of meaning but as objects to place in a row. For instance, Steele's expression *"solemn strong Barriers"* prompts Swift to jeer: "Although I have heard of a *solemn* Day, a *solemn* Feast, and a *solemn* Coxcomb, yet I can conceive no Idea to my self [a parody of Locke] of a *solemn Barrier*" (53). At another point, "our Author tells us, with extreme Propriety, [that something] *seems reasonable to common Sense;* that is, in other Words, it seems *reasonable* to *Reason*" (44). These solecisms arise because, like the *Tale*-denizens, Steele has no cultural memory. Despite his education, which ought to heighten his sensitivity to language, Steele "hath a confused Remembrance of Words since he left the University, but hath lost half of their Meaning, and puts them together with no Regard, except to their Cadence; as I remember a Fellow nailed up Maps in a Gentleman's closet, some sideling, others upside down, the better to adjust them to the Pannels" (36). Neither social nor syntactical context affects Steele's style.

Steele's essay, Swift argues, is not only hackneyed but obscure, an unlikely combination not easily achieved. Swift suggests that when Steele tries to vary his style, he creates verbal monsters that he lacks the wit to delete. According to Swift, Steele's tract is "like a School-Boy's Theme, beaten, general Topicks, where any other Man alive might wander securely; but this Politician, by venturing to vary the good old Phrases, and give them a new Turn, commits an hundred Solecisms and Absurdities" (46). Steele's vocabulary, though pretentious, is limited: he has a stock of "about twenty Polysyllables . . . and hath writ from no other Fund" (41). Steele often uses words in strange ways, divorced from "common acceptations." He says, for instance, on the title page that *The Crisis* is "*A Discourse, representing from the most authentick Records.*" Swift sneers that Steele "hath borrowed this Expression from some Writer, who probably understood the Words, but this Gentleman hath altogether misapplied them" (34–35). Even when Steele plagiarizes, he cannot manage to get "Proper Words in proper Places."

Swift gives some lengthy examples of Steele's prose to illustrate his general *impropriety*, a word that recurs in the discussion. One of Steele's passages is as follows:

> We cannot possess our Souls with Pleasure and Satisfaction except we preserve to our selves that inestimable Blessing which we call Liberty: by Liberty, I desire to b[e] understood, to mean the Happiness of Men's Living, &c.—The true Life of Man consists in conducting it according to his own just Sentiments and innocent Inclinations.—Man's Being is degraded below that of a free Agent, when his Affections and Passions are no longer governed by the Dictates of his own Mind.—Without Liberty, our Health (among other Things) may be at the Will of a Tyrant, employed to our own Ruin and that of our Fellow Creatures.
>
> (46; italics omitted)

Swift satirically translates the passage to suggest Steele's love of inanity and anarchy:

The weighty Truths which he endeavours to press upon his Reader are such as these. That, Liberty is a very good Thing; that, without Liberty we cannot be free; that, Health is good, and Strength is good, but Liberty is better than either; that, no Man can be happy, without the Liberty of doing whatever his own Mind tells him is best; that, Men of Quality love Liberty, and common People love Liberty; even Women and Children love Liberty; and you cannot please them better than by letting them do what they please. Had Mr. Steele contented himself to deliver these and the like Maxims in such intelligible Terms, I could have found where we agreed and where we differed. . . . [But] if there be any of these Maxims, which is not grossly defective in Truth, in Sense, or in Grammar, I will allow them to pass for uncontroulable.

(46; italics omitted)

Thus Swift, in his parting shot, concedes that Steele, like Thomas Shadwell in *MacFlecknoe*, might inexplicably "deviate into sense." On the whole, though, Steele displays a "complicated Ignorance in History, human Nature, [and] Politicks, as well as in the ordinary Proprieties of Thought or of Style" (44). Steele, like the *Tale*-teller, has a "complicated Ignorance" that prevents him from seeing plain truth; he cannot even "furnish out so much as a Title-Page with Propriety or common sense" (35).

As might be expected, Steele hurled comparable charges back at Swift, accusing him of distorting the traditional definitions and associations of such basic ideas as "*Good, Safe, honourable, Advantageous, England, France, Trade, Commerce:* he makes the *Examiner* the Mint-Master for the New Tongue. . . . Nor are his *New* Politicks any better than his *New* Language."[6] Each man saw the other as a radical bent on destroying the common understandings that bind British society together.

In his exegesis of *The Crisis* as in his other stylistic analyses, Swift attempts to show that an ignorance of the common forms reveals an alien nature. Swift depicts Steele and his Whig patrons as foreign visitors who are not fluent in English. At one point Swift attempts to explain a passage in Steele's writing but then pretends to give up, saying that "if there be any thing further in it, than a want of Understanding our Language, I take it to be only a Refinement upon the old levelling Principle of the Whigs" (*Importance of the* Guardian *Considered*, PW 8:24). Swift mockingly concedes, however, that "it is of little consequence to [the Whig's] cause, whether this Defender of it understands Grammar or no" (*Publick Spirit of the Whigs, PW* 8 : 36). A larger question Swift poses is not whether a person "who writes at this Rate . . . be a GENTLEMAN BORN [as Steele liked to designate himself], but whether he be a HUMAN CREATURE" (68), since rational speech is supposedly characteristic of homo sapiens.

Swift's satires of Steele and Tindal are hardly subtle and do not represent the best of his writing, but they are important because they show the intimate linkage of stylistic propriety—"Proper Words in proper Places"— with an acceptance of the fundamental forms that shape the lives of British citizens.

Those Who Possess Propriety

One of the most remarkable examples of Swift's use of style as an index to character occurred when he received a letter from Andrew Fitzherbert, a young man who had been ostracized by his parents. Swift writes the elder Fitzherberts, "I have always thought that a happy genius is seldom without some bent towards virtue, and therefore deserves some indulgence. Most of the great villains I have known (which were not a small number) have been brutes in their understandings, as well as their actions" (*C* 4 : 309). Swift admonishes the parents to relent and chastises them with considerable feeling: "I think," says Swift, "if I had a son, who had understanding, wit, and humour to write such a letter, I could not find in my heart to cast him off, but try what good advice and maturer years would do toward amendment, and, in the meantime, give him no cause to complain of wanting convenient food, lodging, and raiment" (308). After seeking the counsel of his friends, Swift figuratively adopted the young man sight unseen solely because he wrote in a style that reflected humane understanding.[7] Implicit in Swift's reaction is the presumption that style reflects the disposition of an individual's character. If a person is reasonable, in other words, if he understands his communal ties, he will be able to put "Proper Words in proper Places." Conversely, antisocial people, "villains" of various sorts, would naturally fail to express themselves with propriety, thus revealing that they are closer to "brutes" than to human beings.

Swift similarly linked in praise the style and character of Esther Vanhomrigh. Writing to her often in French—a language symbolically apart from the "little language" he shared with Stella, the pun-ridden argot in which he communicated to Sheridan, and the standard English through which he addressed the world at large—he told her that her discourse reflected the perfection of her actions. Part of his extended compliment is as follows: "j'ay toujours remarquè que ni en conversation particuliere, ni

general aucun mot a echappè de votre bouche, qui pouvoit etre mieux ex-
primè; et je vous jure qu'en faisant souvent la plus severe Critique, je ne
pouvois jamais trouver aucun defaut ni en vos Actions ni en vos parolles"
(*C* 2 : 326) [I have always observed that in neither private nor public conversation any word has escaped your mouth that ought to be better expressed;
and I swear to you that in often making the severest criticism, I have been
unable to find any fault with either your actions or your words]. Perhaps
afraid of addressing more personal qualities, yet governed by his obsession
with language, Swift focuses on Vanessa's style in his flattery.

In eulogizing Esther Johnson the night of her funeral, Swift also cited
verbal effectiveness as evidence of general virtue. Almost all of his memorial addressed Stella's ability to discriminate "Proper Words in proper
Places." He obviously valued her judgments on his own writings. In the
Journal to Stella he constantly sought her opinion about his publications
and seems, when practicable, to have solicited her advice while he was
writing: "She had a true taste of wit and good sense, both in poetry and
prose, and was a perfect good critic of style: Neither was it easy to find
a more proper or impartial judge, whose advice an author might better
rely on, if he intended to send a thing into the world" (*On the Death of
Mrs. Johnson, PW* 5 : 231). Her stylistic discrimination was evidence of a
comprehensive reason that allowed her to understand correctly: Swift
notes, "I cannot call to mind that I ever once heard her make a wrong judgment of persons, books, or affairs" (228).

Stella's discourse was always appropriate to the social context in which
it occurred. In conversation she had a knack for making people comfortable with her. Talking in an ordinary way that included rather than ex-
cluded people, she profited from the ideas of "people of all sorts [who]
were never more easy than in her company" (229). She eschewed jargon
and affected expressions, preferring a basic, sensible style. Her simplicity
of expression was one of conscious choice. She had the knowledge and
ability to discourse in an erudite manner if she wished, but she obviously
shared Swift's conviction that the matters of most importance could be
conveyed in everyday language: "Although her knowledge, from books
and company, was more extensive than usually falls to the share of her sex;
yet she was so far from making a parade of it, that her female visitants, on
their first acquaintance, who expected to discover it, by what they call
hard words and deep discourse, would be sometimes disappointed, and
say, they found she was like other women. But wise men, through all her
modesty, whatever they discoursed on, could easily observe that she understood them very well" (236). Not only did she speak straightforwardly, she

interpreted the words of others without skewing their meanings: "She never mistook the understanding of others" (229).

In company Stella was direct but never indecorous—"Her advice was always the best, and with the greatest freedom, mixt with the greatest decency" (228). Like Swift, she would not tolerate bawdy talk: "It was not safe or prudent, in her presence, to offend in the least word against modesty; for she then gave full employment to her wit, her contempt and resentment, under which even stupidity and brutality were forced to sink into confusion; and the guilty person, by her future avoiding him like a bear or a satyr, was never in a way to transgress a second time" (234). Swift's praise is hyperbolic, an emotional response to the loss of someone he loved deeply, yet this is not the stuff of conventional eulogy. Swift defines Stella's virtues as a human being almost exclusively in relation to her stylistic discrimination because, for Swift, style revealed the true principles by which a person lived his or her life.

Andrew Fitzherbert, Esther Vanhomrigh, and Esther Johnson might have epitomized "Proper Words in proper Places," but because they did not write to publish, their beneficial effect on society at large was limited. Authors, on the other hand, could wield influence far beyond their circles and indeed, by producing something of lasting value, might be incorporated into the national fabric as part of the accepted canon of English literature. Famous or not, writers, Swift believed, have an obligation to preserve traditional values and institutions, without which no transcendent meaning could exist.

Toward the end of his life, Swift turned to assess his contributions. His most important legacy, he believed, was his writing. Had his writing strengthened the important common forms? Was he a linguistic weaver who had added to the permanent fabric of British life? Had his writings changed the world for the better? Would he be remembered?

9

Judgment of Himself

ALTHOUGH I have never been once charged with
the least Tincture of Vanity, the Reader will, I
hope, give me Leave to put an easy Question.
What is become of all the King of *Sweden*'s Victories? Where are the Fruits of them at this
Day? . . . I, who have alone, with this Right
Hand, subdued Barbarism, Rudeness, and Rus-
ticity; who have established, and fixed for ever,
the whole System of all true Politeness, and
Refinement in Conversation; should think my
self most inhumanly treated by my Countrymen . . . to be put upon the Level, in Point of
Fame, in after Ages, with [the] . . . late King of
Sweden.

Introduction to *Polite Conversation*,
PW 4 : 122

Toward the end of his life, Swift became increasingly concerned
about what Prince Posterity would think of him, and it became
clear that he wanted, above all, to be remembered as a great
writer, one whose language clarified fundamental truths and improved the
world. But was the accessible, conversational style that typified many of
his works and served as a norm against which to measure his parodies a
sufficient foundation for lasting literary fame? Swift affected indifference
to the opinion of the literary establishment, whoever they may be, and
claimed to "write to the Vulgar, more than to the Learned" (*Faulkner's Preface, PW* 13 : 202; italics omitted). But he must have wondered whether the
approbation of the "Vulgar" would earn him a place in the history of En-

134

glish literature. Had any canonized writer such a broad, popular appeal? Had any canonized writer achieved eminence without writing poetry in an epic, tragic, lyric, or heroic vein? As Swift entered his sixth decade, he seems to have had some doubts about his lifelong stylistic strategies. Arthur H. Scouten points out that in the late 1720s, Swift almost abandoned prose writing altogether and started to experiment with heroic couplets, perhaps in imitation of his friend Alexander Pope, whose place in the history of English literature seemed assured.[1] Swift must have realized his attempts at High Art were failures because he returned to the congenial octasyllabic couplet and began composing, among other things, "Verses on the Death of Dr. Swift."

Swift took a great deal of care in composing the "Verses" and arranging for its publication. Writing to John Gay in 1731, Swift describes his project: "I have been several months writing near five hundred lines on a pleasant Subject, only to tell what my friends and enemyes will say of me after I am dead. I shall finish it soon, for I add two lines every week, and blott out four, and alter eight" (C 4:273). The poem seems to have been substantially completed by 1732. Swift sent a copy of the manuscript to Dr. William King, Principal of St. Mary Hall, Oxford, who, influenced and assisted by Pope and some "others of the Dean's friends" (C 5:137) in England, radically altered the poem and had it published in London, January 1738/39. Large pieces of verse and all of the footnotes were omitted, supposedly so as not to offend the ministry. Swift, annoyed at the mangled London edition, arranged for the full poem with notes to be published in Dublin by Faulkner.[2] Swift's insistence on restoring the long footnotes, many of which recount the tribulations and triumphs of the Drapier, and the care he spent in writing and revising the poem reveal his intense personal investment in it.[3]

The "Proem" of the "Verses" explains the necessity of the task Swift undertakes in commemorating himself. Half in earnest, half in jest, Swift asserts that since no sincere human sympathy is possible, a complimentary evaluation of one's life can be conducted only by oneself. Cynically he observes that, even if they are friends, other people's sorrows bring a measure of joy, and other people's achievements provoke hatred and envy. Swift knows this well, he facetiously claims, from his own experience. With humorous irony he describes how his friends' abilities in the realm he values the most, the literary, turn his love to spite: "If with such Talents Heav'n hath blest 'em / Have I not Reason to detest 'em?" (P 2:555, 65–66). He pretends that the accomplishments of his fellow Scriblerians sting his raw ego like vinegar:

WHAT Poet would not grieve to see,
His Brethren write as well as he?
But rather than they should excel,
He'd wish his Rivals all in Hell.

. . . .

IN POPE, I cannot read a Line,
But with a Sigh, I wish it mine:
When he can in one Couplet fix
More Sense than I can do in Six:
It gives me such a jealous Fit,
I cry, Pox take him, and his Wit.

WHY must I be outdone by GAY,
In my own hum'rous biting Way?

ARBUTHNOT is no more my Friend,
Who dares to Irony pretend;
Which I was born to introduce,
Refin'd it first, and shew'd its Use.

. . . .

To all my Foes, dear Fortune, send
Thy Gifts, but never to my Friend:
I tamely can endure the first,
But, this with Envy makes me burst.
(31−34, 47−58, 67−70)

Swift's exaggerated jealousy of his friends, of course, is an indirect praise of their talents—and his own. Swift writes the lines with tongue in cheek, yet underneath is a basic insecurity about his unique contribution to the world of letters. Given the seeming ubiquity of rampant self-interest, who will remember his efforts to "entertain and improve"? Swift shows, though, using his biased judgment of his friends as an example, that a fair estimation of one's work may not be made by one's colleagues. Clearly the reputations of Pope, Gay, and Arbuthnot do not depend on his opinion. By the agreement of a large number of citizens, they have already achieved a permanent place in England's cultural legacy. Swift also desired to be a lasting memory in the collective mind of the nation, as the "Verses" makes clear, but his achievements are different from those of his Scriblerian fellows. Although he praises his friends for their poetic technique—Pope's couplet art, Arbuthnot's irony, Gay's humor, all intrinsic aesthetic elements characteristic of his poetry as well—Swift encourages an evaluation of his own literary merit using another, extrinsic criterion very different from those usually applied—that works should have as a norm "Proper Words"— an easily and universally understood style used to reinforce social unity and traditional values. Because Swift-as-Drapier achieved this ideal in a highly visible way, Swift highlights the publication of *The Drapier's Letters* in the "Verses." The Drapier, as Chapter 2 illustrates, is the epitome of "Proper Words in proper Places." He is a weaver, literally and figuratively.[4]

After demonstrating the way in which his egoism distorts his assessment of his literary friends, Swift, in the next section of the poem, imagines how the self-love of his friends and enemies will warp their view of him. Just as he envies his friends who were great writers, he hopes others will envy him as a great writer. Throughout, however, he stresses that it is the *power* of his words to affect social realities that makes him so feared. People dare not express their opinions of him while he has his verbal skills, for fear of reprisals, and will feel at liberty only when they see that his wits are fading. He imagines how his acquaintances, full of self-congratulatory pity, will remark, "He recollects not what he says" (87); He "Plyes you with Stories o'er and o'er, / He told them fifty Times before" (89–90); "For Poetry, he's past his Prime, / He takes an Hour to find a Rhime" (99–100). The relief and delight elicited by the decline of his writing ability dramatize Hobbes's observation that, in a state of nature, the death of one's rival is the "only security" against usurpation of one's power, and Swift emphasizes that his power emanates from his use of "Proper Words in proper Places."

Swift's beneficial influence on society is ironically revealed when he depicts the revelry of antisocial forces—in this case, the court and Walpole's ministry—upon hearing news of his death. Lady Suffolk "Runs laughing up to tell the Queen" (180), who expresses happiness that he is gone: "'Tis time he shou'd" (182). Swift suggests that because he had been so successful in satirizing the ruling circle, they could only feel joy at his demise. Even though they represent the pinnacle of temporal power, their opinions, the poem implies, are irrelevant to Swift's lasting reputation, which was won, in part, by active opposition to them. Quite self-consciously in the "Verses," Swift characterizes himself as the "wild Dean," who could not conform to the limiting expectations of authorities he did not respect.

Invariably, he demonstrates that those in power are isolated from common sense and hence fear his efforts to impose it. He flouted, for example, the arrogant advice of his doctors, who snipe that "Had he been rul'd, for ought appears, / He might have liv'd these Twenty Years" (173–74) as well as the opinions of those who believed he should have "spar'd his Tongue and Pen / [and] rose like other Men" (355–56). But he never wanted to be like "other Men" and let conventional attitudes dictate his choices. He respected the high offices of church and state, but he never considered the individuals holding those offices morally or intellectually superior to him: "With Princes [he] kept a due Decorum, / But never stood in Awe before 'em" (338–39).

Swift was proud of the way his life and works dismayed those whose values were alien to his. For instance, he imagines that when his bequest of money for "public Uses" (to endow a mental asylum in Dublin) becomes known, certain people will think the failure to enrich his own circle very odd:

> "And had the Dean, in all the Nation,
> "No worthy Friend, no poor Relation?
> "So ready to do Strangers good,
> "Forgetting his own Flesh and Blood?"
> (161–64)

Such is the tattle around Dublin after "The News thro' half the Town has run" (152). The headlines are broadcast from one urban center to another, "From *Dublin* soon to *London* spread" (177). The significance of Swift's contribution to society cannot be perceived by those isolated in the *Tale*-like world of the metropolis, where wealth and fashion are all-important. Swift characterizes himself as a man the shortsighted materialistic urbanities cannot comprehend: he is an idealist who fights to enlarge individual freedoms by shoring up the traditional institutions and beliefs that shelter them.

Swift shows that his reputation does not depend on the ephemeral London clique and the booksellers who service them. One of this crowd asks after his death, "Where's now this Fav'rite of *Apollo?*" to be answered,

> Departed; *and his Works must follow:*
> Must undergo the common Fate;
> His kind of Wit is out of Date
> (249–52)

Even though his wit may be "out of Date" with city Moderns who confuse "new" with "true," Swift implies in the "Verses" that he will not share "the common Fate" of being forgotten because he is valued by common men who are able to appreciate the binding truths that Swift's writing reinforces. Unlike members of the self-proclaimed elite, who parade themselves in the latest linguistic fashions, common men, in Swift's view, are suspicious of trendy jargon and can recognize deviations from the verbal norm. Not accidentally, Swift has a "Country Squire" seek "*Swift* in Verse and Prose" a year after Swift's death. The bookseller, at that point, has only a hazy memory of the Dean and tells the squire,

> "I find you're but a Stranger here.
> "The Dean was famous in his Time;
> "And had a Kind of Knack at Rhyme:
> "His way of Writing now is past;
> "The Town hath got a better Taste:
> "I keep no antiquated Stuff;
> "But, spick and span I have enough.
> "Pray, do but give me leave to shew 'em;
> "Here's *Colley Cibber's* Birth-day Poem.
> "This Ode you never yet have seen,
> "By *Stephen Duck*, upon the Queen."
> (262–72)

In a place perverted to lionize Colley Cibber and Stephen Duck, objects of scorn to the Scriblerians, the common sense valued by both Swift and the country squire is a "Stranger." Swift clearly shows that the bookseller's estimation of his fame is not to be trusted.

The urban bookseller's shop as a Hall of No Fame is an image Swift used in one of his first works, *A Tale of a Tub.* In the "Dedication to Prince Posterity," the *Tale*-teller tries to prove that Modern productions are worthy of preservation. He prepares a list of publications as evidence, but before he can complete his essay—a matter of hours—the originals have disappeared. "I enquired after them among Readers and Booksellers, but I enquired in vain, the *Memorial of them was lost among Men, their Place was no more to be found:* and I was laughed to scorn, for a *Clown* [usually meaning a country bumpkin] and a *Pedant*, without all Taste and Refinement, little versed in the Course of *present* Affairs, and that knew nothing of what had pass'd in the best Companies of Court and Town" (*Tale, PW* 1:21). In this exaggerated scenario, a person with any memory at all is seen as a rustic troglodyte, who is laughed at by snobby booksellers, men who judge books as butchers judge meat—only the freshest will do! Meat rots, but the contents of a good book, an embodiment of the human spirit, will live on. Good books do not cease to exist when they are removed from the bookseller's shelves and sent "to the Pastry-cooks" (*P* 2:563, 260) for pie-pan liners. Good books, however, will end up in the "Abyss of Things" if the language in which they are written becomes obsolete or if the world becomes so debased that traditional definitions of enlightenment and entertainment disappear. Swift is both serious and self-mocking when in the "Apology" to the *Tale*, he predicts that his "Book seems calculated to live at least as long as our Language, and our Tast admit no great Alterations" (*PW* 1 : 1; italics omitted).

The basis of literary fame was a theme to which Swift returned, with renewed emphasis, in the "Verses." What mechanism incorporates a writer permanently into the cultural memory? Swift suggests that the common-sense judgment of ordinary people is needed to determine ultimate significance. How is this common sense ascertained? Through everyday discourse. With this in mind, Swift switches the scene in the "Verses" from the vicious haunts of Grubstreet to the humane warmth of the Rose Tavern, where in the midst of a lively, congenial conversation, Swift imagines that "from Discourse of this and that, / I grow the Subject of their Chat" (*P* 2 : 565, 301–2). Talking in an ideal manner, the participants bring forth all sides of the issue until a consensus, presented by "One quite indiff'rent in the Cause," is created. As opposed to the self-interested speakers who comment earlier in the poem, this one is said to be "impartial." He offers his summation of Swift:

> "As for his Works in Verse and Prose,
> "I own my self no Judge of those:
> "Nor, can I tell what Cricks thought 'em;
> "But, this I know, all People bought 'em;
> "As with a moral View design'd
> "To cure the Vices of Mankind:
> "His Vein, ironically grave,
> "Expos'd the Fool, and lash'd the Knave."
>   (309–16)

The speaker is obviously not well educated, but he expresses the rational opinion that Swift's works must have some universal, lasting appeal since they were so popular with "all People." That Swift may have been dismissed by the quadrille club, the court, and Grubstreet is insignificant because these are isolated realms not contiguous to the real world. In contrast to those who, with their own ends in mind, purposefully skew their judgments of Swift's motives and values, the "impartial" speaker at the Rose Tavern, this representative of the people, this honest observer, recognizes what Swift was trying to accomplish: to expose foolishness and to lash knavery—to strengthen the common forms of civilized life. The "impartial" speaker's supposedly candid summary of Swift's accomplishments fills the last section of the poem.

Many contemporary and modern readers are troubled by the tone of this eulogy put in the mouth of the "impartial" speaker, and with good cause. Swift is very serious about memorializing himself as a great writer whose fame is not dependent on "private ends," his own and others, but on the lasting contribution he made to the public by his words and deeds, yet he cloaks this serious intent with humorous hyperbole that qualifies the boasts he ascribes to the narrator. Truths are mixed with outright untruths. For example, the first claim from the speaker's lips is a known lie—"The Dean, if we believe Report, / Was never ill receiv'd at Court" (307–8). Indeed, earlier in the poem Swift had reported Queen Caroline's callous treatment of him. Throughout the "Verses," the reader is forced to winnow out the truth of the matter from a mass of contradictory statements. The poem is a "test of the reader's discrimination,"[5] for as usual, Swift relies on his audience's abilities to separate proper words from improper words, much as one has to do in any discourse. From a series of oversimplified and erroneous statements by various speakers, including the "impartial" speaker and Swift when he claims to speak *in propria persona*, the reader, using his common sense, must arrive at a complex synthesis that comes closer to the truth than any of the false ultimatums that the "Verses" puts forth. In this method of provoking the reader's active participation to determine the meaning of the work, "Verses on the Death of Dr. Swift" operates like others of Swift's satires, in which norms are not articulated but must be supplied by the reader after he rejects the extreme positions presented to him. Gulliver is neither Yahoo nor Houyhnhnm. Celia is neither an ethereal goddess nor a mere shitter. Swift is neither the narrow seeker of private ends, as he appears at the beginning of the "Verses," nor the totally altruistic supporter of "Public Uses" he depicts at the poem's end. Similarly, he is neither an establishment icon nor a renegade iconoclast, both of which characterizations are offered by the poem. And although Swift creates a portrait of himself as a man of the people, he does so in carefully crafted, witty couplets that would please the most educated literati. Swift never wanted to foreclose any possibilities.

Swift as the Drapier

Swift accentuates his identity as a writer in "Verses on the Death of Dr. Swift" but strangely fails to mention *Gulliver's Travels*, *The Conduct of the Allies*, or *A Tale of a Tub*, all of which were widely known. Instead, Swift repeatedly calls attention to the *The Drapier's Letters* and stresses his identity as M.B., Drapier. Why the Drapier? Both *A Tale of a Tub* and *Gulliver's Travels* are intricate and ironic. What *Gulliver* and the *Tale* "are about" varies from reader to reader and often incites testy controversy, even among mild-mannered professors on liberal arts faculties. The themes and norms of these two works are difficult to determine, although both produce immense aesthetic delight. Swift might have feared that he had a reputation for being too entertaining and that he might be dismissed as an amoral jester. Neither Gulliver nor Martin (in *A Tale of a Tub*) is the Red-crosse Knight. *The Conduct of the Allies*, on the other hand, is an accessible document with a clear thesis, yet its concerns are transitory—the jockey-ing of various interests at the end of the War of the Spanish Succession. No high or transcendent principles are expressed; indeed, Ehrenpreis suggests that *The Conduct* is a brief for a particular policy of the Tory ministry—"Though the author seems explicitly to be recommending only peace in general, he is really recommending the specific treaty envisaged by St. John."[6] For writing this and other Tory propaganda, Swift's enemies branded him a mercenary party hack, a characterization anathema to him.

Although *The Drapier's Letters* were generated in response to a particular political event—the imposition of Wood's Half Pence on Ireland—they sound the noble theme of liberty through unity. M.B., Drapier, epitomizes the best in British civilization—he is independent, high-minded, and brave. Rousing his compatriots with a stirring call to action, he binds the Irish people together to prevail against oppression. It was a decisive vic-tory that made a hero out of Swift (a role he relished) and gave the people a glimpse of a free Ireland.[7] But Swift, like his ironic persona Simon Wagstaff, does not desire to be remembered for political triumphs—"What is become of all the King of *Sweden's* Victories? Where are the Fruits of them at this Day?" (*PW* 4:122), he asks in the Introduction to *Polite Conversation*. The land taken in a successful military assault will inevitably be retaken by someone else later on, but "Proper Words," once committed to print, can be incorporated in the permanent fabric of culture and serve to unify past and present.

Ironically, of course, the Drapier is a rebel, an enemy to the status quo—hardly an appropriate vehicle, one might think, to preach the com-mon forms. Swift implies by his life and art, though, that the common forms become debased by those in power. Purity and power are antitheti-cal in his view, although he wanted both and achieved the synthesis in the Drapier. In the realms of church, state, and letters, he pursued eminence in traditional ways at times, but in the end could not change his funda-mental belief that historical values would be preserved by the common mass of humanity, not by an enshrined elite, and that conventional ex-pressions of the common forms were bankrupt and depleted. In his own radically innovative elegy, Swift celebrates himself as an outcast who was crucified for his unswerving adherence to the basic principles and traditional institutions that shaped British life—principles and institutions strangled by the powerful people who ought most to nurture them. In many ways the Drapier was Swift's alter ego, an expression of the subversive tendencies that Swift felt so strongly.

While rejecting the status quo, however, Swift still sought to become part of it. His efforts to win a place in the English establishment—as creator of the English academy or bishop of an English see—had come to nothing. Ironically, he became ensconced in the establishment of a country to which he hoped never to return, a country he repeatedly referred to as a "Land of Slaves and Fens" (396). As Dean of St. Patrick's he had a certain responsibility to support the status quo, and yet he was impelled toward sedition at the same time. Swift, like the public at large, had trouble reconciling his identities, not knowing whether "To *curse* the *Dean,* or *bless* the *Drapier*" (168).

Swift encourages the reader to sort out the ambivalences and contradictions in his personality, but he does not allow any uncertainty to exist about his reputation as a socially effective writer. The "Verses" is clear on this point, but to make sure, Swift carefully educates the reader with extensive footnotes, the omission of which in the London edition of the "Verses" propelled him to supervise the publication of an unexpurgated version in Dublin. These footnotes specifically enhance his identity as the Drapier, for it was in this role that he most dramatically demonstrated the power of his writing. With it he reversed the policy of one of the most powerful nations on earth.[8] Thus in his annotation to the lines,

> Two Kingdoms, just as Faction led,
> Had set a price upon his Head;
> But, not a Traytor cou'd be found,
> To sell him for Six Hundred Pound
> (351–54)

he first mentions the bounty offered in England because he wrote *The Publick Spirit of the Whigs,* and then he describes how "in the Year 1724, my Lord Carteret at his first coming into the Government, was prevailed on to issue a Proclamation for promising the like Reward of Three Hundred Pounds, to any Person who could discover the Author of a Pamphlet called, The Drapier's Fourth Letter, &c. writ against that destructive Project of coining Half-pence for Ireland; but in neither Kingdoms [*sic*] was the Dean discovered" (566–67; italics omitted). Swift, in his self-portrait, stresses how the current establishment time-servers "sought [the

Drapier's] Blood" (414), whereas the commonality loved and supported him. In another footnote, Swift points out that "All the Kingdom took the Drapier's Part, except the Courtiers, or those who expected Places. The Drapier was celebrated in many Poems and Pamphlets: His Sign was set up in most Streets of Dublin (where many of them still continue) and in several Country Towns" (569; italics omitted).

Earlier in the "Verses," when Swift first alludes to the Drapier, he provides a lengthy note that emphasizes the schism between the "Scriblers," who feared and therefore hated him, and persons of common sense summoned by his call:

> The Author imagines, that the Scriblers of the prevailing Party, which he always opposed, will libel him after his Death; but that others will remember him with Gratitude, who consider the Service he had done to Ireland, under the name of M.B. Drapier, by utterly defeating the destructive Project of Woods Half-pence, in five Letters to the People of Ireland, at that Time read universally, and convincing every Reader.
> (558; italics omitted)

Rallying the Irish nation against the English juggernaut to defeat Wood's Half Pence was conclusive evidence of Swift's rhetorical power. It validated his belief in the liberating effect of proper words in proper places to bind people together against the irrationality that always threatens to crush them. As the "impartial" speaker relates it,

> "The Dean did by his Pen defeat
> "An infamous destructive Cheat.
> "Taught Fools their Int'rest how to know;
> "And gave them Arms to ward the Blow."
> (407–10)

As the Drapier, Swift was showered with adulation, a rare reward for a living author. Eight years after *The Drapier's Letters* Swift writes of the effect he had and continues to have, disguising his pride as mock dismay: "I . . . have in twenty years drawn above one thousand scurrilous Libels on myself, without any other Recompence than the Love of the *Irish* Vulgar, and two or three Dozen Sign-Posts of the *Drapier* in this City, besides those that are scattered in Country Towns, and even these are half worn out. So that, whatever little Genius God hath given me, I may justly pretend to have been the worst Manager of it to my own Advantage of any Man upon Earth" (*C* 4:54). The Irish populace recognized and appreciated Swift's efforts and still do, even today. (His portrait currently appears on the ten pound bill.) But Swift wondered whether their regard could ensure the literary immortality he craved.

Swift worried about this when writing to Pope in February 1736–37: "My popularity that you mention is wholly confined to the common people, who are more constant than those we miscal their betters. I walk the streets, and so do my lower friends, from whom and from whom alone, I have a thousand hats and blessings upon old scores, which those we call the gentry have forgot" (*C* 5:4). Swift seems bitter here that only the common people, the illiterate mass, remember his efforts. Since Swift believed that print was the only means by which men and their ideas could be conveyed into succeeding ages, no doubt he wondered whether his memory would outlive the present generation. In the *Proposal*, he tells Harley that he has "always disapproved that false Compliment to Princes: That the most lasting Monument they can have, is the Hearts of the Subjects. It is indeed their greatest present Felicity to reign in their Subjects Hearts; but these are too perishable to preserve their Memories, which can only be done by the Pens of able and faithful Historians" (*PW* 4:17). Swift had the "present Felicity" of being loved for his leadership but was unsure whether that was enough for his writings to be perceived as a "lasting Monument." Leaving nothing to chance, Swift acted as his own historian.

After his tumultuous triumph as the Drapier, Swift referred to himself that way and sought immortality in that role. In "The Life and Character of Dr. Swift," he has someone question, "Must we the *Drapier* then forget? / Is not our *Nation* in his Debt?" (*P* 2:547, 95–96). The theme of immortality or remembrance as the Drapier also figures in "Drapier's Hill." The conceit of the poem is that Sir Arthur Acheson names a parcel of land he sold to Swift "Drapier's Hill" so

> That when a Nation long enslav'd,
> Forgets by whom it once was sav'd;
> When none of the DRAPIER's Praise shall sing;
> His Signs aloft no longer swing;
> His Medals and his Prints forgotten,
> And all his Handkerchiefs are rotten;
> His famous LETTERS made waste Paper;
> This Hill may keep the Name of DRAPIER:
> In Spight of Envy flourish still,
> And DRAPIER's vye with COOPER's Hill.
> (*P* 3:875, 11–20)

Though seeming to assert the transience of the Drapier's fame, Swift is actually boasting about his explicit victory and the pervasive influence of his writing. The hill itself is mere matter, another object in the "Abyss of Things"; the memory of the hill will persist because the memory of the Drapier will persist—not just in the hearts of Irishman but in the literary canon. Just as John Denham endowed Cooper's Hill with lasting meaning, Swift's writing, in particular "The Dean's Reasons," will distinguish one bit of Irish geography from all the rest by reminding readers of its associations.

As one can see from "Verses on the Death of Dr. Swift," Swift merged his identity with that of M.B., Drapier. The Drapier, albeit distinctly different from Swift, embodied the virtues for which Swift would like to be remembered: in particular, he shared with Swift a belief that liberty is the birthright of every British citizen and that the force of clear, honest discourse can produce a consensus to overthrow tyranny. Like Swift, he had a great faith in the ability of the average person to be convinced by reason if it is clearly presented to him. But the Drapier's medium was exclusively prose, and Swift wanted to demonstrate, in part by writing poetry about himself-as-Drapier, that he was the master of both.

With an eye to how the future would view him, Swift collected his works in the 1730s and fastidiously supervised their publication by George Faulkner, although he pretended not to be involved. He may have been embarrassed to let others know how important the preservation of his canon was to him. Yet, as Arthur Scouten points out, at the same time he was manipulating his public image for posterity, he was writing poems that were guaranteed to offend—for example, "The Legion Club" and the scatological poems.[9] Perhaps he was asserting his freedom to him and expressing the hope that his effect as a writer was so great that the disapproval of conventional readers would not matter. No doubt he would be delighted to know that "our Language, and our Tast [have admitted] no great Alterations" (*Tale, PW* 1 : 1; italics omitted), so that his immortal longings have been fulfilled. *Swiftian* and *Swiftianism*, according to the *Oxford English Dictionary*, have been current since the late eighteenth century. *Gulliver's Travels* is a cultural fixture, manifesting itself in animated videos, *Classic Comic Books*, and high school anthologies. Nevertheless, Swift would be very disappointed that despite his efforts, society still has not arrived at the point it might have if we allowed our best qualities free reign. Unfortunately, the word *yahoo* has become part of the lexicon because it serves a constant need.

No More Words

Swift self-consciously associated the end of his writing ability with the end of his life. In March 1732–33 he declares that his flatterers say he has "retained more spirits than hundreds of others who are richer, younger, and healthier than myself" (*C* 4:126), but by February 1735–36, he proclaims himself to be an old man, *sans* health, spirits, or verbal powers: "My state of health is not to boast of; my giddiness is more or less too constant . . . I can as easily write a poem in the Chinese-language as my own. I am as fit for Matrimony as invention; and yet I have daily schemes for innumerable Essays in prose, and proceed sometimes to no less than half a dozen lines, which the next morning become waste paper" (*C* 4:458). Swift's complaints about his artistic barrenness ring through his letters of the mid- to late 1730s. The expression of his despair is somewhat rhetorical, of course, because several of his finest poems were composed during this time, yet by the end of the decade, his literary output had almost ceased.

During this period, the fight that supplied Swift with so much vigor—Irish rights—began to appear futile to him. So much of his life was invested in the betterment of Ireland that the death of his hopes may have been correlated to his deteriorating health. In a letter to Pope, May 12, 1735, he writes, "This condition of things both publick and personal to my self, hath given me such a kind of despondency, that I am almost unqualified for any company, Diversions, or Amusement" (*C* 4:334). He claimed in June 1735 that he could no longer rouse himself to give battle: "I have utterly waved intermeddling even in this enslaved kingdom, where perhaps I might have some influence to be troublesome; yet I have long quitted all such thoughts, out of perfect despair" (*C* 4:346). This statement is disingenuous because he wrote a few pamphlets after 1735, but he did, in fact, increasingly withdraw from public affairs. As the Drapier, Swift had "saved" the Irish from ruin, yet that salvation, as it later seemed to him, was only temporary, a realization that depressed him greatly because he may have believed that his own fate was bound with Ireland's.

By 1739, Mrs. Whiteway, Swift's cousin and caretaker in his last years, reported that the condition of Ireland killed him daily; that even though "he is better both in health and hearing than I have known him these twelve months, [he is] so indolent in writing, that he will scarce put his name to a receipt for money" (*C* 5:142). A few years later, in 1742, after Swift apparently suffered a series of strokes, Mrs. Whiteway must write Lord Orrery that "the Dean's understanding was quite gone" (*C* 5:207) and that he had been declared non compos mentis. Although Swift sank into laconic isolation, his urge "to talk, as talk [he] must," occasionally resurfaced. Writing Lord Orrery in 1744, for instance, Deane Swift describes Swift's seeming desire to speak to him during one visit. To promote the conversation, the housekeeper had asked Swift to offer the wine, at which "he shrugged his shoulders, just as he used to do when he had a mind that a friend should spend the evening with him. Shrugging his shoulders, your Lordship may remember, was as much to say, 'You'll ruin me in wine.' I own, I was scarce able to bear the sight. Soon after, he again endeavoured, with a good deal of pain, to find words to speak to me: at last, not being able, after many efforts, he gave a heavy sigh" (*C* 5:214–15). Occasionally breaking his silence in his last days, Swift would mutter, "*I am what I am, I am what I am*" (*C* 5:214). He died October 19, 1745.

In his will, Swift specified an inscription for his tomb that carefully managed how he wished the world to view him: as a social reformer. An English translation of Swift's Latin runs as follows: "The body of Jonathan Swift, Doctor of Divinity, Dean of this Cathedral Church, is buried here, where savage indignation can lacerate his heart no more. Go, traveler, and imitate if you can one who strove his utmost to champion liberty." Swift commanded the epitaph to be written in "large Letters deeply cut and strongly gilded" (*Dr. Swift's Will*, PW 13:149) to make sure the words would be physically explicit, for he never could tolerate vagueness. In death as in life, too, he forces a response from his audience, which is egged into moral action by a sly taunt—"imitate if you can." The inscription presents the unique combination of heterodoxy and orthodoxy that characterized Swift and his writing: he describes himself both as "Dean of this Cathedral" and as "wild," one ripped by "savage indignation." Nothing aroused his "savage indignation" more than linguistic corruption, which he viewed as the tyrannic imposition of a self-styled elite upon the common sense of the majority. Preservation of the English language and the common forms it expresses can free people from lives that are "solitary, poore, nasty, brutish, and short." Encouraging "Proper Words in proper Places" was the primary way Swift chose "to champion liberty."

Notes

Introduction

    1. The use of the terms *linguist* and *linguistic* in this book is derived from *linguistics* in its most general meaning: the study of human speech in all its aspects. *Linguistics* as a scientific discipline did not emerge until the nineteenth century.

    2. Thomas Hobbes, *Leviathan*, ed. A. R. Waller (Cambridge: Cambridge University Press, 1935), 84.

Chapter 1

    1. This is one of the main themes of David Nokes's biography of Swift, *Jonathan Swift, A Hypocrite Reversed: A Critical Biography* (Oxford: Oxford University Press, 1985).

    2. The mixed reactions of readers to Houyhnhnmland—some see it as peaceful and enlightened, others as boring and oppressive—may derive from Swift's own ambivalences.

    3. A good survey of these linguistic activities is provided in the Introduction to Vivian Salmon's *The Works of Francis Lodwick* (London: Longman, 1972).

    4. Philip Griffith points out that Samuel Johnson used Swift's *Directions to Servants* as a valuable repository of "downstairs" terms ("Dr. Johnson's 'Diction of Common Life' and Swift's *Directions to Servants*," in *Jonathan Swift: Tercentenary Essays* [Tulsa: University of Tulsa Press, 1967], 10–30). One can also see the language of the servant class captured, for instance, in Swift's dramatic monologue "Mrs. Harris's Petition."

    5. John Boyle, Earl of Orrery, *Remarks on the Life and Writings of Jonathan Swift* (London: 1752), 34.

    6. A discussion of Swift's knowledge of Hibernicisms is contained in Alan Bliss's introduction to *A Dialogue in Hybernian Stile Between A and B* and *Irish Eloquence*, in *Irish Writings from the Age of Swift*, Vol. 6 (Dublin: Cadenus Press, 1977).

    7. According to Andrew Carpenter and Alan Harrison, Swift himself did not translate the "Irish Feast" but rather worked from a translation prepared by Dr. Anthony Raymond, a friend and fellow churchman. See "Swift, 'O'Rourke's

Feast,' and Sheridan's 'Letter,'" in *Proceedings of the First Münster Symposium on Jonathan Swift*, ed. Hermann Real and Heinz J. Vienken (Munich: Wilhelm Fink Verlag, 1985), 27-46.

8. Carole Fabricant in *Swift's Landscape* (Baltimore: Johns Hopkins University Press, 1982), 245–49, discusses Swift's attitude toward the Irish language and his knowledge of it, as do Carpenter and Harrison, cited above.

9. For a discussion of the connotations of "wild" in the eighteenth century, see Maximilian E. Novak, "The Wild Man Comes to Tea," in *The Wild Man Within*, ed. Edward Dudley and Maximilian Novak (Pittsburgh: University of Pittsburgh Press, 1972), 183–222.

10. This ongoing argument is manifest, for instance, in J. A. Downie's review of F. P. Lock's *Tory Politics* in *Eighteenth-Century Studies* 19 (1985): 113–15.

11. The antitheses in Swift's life and thought have, of course, been noticed by many critics, including George Orwell, who coined the label "Tory Anarchist" in "Politics vs. Literature: An Examination of *Gulliver's Travels*," in *Shooting an Elephant, and Other Essays* (New York: Harcourt, Brace, 1950), 53–76, a term later used by Edward Said ("Swift's Tory Anarchy," *Eighteenth-Century Studies* 3 [1969]: 48–66); Peter Steele, *Jonathan Swift: Preacher and Jester* (Oxford: Oxford University Press, 1978); Claude Rawson, *Gulliver and the Gentle Reader: Studies in Swift and Our Time* (London: Routledge & Kegan, Paul, 1973); J. A. Downie, *Jonathan Swift: Political Writer* (London: Routledge & Kegan Paul, 1984); and most recently, Nokes, *Swift*. Irvin Ehrenpreis, in his comprehensive biography *Swift: The Man, His Works, and the Age*, 3 vols. (Cambridge, Mass.: Harvard University Press, 1962–83), does not accentuate Swift's dualities per se, but I would like to acknowledge here the massive debt I (and indeed any Swift scholar) owe to Ehrenpreis's research.

12. Thomas Sprat, *History of the Royal Society*, facsim., ed. Jackson I. Cope and Harold W. Jones (St. Louis: Washington University Press, 1958), 113.

13. Swift's faith in the common man is suggested by James Preu, "Jonathan Swift and the Common Man," *Florida State University Studies* 11 (1953): 19–24, and developed at length by Ehrenpreis and Fabricant.

14. *Reflections on Dr. Swift's Letter to Harley*, facsim., rpt. in *Poetry and Language*, ed. Louis Landa (Ann Arbor, Mich.: Augustan Reprint Society, 1948), 4–5, 15–16.

15. Frederik Smith, *Language and Reality in Swift's* A Tale of a Tub (Columbus: Ohio State University Press, 1979), 28. The study Smith cites is the Ph.D. dissertation of Lewis Freed, "Sources of Johnson's Dictionary" (Cornell University, 1930).

16. Joseph Addison, "Essay #61," in *The Spectator*, ed. Donald Bond, 5 vols. (Oxford: Clarendon Press, 1965), 1:259.

17. See Smith's discussion of wordplay, *Language and Reality*, 27–47; George Mayhew's discussion of Swift's Anglo-Latin games, *Rage or Raillery: The Swift Manuscripts at the Huntington Library* (San Marino, Calif.: Huntington Library,

1967), 131–48; Maurice J. Quinlan, "Swift's Use of Literalization as a Rhetorical Device," *PMLA* 82 (1967):516–21; and David Nokes, "'Hack at Tom Poley's': Swift's Use of Puns," in *The Art of Jonathan Swift*, ed. Clive Probyn (New York: Barnes and Noble, 1978), 43–56.

18. See, for example, Johannes Soderlind, "The Word *Lilliput*," *Studia Neophilogica* 40 (1968):75–79; M. W. Buckley, "Key to the Language of the Houyhnhnms in *Gulliver's Travels*," in *Fair Liberty Was All His Cry*, ed. A. Norman Jeffares (London: Macmillan, 1967), 270–78; Pierre Henrion, *Le Secret de Gulliver* (1962, rpt. Norwood, Pa.: Norwood Editions, 1975); and many more.

19. Smith, *Language and Reality*, 93–94.

20. Fabricant, *Swift's Landscape*, 17.

21. Maurice Johnson provides background to the Schomberg incident in "Swift and the Greatest Epitaph in History," *PMLA* 68 (1953):814–27.

Chapter 2

1. A good overview of humanist ideas on language is contained in Jane Donawerth, *Shakespeare and the Sixteenth-Century Study of Language* (Urbana: University of Illinois Press, 1984).

2. The relationship of tyranny to Babel is treated by Daniel Eilon, "Swift Burning the Library of Babel," *Modern Language Review* 80 (1985):269–82. Ricardo Quintana, *The Mind and Art of Jonathan Swift* (1936; rpt. Gloucester, Mass.: Peter Smith, 1965), 216–17, also discusses how Swift associates national welfare with linguistic stability.

3. Fabricant has a fascinating discussion of Swift's perspective. Instead of putting himself in the elevated vantage assumed by most of the Augustan authors, Swift preferred to be on the same level and close up to the objects he described (*Swift's Landscape* [Baltimore: Johns Hopkins University Press, 1982], 173–209).

4. Although Swift ardently supported the Established Church, the constitutional monarchy, the perpetuation of the English literary tradition, and other common forms of British life, he had very little good to say about the caste system. Typical views are contained in the satire on the aristocracy when Gulliver visits Glubbdubdrib (*PW* 11:200).

5. Frederik Smith, *Language and Reality in Swift's* A Tale of a Tub (Columbus: Ohio State University Press, 1979), has a list of comparisons of discourse to clothing or cloth (25, n. 32). James Thompson, in *Language in Wycherley's Plays: Seventeenth-Century Language Theory and Drama* (University, Ala.: University of Alabama Press, 1984), explores the trope in chapter 4.

6. Paul Fussell, *The Rhetorical World of Augustan Humanism: Ethics and Imagery from Swift to Burke* (London: Oxford University Press, 1965), 222.

7. I.i–ii.2, trans. H. M. Hubbell, Loeb Classical Library, 1944, p. 5.

8. In *Form and Frenzy in Swift's* Tale of a Tub (Ithaca: Cornell University Press, 1970), John R. Clark discusses three (dis)organizing premises of the Modern world: no memory, no past, no duration, 117–141.

9. In *The Mechanical Operation of the Spirit*, Swift describes Modern discourse as fragmentary, stressing letters (things) rather than sentences (ideas): "The Force, or Energy of this Eloquence, is not to be found, as among antient Orators, in the Disposition of Words to a Sentence, or the turning of long Periods; but agreeable to the Modern Refinements in Musick, is taken up wholly in dwelling, and dilating upon Syllables and Letters" (*PW* 1:183).

10. Frances Louis's chapter in *Swift's Anatomy of Misunderstanding: A Study of Swift's Epistemological Imagination in* A Tale of a Tub *and* Gulliver's Travels (Totowa, N.J.: Barnes and Noble, 1981), 80–89, discusses the fragmenting and reductive effect of false linguistic concepts.

11. It has been suggested that the Drapier's initials, M.B., stand for Marcus Brutus, an idea consonant with the Drapier's hatred of tyranny and his understanding of the principles of classical rhetoric. Denis Donoghue stresses the classical mode in *The Drapier's Letters* in *Jonathan Swift: A Critical Introduction* (Cambridge: Cambridge University Press, 1969), 145–46.

12. I disagree with C. J. Rawson's suggestion that the values for which the Drapier stands are blurred and ambivalent ("The Injured Lady and the Drapier: A Reading of Swift's Irish Tract," *Philological Society Transactions* 3 [1980]: 15–43).

13. Thomas Maresca also demonstrates, with different emphasis, Swift's association of bad discourse with the Epicurean, or Lucretian, universe in "Language and Body in Augustan Poetic," *ELH* 37 (1970): 374–88.

Chapter 3

1. I suggest the links between Swift's ideas of conversation and those of the Renaissance courtesy writers in "Swift's *Polite Conversation:* An Eschatological Vision," *Studies in Philology* 73 (1976): 204–24. The point is made in a more general way by Herbert Davis in "The Conversation of the Augustans," in *The Seventeenth Century: The History of English Thought and Literature from Bacon to Pope*, ed. Richard Foster Jones (Stanford, Cal.: Stanford University Press, 1951), 181–97.

2. Davis, "Conversation of the Augustans," 186. See also Leland E. Warren, "Turning Reality Round Together: Guides to Conversation in Eighteenth-Century England," *Eighteenth-Century Life* 8 (May 1983): 65–87.

3. William Piper, *The Heroic Couplet* (Cleveland: Case Western Reserve University Press, 1969), 144.

4. Thomas Sprat, *History of the Royal Society*, facsim., ed. Jackson I. Cope and Harold W. Jones (St. Louis: Washington University Press, 1958), 64.

5. Ibid., 65.

6. [Alexander Pope and Jonathan Swift] (anonymous), *Miscellanies in Prose and Verse*, 3 vols. (London: 1727/28), 2:354.

7. Davis, "Conversation of the Augustans," 186.

8. John Bullitt, *Jonathan Swift and the Anatomy of Satire* (Cambridge, Mass.: Harvard University Press, 1966), 127.

9. Further description of conversation cookbooks is contained in my article "Swift's Polite Conversation," and Warren's, cited above.

10. Thomas Hobbes, *Leviathan*, ed. A. R. Waller (Cambridge: Cambridge University Press, 1935), 83.

11. John Boyle, Earl of Orrery, *Remarks on the Life and Writings of Jonathan Swift* (London: 1752), 33.

12. Peter Dixon, "'Talking on paper': Pope and Eighteenth Century Conversation," *English Studies* 66 (1965): 36–44.

13. Swift's attempt to create a *private* world by the use of little language is analyzed by E. M. Whitley, "Contextural Analysis and Swift's Little Language of *The Journal to Stella*," in *In Memory of J. R. Firth*, ed. C. E. Bazell et al. (London: Longmans, 1966), 475–500; and Virginia Woolf, "Swift's Journal to Stella," in *Fair Liberty Was All His Cry: A Tercentenary Tribute to Jonathan Swift*, ed. A. Norman Jeffares (London: Macmillan, 1967), 107–15, reprinted from *The Second Common Reader* (New York, Harcourt, Brace and World, 1932), 58–67. Also see A. B. England, "Private and Public Rhetoric in the *Journal to Stella*," *Essays in Criticism* 22 (1972): 131–41; and Irvin Ehrenpreis, "Swift's 'Little Language' in the *Journal to Stella*," *Studies in Philology* 45 (1948): 80–88.

14. See Frederik Smith, "Dramatic Elements in Swift's *Journal to Stella*," *Eighteenth Century Studies* 1 (1968): 332–52.

15. Johannes Soderlind, "Swift and Linguistics," *English Studies* 51 (1970): 137–40, sees the language of the journal as being "modelled on nursery language" (140), as does Williams in his Introduction to *Journal to Stella* (1 : 1v). But this is not the world of the nursery; see discussion of sexuality below.

16. Irvin Ehrenpreis, in *Swift: The Man, His Works, and The Age*, 3 vols. (Cambridge, Mass.: Harvard University Press, 1962–83), remarks on the titillating nature of *The Journal*, 2:659. Jean Hagstrum agrees that "this language is full of psychosexual meaning. . . . Swift and Stella were bound together by more than the virtuous, rational, and adult rapport revealed in the poems addressed to her" (*Sex and Sensibility* [Chicago: University of Chicago Press, 1980], 156).

17. Ibid., 153–55.

18. For further discussion of the Anglo-Latin games Swift played with Sheridan, see George Mayhew's *Rage or Raillery: The Swift Manuscripts at the Huntington Library* (San Marino, Calif.: Huntington Library, 1967), 131–48; and James Woolley, "Thomas Sheridan and Swift," *Studies in Eighteenth Century Culture* vol. 9, ed. Roseann Runte (Madison: University of Wisconsin Press, 1979), 93–114.

19. Steeven Guazzo, *Civil Conversation*, trans. George Pettie, ed. Charles Whibley (New York: Knopf, 1925), 35.

Chapter 4

1. Paul Pellisson-Fontanier, *The History of the French Academy* (London: 1657), 26.

2. Thomas Hobbes, *Leviathan*, ed. A. R. Waller (Cambridge: Cambridge University Press, 1935), 254.

3. Samuel Butler, *Hudibras*, ed. John Wilders (Oxford: Clarendon Press, 1967), 1, 1–4.

4. John Locke, *An Essay Concerning Human Understanding*, ed. Peter Nidditch (Oxford: Oxford University Press, 1975), 486.

5. Stephen Zwicker, in *Politics and Language in Dryden's Poetry* (Princeton: Princeton University Press, 1984), 6–10, discusses the effect of the late seventeenth-century perception that both language and politics result from a social contract and therefore are negotiable.

6. The Lock-Downie controversy illustrates that the meaning of these words is still debatable. See Chapter 1, note 10.

7. Hugh Sykes Davis discusses in a general way Swift's association of linguistics and politics ("Irony and the English Tongue," in *The World of Jonathan Swift: Essays for the Tercentenary*, ed. Brian Vickers [Oxford: Blackwell, 1968], 129–38). Steven Blakemore shows that the association of political turmoil with linguistic confusion is expressed later in the century by Edmund Burke (see "Burke and the Fall of Language: The French Revolution as a Linguistic Event," *Eighteenth Century Studies* 17 [1984]:284–307).

8. Louis Landa in his Introduction to the sermons in *The Prose Works* emphasizes that the sermons often contained violent partisan rhetoric (9:116–26).

9. For a discussion of Swift's strategies in *The Examiner* and elsewhere, see Richard I. Cook, *Jonathan Swift as a Tory Pamphleteer* (Seattle: University of Washington Press, 1967), 31–53.

10. I analyze in more detail Swift's attacks on etymologizing for disreputable purposes in "Swift's Satire against Modern Etymologists," *South Atlantic Review* 48 (May 1983):32–33.

11. The belief that individual reason is sufficient to guide one toward salvation is examined by Phillip Harth, *Swift and Anglican Rationalism: The Religious Background of* A Tale of a Tub (Chicago: University of Chicago Press, 1961), 27–29.

12. J. A. Downie, in *Jonathan Swift, Political Writer* (London: Routledge & Kegan Paul, 1984), discusses the importance of history writing to Swift, 192–94.

13. For more discussion of Swift's satires against critics, see Miriam Kosh Starkman, in *Swift's Satire on Learning in* A Tale of a Tub (Princeton: Princeton University Press, 1970), 87–105.

Chapter 5

1. William Camden, *Remains Concerning Britain*, ed. R. D. Dunn (Toronto: University of Toronto Press, 1984), 22.

2. The linguistic environment in which Swift wrote has been extensively analyzed by Richard Foster Jones, *The Triumph of the English Language: A Survey of Opinions Concerning the Vernacular from the Introduction of Printing to the Restoration* (Stanford: Stanford University Press, 1953); James Knowlson, *Universal Language Schemes in England and France, 1600–1800* (Toronto: University of Toronto Press, 1975); Hans Aarsleff, *The Study of Language in England, 1780–1860* (Princeton: Princeton University Press, 1967); Stephen K. Land, *From Signs to Propositions: The Concept of Form in Eighteenth Century Semantic Theory* (London: Longman, 1974); M. M. Slaughter, *Universal Languages and Scientific Taxonomy in the Seventeenth Century* (Cambridge: Cambridge University Press, 1982); and most valuable for my purposes, Murray Cohen, *Sensible Words: Linguistic Practices in England, 1640–1785* (Baltimore: Johns Hopkins University Press, 1977), and Vivian Salmon's Preface to *The Works of Francis Lodwick* (London: Longman, 1972). Paul J. Korshin's "Deciphering Swift's Codes," in *Proceedings of the First Münster Symposium on Jonathan Swift* (Munich: Wilhelm Fink Verlag, 1985), 123–34, examines the importance of codes in seventeenth- and eighteenth-century England and Swift's reaction to them.

3. Francis Bacon, *Of the Advancement of Learning*, in *The Philosophical Works of Francis Bacon*, trans. John M. Robertson, ed. James Ellis and Robert Spedding (London: Routledge and Sons, 1905), 121.

4. John Locke, *An Essay Concerning Human Understanding*, ed. Peter Nidditch (Oxford: Oxford University Press, 1975), 522.

5. In this overview I am indebted to Vivian Salmon.

6. John Bulwer, *Chirlogia: or the Natural Language of the Hand* and *Chirnomia: or the Art of Manual Rhetoric*, facsim., ed. James W. Cleary (Carbondale: Southern Illinois University Press, 1974), 19.

7. Ibid.

8. See, for instance, Quintilian, *Instituto Oratoria* XI.iii.9.

9. *The Works of Francis Lodwick*, facsim., ed. Vivian Salmon (London: Longman, 1972), 224.

10. John Wilkins, *An Essay towards a Real Character and a Philosophical Language* (London, 1668), b1v.

11. Benjamin DeMott, "Comenius and the Real Character in England," *PMLA* 70 (1955):1068–81.

12. Johan Comenius, *The Way of Light*, trans. E. T. Campagnac (London: Hodder and Stoughton, 1938), 183.

13. For more on the language of gesture, see my "After Eden: Gulliver's (Linguistic) Travels," *ELH* 45 (1978):33–54, as well as John Sena, "The Language of Gesture in *Gulliver's Travels*," *Papers in Language and Linguistics* 19 (1983):145–66.

14. Bulwer, *Chirlogia*, 18.

15. For additional background, see Paul Cornelius, *Languages in Seventeenth- and Early Eighteenth-Century Imaginary Voyages* (Geneva: Librairie Droz, 1965). Also of interest is Edward Seeber, "Ideal Languages in the French and English Imaginary Voyage," *PMLA* 60 (1945):586−97, and Knowlson, *Universal Language Schemes*, 112−38.

16. Thomas Sprat, *History of the Royal Society*, facsim., ed. Jackson I. Cope and Harold W. Jones (St. Louis: Washington University Press, 1958), 113.

17. *Works of Lodwick*, 224.

18. Wilkins, *Essay towards a Real Character*, 399. It is interesting to note that Roget used Wilkins's tables as a basis for his *Thesaurus*.

19. Lewis Walker believes the forty handles on the Lagadan machine allude to the forty genuses of Wilkins's scheme ("A Possible Source for the Linguistic Projects in the Academy of Lagado," *Notes and Queries* 20 [1973]:413−14), a connection also made by Denis Donoghue. The idea of Lagado as a satire on Wilkins is developed by Clive Probyn, "Swift and Linguistics: The Context behind Lagado and around the Fourth Voyage," *Neophilologus* 58 (1974):425−39. Although Wilkins's scheme is widely assumed to be behind Swift's satire, Vivian Salmon shows that his inspiration may have come from universal language theorists in Ireland ("William Bedell and the Universal Language Movement in Seventeenth-Century Ireland," *Essays & Studies* 36 [1983], 27−39).

20. By issuing the Act of Oblivion, which forbade the use of "any reproach or term of distinction," Charles I tried to eliminate dissension by eliminating dissentious terms (quoted in Stephen Zwicker, *Politics and Language in Dryden's Poetry* [Princeton: Princeton University Press, 1984], 9).

21. Robert M. Philmus, "Swift, Gulliver, and 'The Thing Which Was Not,'" *ELH* 38 (1971):67, discusses the failure of the Houyhnhnm language to convey reality.

22. Benjamin DeMott discusses the irenic impulse behind many seventeenth-century linguistic theories ("Comenius and the Real Character," 1070−77).

23. Wilkins, *Essay towards a Real Character*, b1r.

24. George Dalgarno, Introduction, *Didascalocophus* (1680; facsim. rpt. Menston: Scolar Press, 1971), n.p.

25. Comenius, *Way of Light*, 183.

26. For further development of the idea that the Houyhnhnms are limited and oppressive, see my "Swift's Explorations of Slavery in Houyhnhnmland and Ireland," *PMLA* 91 (1976):846−55.

27. Cohen, *Linguistic Practices in England*, xxiv.

28. That custom, both in the past and present, determines usage is an idea expressed earlier, in classical literature and again in the English Renaissance, by, among others, Ben Jonson in *Timber, or Discoveries*, in *Ben Jonson's Literary Criti-*

cism, ed. James Redwine, Regents Critics Series (Lincoln: University of Nebraska Press, 1970), 20–21.

29. Cohen, *Linguistic Practices in England*, 143, n. 11.

30. Francis Bacon, *Novum Organum*, in *The Works of Francis Bacon*, trans. Basil Montague, 3 vols. (Philadelphia: Carey and Hart, 1846), 3:375.

31. Ibid., 347.

32. Swift's aversion to Bacon and his frequent, often unsignaled parody of Bacon is documented by Brian Vickers in "Swift and the Baconian Idol," in *The World of Jonathan Swift: Essays for the Tercentenary*, ed. Brian Vickers (Oxford: Blackwell, 1968), 87–128.

33. Bacon, *Novum Organum*, 348.

34. Cohen stresses the shift in emphasis that Locke's popularization of the ideas of Port-Royal effected (*Sensible Words*, 38–42). James Thompson has a good analysis of the differences between Wilkins and Locke in *Language in Wycherley's Plays: Seventeenth-Century Language Theory and Drama* (University, Ala.: University of Alabama Press, 1984), 17–24.

35. Locke, *Essay Concerning Human Understanding*, 395.

36. Ibid.

37. Matthew Prior, "A Dialogue between Mr. John Lock and Seigneur de Montaigne," in *The Literary Works*, 2d. ed., ed. H. Bunker Wright and Monroe Spears, 2 vols. (Oxford: Clarendon Press, 1971), 2:615.

38. Locke, *Essay Concerning Human Understanding*, 521.

39. W. B. Carnochan discusses, in a different light, Swift's satire on Lockean linguistics in *Gulliver's Travels* in *Lemuel Gulliver's Mirror for Man* (Berkeley and Los Angeles: University of California Press, 1968), 147–50.

40. John T. Waterman, *Perspectives in Linguistics* (Chicago: University of Chicago Press, 1970), 13.

41. Dalgarno, in *Didascalocophus*, 102.

42. The impact of Chinese on English writers and linguists is a major theme of Cornelius' book.

43. Waterman, *Perspectives in Linguistics*, 43.

44. See A. L. Owen, *The Famous Druids: A Survey of Three Centuries of English Literature on the Druids* (Oxford: Clarendon Press, 1962), 59–82.

45. Butler, I.i.59–62 and I.i.177–78.

46. Paul Pezron, *The Antiquities of Nations*, trans. Mr. Jones (London, 1706), x.

47. Ibid., viii.

48. Ibid., xiii.

49. Richard Verstegan, *A Restitution of Decayed Intelligence* (London, 1673), 161.

50. Ibid., 211.

51. William Camden, *Commentarioli Brytannicae Descriptionis Fragmentum* (Cologne, 1572), quoted by Owen, *Famous Druids*, 68.

52. Camden, *Remains*, 34–35.

53. James Sledd and Gwin J. Kolb, *Dr. Johnson's Dictionary: Essays in the Biography of a Book* (Chicago: University of Chicago Press, 1955), 39.

Chapter 6

1. "Dedication," *Troilus and Cressida* in *The Works of John Dryden*, ed. H. T. Swedenberg et al., 20 vols. (Berkeley and Los Angeles: University of California Press, 1956–84), 13:221–22.

2. Paul Pellisson-Fontanier, *The History of the French Academy* (London, 1657), 26. Italics omitted.

3. Thomas Sprat, *History of the Royal Society*, facsim., ed. Jackson I. Cope and Harold W. Jones (St. Louis: Washington University Press, 1958), 66.

4. Murray Cohen, *Linguistic Practices in England, 1640–1785* (Baltimore: Johns Hopkins University Press, 1977), 99.

5. "Dedication" to *The Rival Ladies*, *Works of Dryden*, 8:98.

6. Samuel Johnson, "Preface," *A Dictionary of the English Language* (London, 1755), Ar.

7. Ibid., Ar and Av.

8. William Camden, *Remains Concerning Britain*, ed. R. D. Dunn (Toronto: University of Toronto Press, 1984), 32.

9. Ibid., 33.

10. See Susie I. Tucker, *English Examined: Two Centuries of Comment on the Mother-Tongue* (Cambridge: Cambridge University Press, 1961).

11. Charles Butler, *English Grammar*, ed. A. Eichler (1634; rpt. Vienna: Neimeyer, 1910), 9.

12. Cohen, *Sensible Words*, 48–49.

13. For the debate in the Renaissance, see Jane Donawerth, *Shakespeare and the Sixteenth-Century Study of Language* (Urbana: University of Illinois Press, 1984), 32–33, and in the restoration and eighteenth century, see James Thompson, *Language in Wycherley's Plays: Seventeenth-Century Language Theory and Drama* (University, Ala.: University of Alabama Press, 1984), 31–33.

14. Louis Landa, Introduction, *Reflections on Dr. Swift's Letter to Harley*, facsim. rpt. in *Poetry and Language*, ed. Landa (Ann Arbor, Mich.: Augustan Reprint Society, 1948), 3.

15. Irvin Ehrenpreis, *Swift: The Man, His Works, and the Age*, 3 vols. (Cambridge, Mass.: Harvard University Press, 1962–83), 2:542–43.

16. [John Gay], *The Present State of Wit* (1711), facsim., rpt. in *Essays on Wit: Number Three* (Ann Arbor, Mich.: Augustan Reprint Society, 1947), 2.

17. Introduction, *The Memoirs . . . of Martinus Scriblerus* (New Haven: Published for Wellesley College by the Yale University Press, 1950), 9. Henry Sams links Swift's *Proposal* to his desire to be Historiographer Royal ("Jonathan Swift's

Proposal Concerning the English Language: A Reconsideration," *Studies in Philology* 4 [1967]:76–87).

18. For a fuller discussion of this issue, see my "Why Did Swift Sign His Name to *A Proposal for Correcting . . . The English Tongue?*" *Neophilologus* 63 (1979): 469–80, where sections of this chapter originally appeared.

19. Daniel Defoe, *An Essay on Projects* (London, 1697), 235–36.

20. Ibid., 234–35.

21. Ehrenpreis, *Swift*, 2:544.

22. Herbert Davis, "The Textual Notes," *PW* 4:285.

23. Pellisson-Fontanier, *History of the French Academy*, 251.

24. Robert Fitzgerald suggests that the Struldbruggs are a satire on the isolation of the French Academicians, who called themselves "Immortals," and that though Swift was enthusiastic about the *Proposal* when it came out, he subsequently had doubts about it. See "The Allegory of Luggnagg and the Struldbruggs in *Gulliver's Travels*," *Studies in Philology* 65 (1968):657–76.

Chapter 7

1. James Thompson, *Language in Wycherley's Plays: Seventeenth-Century Language Theory and Drama* (University, Ala.: University of Alabama Press, 1984), 39–40.

2. For example, in *The Dunciad* (1742), Alexander Pope refers to "native Anarchy, the mind," a concept he illuminates as follows: "*The native* Anarchy *of the mind* is that state which precedes the time of Reason's assuming rule of the Passions" (*The Poems of Alexander Pope*, ed. John Butt Sutherland, 12 vols. [London: Methuen, 1939–69], 5:270, 15, 16 n.). Dryden describes his experience with the "native anarchy of the mind" in the Preface to *The Rival Ladies*, when he remembers the time "long before it was a Play; When it was only a confus'd Mass of Thoughts, tumbling over one another in the Dark: when the Fancy was yet in its first Work, moving the Sleeping Images of things toward the Light, there to be distinguished" in words (*The Works of John Dryden*, ed. H. T. Swedenberg et al., 20 vols. [Berkeley and Los Angeles: University of California Press, 1956–84], 13:95).

3. Murray Cohen, *Sensible Words: Linguistic Practices in England, 1640–1785* (Baltimore: Johns Hopkins University Press, 1977), 37–42.

4. In his *Essay on Projects* (London: 1697), Daniel Defoe also stresses verbal discrimination as a particularly human attribute: "*Words* without [sense], are only Noise, which any Brute can make as well as we, and Birds much better . . . 'tis the proper Position of *Words*, adapted to their Significations, which makes them intelligible, and conveys the Meaning of the Speaker to the Understanding of the Hearer; the contrary to which we call *Nonsense*," 244–45.

5. Frederik Smith, *Language and Reality in Swift's* A Tale of a Tub (Columbus: Ohio State University Press, 1979) also makes this point, 99.

6. Samuel Johnson, *The Life of Swift*, in *Samuel Johnson, Selected Poetry and Prose*,

ed. Frank Brady and W. K. Wimsatt (Berkeley and Los Angeles: University of California Press, 1977), 467.

7. Louis Milic, in *A Quantitative Approach to the Style of Jonathan Swift* (The Hague: Mouton, 1967), shows that certain generalizations can be made about Swift's style, regardless of context.

8. William Wotton, "A Defense of the Reflections upon Ancient and Modern Learning," in *A Tale of a Tub*, ed. A. C. Guthkelch and D. Nichol Smith (1920; rpt. Oxford: Clarendon Press, 1973), 323.

9. The degree to which Swift satirized occult philosophies in *A Tale of a Tub* is documented by Guthkelch and Smith in "Notes on Dark Authors," ibid., 352–60. Smith, Louis, and Starkman all treat Swift's satire on mysticism, and excellent background is provided by Ronald Paulson's *Theme and Structure in* A Tale of a Tub (New Haven: Yale University Press, 1960), 87–144.

10. Richard Steele, *The Guardian*, ed. John Calhoun Stephens (Lexington: University Press of Kentucky, 1982), 84.

11. Barbara Strang, "Swift and the English Language: A Study in Principles and Practice," in *To Honor Roman Jakobson: Essays on the Occasion of His Seventieth Birthday* (The Hague: Mouton, 1967), 3:1947–59.

12. In the Preface to his translation of the *Aeneid* and elsewhere, Dryden, for example, complains about the preponderance of monosyllables in English, and in *Characteristics of Men, Manners, Opinions, Times* (3 vols.), Anthony Ashley Cooper, the third Earl of Shaftesbury, speaks of "the shocking Consonants and jarring Sounds to which [English] is so unfortunately subject" ([London, 1732], 3:264).

13. How much jarring sound bothered Swift in poetry can be seen in his line-by-line analysis of a poem that Thomas Beach sent him (*C* 4:320–21).

Chapter 8

1. Morris Tilley, *A Dictionary of Proverbs to the Sixteenth and Seventeenth Centuries* (Ann Arbor: University of Michigan Press, 1950), S735, M75.

2. Ben Jonson, *Timber, or Discoveries*, in *Ben Jonson's Literary Criticism*, ed. James Redwine, Regents Critics Series (Lincoln: University of Nebraska Press, 1970), 24.

3. Swift is heir to the classical idea that the good man speaks well. See Jane Donawerth, *Shakespeare and the Sixteenth-Century Study of Language* (Urbana: University of Illinois Press, 1984), 110.

4. Martin Price, *Swift's Rhetorical Art: A Study in Structure and Meaning* (New Haven: Yale University Press, 1953), 14.

5. In the end, Swift did not publish these *Remarks upon Tindall's Rights of the Christian Church, etc.* He tells Charles Ford that "the Report of my Answering Tindall's Book is a Mistake; I had some thoughts that way, but they are long layd aside" (*C* 1:126). Instead, according to Herbert Davis, Swift created a more general satiric attack against freethinking, *An Argument against Abolishing Christianity* (Introduction, *PW* 2:xix).

6. Richard Steele, *The Importance of Dunkirk Consider'd* (London, 1713), F4v, G2r.

7. Swift also gave the boy a small amount of money. See Irvin Ehrenpreis, *Swift: The Man, His Works, and the Age*, 3 vols. (Cambridge, Mass.: Harvard University Press, 1962–83), 3:812.

Chapter 9

1. Arthur H. Scouten, "Jonathan Swift's Progress from Prose to Poetry," in *The Poetry of Jonathan Swift: Papers Read at a Clark Library Seminar, 20 January 1979*, ed. Maximillian Novak (Los Angeles: Clark Memorial Library, 1981), 33.

2. The textual history of this poem is very complicated and controversial. Arthur H. Scouten and Robert D. Hume summarize the tangled history of the "Verses" in "Pope and Swift: Text and Interpretation of Swift's Verses on His Death," *Philological Quarterly* 52 (1973): 205–11.

3. The mixed assertions and mixed modes in the "Verses" have generated reams of critical discussion, some of which focus on Swift's seeming attempt at final self-definition: Barry Slepian, "The Ironic Intention of Swift's Verses on His Own Death," *Review of English Studies* 14 (1963): 249–56; Ronald Paulson, *The Fictions of Satire* (Baltimore: Johns Hopkins Press, 1967), 189–94; Edward Said, "Swift's Tory Anarchy," *Eighteenth-Century Studies* 3 (1969): 48–66; David M. Vieth, "The Mystery of Personal Identity: Swift's Verses on His Own Death," in *The Author in His Work: Essays on a Problem in Criticism*, ed. Louis Martz and Aubrey Williams (New Haven: Yale University Press, 1978), 245–62; James Woolley, "Autobiography in Swift's Verses on His Death," in *Contemporary Studies of Swift's Poetry*, ed. John Irwin Fischer and Donald C. Mell (Newark: University of Delaware Press, 1981), 112–22; Carole Fabricant, *Swift's Landscape* (Baltimore: Johns Hopkins University Press, 1982), 239–41. Although I am indebted to all of the authors listed above, my reading of "Verses" differs from theirs in many ways.

4. I disagree with W. B. Ewald, *The Masks of Jonathan Swift* (Oxford: Blackwell, 1954), and others who suggest that the Drapier's voice represents merely a rhetorical strategy for Swift. With specific attention to Swift's Irish perspective in the poem, Carole Fabricant stresses the intricate interrelationship of Swift and Drapier and Swift's psychic investment in his creation (*Swift's Landscape*, 249–68).

5. This is a phrase Maurice Johnson used to describe Swift's satire and one I have found perennially useful.

6. Ehrenpreis, *Swift*, 2:486.

7. Scouten ("Jonathan Swift's Progress," 28) quotes John Middleton Murry on this point (*Jonathan Swift: A Critical Biography* [London: Jonathan Cape, 1954], 383).

8. The impact of the Drapier on Ireland is documented by Oliver Ferguson, *Swift and Ireland* (Urbana: University of Illinois Press, 1962), 83–138.

9. Scouten, "Jonathan Swift's Progress," 46.

Index

Abbreviations: academy might control, 91–92; tendency of northern nations toward, 114. *See also* Fragmentation, of words and meaning

Académie Française: censorship powers of, 102; desire of English to imitate, 8; elitism of, 103; isolation of members, 159n24

Academy, linguistic: advocated in 17th and 18th centuries, 8, 57, 89; affected Swift with mixed feelings, 4, 100–1; functions of, 90–97; need to establish immediately, 89–90; Swift's reasons for proposing, 97–101, 118. *See also* Académie Française; Alteration (linguistic); Swift, Prose Works, *Proposal for Correcting, Improving, and Ascertaining the English Tongue*

Adamic language. *See* Original language

Addison, Joseph: advocated a linguistic academy, 57; cited in Johnson's dictionary, 18; disapproved of punning, 18; Swift converses with despite political differences, 49

Additions, to language: necessary for cultural progress, 80; should be controlled by an academy, 93

Alteration (linguistic): academy might prevent, 89–97; cultural memory could be obliterated by, 68–69; feared by 17th and 18th centuries, 2; printing multiplies, 92; promoted by anti-establishment religious leaders, 66–68, by politicians, 62–63, by lawyers, 65, by literary hacks, 68–72; Struldbruggs

dramatize effects, 42–43. *See also* Abbreviations; Academy, linguistic; Additions, to language; Coinage, of words; Fragmentation, of words and meaning; Omission, of words; Reduction, or literalness; Standard, linguistic

Anne, Queen: dislike of *A Tale of a Tub*, 24; reign ought to be commemorated, 94

Arbuthnot, John: envied by Swift for writing ability, 136; missed Swift's conversation, 50

Bacon, Francis: on errors embedded in language (Idols of the Marketplace), 80; on methods of empirical definition, 82; on real character, 74; Swift's satires of, 82–83, 157n32

Bawdiness: absent in Stella's conversation, 133; absent in Swift's conversation, 111; in *Journal to Stella*, 53–54, 152n15, 152n16; in poems of the 1730s, 146

Becanus, Goropius: advocated Dutch as the original language, 86

Beck, Cave: proposal for a real character, 75

Bolingbroke, Henry St. John, 1st Viscount. *See* Tory administration

Buffon, Georges Louis Leclerc (Comte): on style revealing character, 120

Bulwer, John: on gesture as a real character, 75

Burnet, Gilbert (Bishop of Sarum): condemned by Swift for euphemism, 21–23, for lack of grammar, 114, for lack of stylistic variety, 115

Butler, Charles: on spelling reform, 95
Butler, Samuel: satire on coined words, 60;
  on search for the original language, 86

Cadence: inappropriate use of, by Steele,
  129, by Tindal, 124; should not obscure sense, 129. *See also* Euphony
Camden, William: as object of Swift's satire
  for specious etymologizing, 87–88; on
  prevalence of linguistic theorizing, 73;
  on spelling, 95
Caroline, Queen: enraged by Swift's explicitness, 22; slighted Swift, 141;
  wanted to see "wild Dean," 10
Chesterfield, Philip Dormer Stanhope, 4th
  Earl: on style as dress of thoughts, 26
Cicero: on relation of language and civilization, 27; on using ordinary speakers as
  standard, 96
Clarendon, Edward Hyde, Earl of: condemned for euphemism, 21; on problems of meaning, 1
Coinage, of words: associated with political
  turmoil, 60–61; could be controlled by
  an academy, 91–92; produced in quantity by Swift, 18. *See also* Ersatz languages; Jargon
Comenius, Johan: on philosophical language, 76, 81
Common forms: common man, preserver
  of, 12–15, 61–62, 91, 139–40, 142,
  150n13; definition of, 3, 11, 17; Drapier's reinforcement of, 31–34; interrelationship of, 4, 10, 29–30, 151n4;
  reinforcers of, designated as "weavers,"
  26; Swift's life partially governed by,
  11–12; urban elite lacking in, 13–14.
  See also Cultural memory; Drapier; English language; Proper Words in proper
  Places; Uncommon forms
Conversation: aims of, 37–38; bad conversation, causes and effects of, 43–48;
  dependent on common language, 42;
  Drapier's use of, 34; epistemological
  necessity of, 22, 39, 140; humanism, as
  source of Swift's ideas on, 56; letter-
  writing, as substitute for, 50–51; reading, as form of, 38; Swift's, condemned
  by Lord Orrery, 49; Swift's enjoyment

of, 49–50; variety needed in, 40;
  utopian model of, 41–42. *See also* Conversational style
Conversational style: as ideal, 10, 107–9; as
  possible barrier to literary fame,
  134–35. *See also* Proper Words in
  proper Places; Style
Critics: Swift's satires against bad, 71–72,
  154n13
Cultural memory: common man, preserved
  by, 12–15, 136–40; in *Drapier's Letters*,
  32–43; in *Tale of a Tub*, lacking, 30–31,
  139; meaning dependent on, 28, 59;
  Steele, lacks, 129; Swift's desire to be a
  part of, 145; Swift's wish fulfilled, 146.
  See also Common forms

Dalgarno, George: proposed real character,
  75
Definition: established by consensus,
  96–97; new methods of, Swift satirizes, 82–83; seventeenth-century
  ideas on, 82–85. *See also* Bacon,
  Francis; Locke, John
Defoe, Daniel: advocated linguistic academy, 8, 57, 101–2; linked verbal discrimination and reason, 159n4
Dialect. *See* Gaelic
Donne, John: on incoherence, 1; on individualism, 17
Drapier: model of Proper Words in proper
  Places, 28, 32–35, 137, 152n11; Swift's
  identity with, 5, 141–45, 161n4
Dryden, John: on lack of euphony in English, 160n12; on linguistic academy, 8,
  90; on linguistic pollution, 57; on linguistic standard using the "best"
  speakers, 96
Dyche, Thomas: spelling book widely
  used, 95

English language: adequacy, 4, 71; corruption since Elizabethan era, 12–13;
  euphony, lack of, 114–15, 160n12; fra-
  gility, 27–28, 120; interrelationship
  with other common forms, 10, 28–32,
  64, 74, 121. *See also* Alteration (linguistic); Common forms; Language
Ersatz languages: in *Gulliver's Travels*, 19,

79–82, 151n18; as solution to linguistic corruption, 73–74. *See also* Real character; Philosophic language

Established Church. *See* Common forms

Etymology: anchor of common linguistic forms, 92–93, 95–96; specious use of, by lawyers, 65, by proponents of an original language, 86–87, 154n10

Euphony: importance of in written discourse, 114–16; lack of, in English, 114, 160n12; Steele's neglect of, 127; Tindal's neglect of, 124–25

Evelyn, John: advocated linguistic academy, 8

Explicitness: of religious truth, 66–67, 154n11; as stylistic touchstone, 12–15, 106–9; Swift's need for, 21–23. *See also* Proper Words in proper Places

Faulkner, George: collected works, 146; described Swift's editing, 13, 114; published Swift's "Verses on the Death," 135

Fitzherbert, Andrew: example of Proper Words in proper Places, 131

Fleetwood, William (Bishop of Asaph): stylistic improprieties, 115

Forms. *See* Common forms; Uncommon forms

Fragmentation, of words and meaning: compared to Epicurean universe, 36, 48, 65, 83; by Lagadan word machine, 35–36; in *Mechanical Operation of the Spirit*, 152n9; by Peter (in *Tale of a Tub*), 30; in politics, 62–63. *See also* Abbreviations; Redefinition

Gaelic: Swift's knowledge of, 9–10, 148–49n7, 149n8

Gay, John: Swift praises satire of, 69, 136

George I, King: as non-English speaker, 64

Gesture: as real character, 75; Swift's satires on, 76–77, 155n13

Grammar: academy would regulate, 93; importance of in written discourse, 114; Steele's lack of, 127–28

Guazzo, Steeven: on purpose of conversation, 56

Harley, Robert. *See* Oxford, Robert Harley, 1st Earl of; Tory administration

Hobbes, Thomas: on dangers of coined words, 60; on world without Proper Words, 4, 48

Hooker, Richard: style as ideal, 12

Humanism, classical and Renaissance: Drapier, the epitome of, 32, 152n11; source of Swift's ideas, 3, 25, 37, 56, 151n1, 152n1

Ireland: effect on Swift's perception, 20, 151n2; Swift's efforts in, 24, 142–43; Swift's impact on, 161n8; Swift's isolation in, 50; Swift's sympathy for, 10. *See also* Gaelic

Irony: Swift's use of, 7, 22. *See also* Parody; Satire

Jargon: Swift's interest in, 8–9; used by mystics, 109–10, by doctors, 13, by philosophers, 71, by Steele, 126–27, by *Tale*-denizens, 31, by Tindal, 124

Johnson, Esther (Stella): conversational ability, 49; an example of Proper Words in proper Places, 132–33; problems with spelling, 113; Swift's relationship to, 16; Swift's use of private language with, 4. *See also* Private language; Swift, Prose Works, *Journal to Stella*

Johnson, Samuel: quoted Swift in *Dictionary*, 18, 149n4; on standardizing English language, 92, 94; on Swift's style, 108; on Tory ideas, 64; used etymology, 96

Jonson, Ben: on linguistic standard established by "best" usage, 96; on style revealing character, 120

Lagado, Academy of: linguistic practices in, 35, 62–63, 77–79, 100, 156n19; resistance of common people against, 12, 103

Language, compared to cloth, 25–36, 151n5; contemporary ideas on, 1–2, 26, 57, 73–88, 155n2; necessity of standard for, 3, 8, 42, 90–95; nonstandard, Swift's fascination with, 8–9, 149n4. *See also* English language;

Language (*continued*)
Ersatz language; Original language;
Private language; Public language;
Universal language
Locke, John: analysis of interpretation, 106;
danger of linguistic pollution, 61; dictionary of real characters, 74; ideas
contrasted to Wilkins', 157n34; method
of definition, 83–84; Port-Royal linguists, relation to, 157n34; Swift's
satire on, 84–85
Lodwick, Francis: philosophic language,
75–76, 78

Meaning: corruption of, 30–31; dependent
on continuity of common forms, 28;
methods of ascertaining, 82–85; problems of determining, 1, 4; Swift's
search for, 5. *See also* Definition;
Redefinition
Moderns: as enemies to common forms, 12.
See also Uncommon forms
Monarchy: English should be language of,
12, 64. *See also* Common forms
Mysticism: as epitome of obscure discourse,
109–10; as influence on universal language, 76; as object of Swift's parody,
160n9

Oldmixon, John: criticizes Swift's style, 17
Omission, of words: as solution to social
problems, 79–81, 156n20
Original language: nature of, 73–74; search
for, 85–86; Swift's satire of, 86–88
Orwell, George: influenced by Swift, 60
Oxford, Robert Harley, 1st Earl of: as addressee of *Proposal*, 17, 89–102 passim;
offers Swift money, 98. *See also* Tory
administration

Parody: Swift's use of, 10, 71; in *Tale of
a Tub*, 17–18, 119, 160n9
Pezron, Paul: advocates "Gaulish" as original language, 87
Philosophic language: described, 75–76;
satirized by Swift, 78–80
Pope, Alexander: conversation with Swift,
50; on critics, 17–21; effectiveness of

satire, 69; on linguistic change, 2, 8; on
nature of mind, 159n2; on punning,
18; satirizes linguistic pollution in
Dunciad, 57; Swift criticizes style of,
13, 115; Swift's desire to imitate,
135–36; on wit, 26
Port-Royal linguists: ideas popularized by
Locke, 157n34; relation of meaning to
mind, 105
Private language: Proper Words in, 4;
Swift's use of with Esther Johnson
("little language"), 51–54, 153n13,
with Esther Vanhomrigh, 54–55, with
Sheridan, 55–56. *See also* Swift, Prose
Works, *Journal to Stella*; Uncommon
forms
Pronunciation: basis of "little language" in
Journal to Stella, 52; inappropriate as
spelling standard, 94–96. *See also*
Cadence
Proper Words in proper Places: defined and
described, 2, 4, 104–12; determined
by accessibility, 13, 67, 85, 107–8,
123; examples, 131–33; impediments,
110–12; liberating power of, 144, 148;
requirements for written discourse,
112–16; social function of, 3, 107–8;
Steele as violator of, 121, 125–31; syn-
onymous with reason, 105–6; Tindal
as violator of, 121–25. *See also* Style;
Writing
Public language: in literary tradition, 68–
72; Proper Words necessary in state,
62–66; relation to social welfare, 4,
57–62, 151n2, 154n5, 154n7; in religion, 66–67. *See also* Common forms;
Proper Words in proper Places
Punning: dual nature of, 18; Swift's enjoyment of, 18–19, 55–56, 150–51n17.
See also Sheridan, Thomas

Quintilian: "best" speakers should be used
as linguistic standard, 96

Real character: defined and described, 74–
76; Swift's satire of, 76–79. *See also*
Gesture; Wilkins, John
Redefinition: corrupts meaning, 30–31;

DATE DUE

MAR 14			
FEB 1 1 1992			
GAYLORD			PRINTED IN U.S.A.